THE

ELEMENTS OF LAW;

BEING

A COMPREHENSIVE SUMMARY

OF

AMERICAN CIVIL JURISPRUDENCE.

FOR THE USE OF STUDENTS, MEN OF BUSINESS, AND GENERAL READERS.

By FRANCIS HILLIARD,
COUNSELLOR AT LAW.

THE LAWBOOK EXCHANGE, LTD.
Union, New Jersey
2002

ISBN 1-58477-188-7

Printed in the United States of America
On Acid-Free Paper

The Lawbook Exchange, Ltd.
965 Jefferson Avenue
Union, New Jersey 07083-8605

Please see catalogue at rear of this volume
or our website
www.lawbookexchange.com
for a selection of our other fine facsimile reprints
of classic works of legal history.

Library of Congress Cataloging-in-Publication Data

Hilliard, Francis, 1806-1878.
The elements of law : being a comprehensive summary of American civil jurisprudence, for the use of students, men of business, and general readers / by Francis Hilliard.
p. cm.
Originally published: Boston: Hilliard, Gray, and co. ; New York : Halsted and Voorhies, 1835.
Includes bibliographical references and index.
ISBN 1-58477-188-7 (cloth: alk. paper)
1. Civil law—United States.I. Title.

KF380 .H55 2001
346.73—dc21

2001041395

THE

ELEMENTS OF LAW;

BEING

A COMPREHENSIVE SUMMARY

OF

AMERICAN CIVIL JURISPRUDENCE.

FOR THE USE OF STUDENTS, MEN OF BUSINESS,
AND GENERAL READERS.

By FRANCIS HILLIARD,
COUNSELLOR AT LAW.

BOSTON:
HILLIARD, GRAY, AND COMPANY.
NEW YORK:
HALSTED AND VOORHIES.
1835.

CAMBRIDGE:
CHARLES FOLSOM, PRINTER TO THE UNIVERSITY.

PREFACE.

The general nature and object of the following work will probably appear, to most readers, from its title. The author may, without incurring the imputation of vanity, remark, that the plan of it is *original.* Mere originality is no merit; for it is likely to be the prominent feature in the productions of a visionary or a madman; and only when combined with *wisdom, utility,* and *a perfect execution,* constitutes a suitable subject of praise. The originality, or, to use a less ambitious word, *novelty,* of the plan, however, requires, or at least justifies, a few words of explanation and defence.

The only general, elementary treatises upon our law, are Blackstone's "Commentaries" and Kent's "Commentaries." I put out of view the large "Abridgments" or "Digests" of Comyns, Bacon, and Dane; because their great magnitude manifestly distinguishes them from every thing in the nature of a brief and compendious abstract, and precludes them from popular use. In regard to the "Commentaries" of Blackstone and Kent, it will be attempted, without implying the slightest pretension to rival these invaluable productions, to point out wherein they differ from the present work.

These are *large works,* usually occupying four large volumes, and costing from ten to sixteen dollars; the following work is *a small and cheap one,* making a single octavo volume of about three hundred and fifty pages, and costing but three dollars.

Blackstone's Commentaries, it is well known, contain a large amount of matter, which is either in its nature not *legal,* but *historical* and *political*, or has no applicability, and even to the professional reader is of little use, in this country. As an elegant and philosophical sketch of the English common and statute law, the work cannot be overrated; but as little can it be depended upon, either by the legal or the general student, for a view of *American law* in its present condition. The "Commentaries" of Chancellor Kent, — admirable as they are, and honorable alike to the author and to his country, — are occupied, to the extent of one entire volume, with *the Law of Nations* and *Constitutional Law*; both of which have more of a political than a strictly legal aspect, and are therefore wholly omitted in the present work. Kent is also, like Blackstone, speculative, historical, and discursive, enlarging at great length upon a few interesting titles, and consequently passing by, for want of room, several important legal topics. The present work is designed to present *American law*, technically so called, *as it is*, in its various branches of *rights*, *wrongs*, and *remedies*. To effect this object in so small a compass, it carefully abstains from all *criticism*, *speculation*, or *history*; and confines itself to a plain, brief statement of *principles now in force*, with occasional *illustrations*.

The title of this book will probably provoke a criticism like the following; — that it is an attempt to compress into a nut-shell that which is *in extent infinite*; to teach briefly and familiarly, that which is *in its nature mysterious and obscure*; and to impose upon the community as useful, that which is, for all but a handful of men, *wholly unprofitable*. This threefold accusation imposes upon the author the corresponding duty of showing, not that the present work is, but that such a work may be, at once *comprehensive*, *intelligible*, *and useful*.

1. I do not question the notorious and proverbial fact, that the science of law branches out into the most extensive and complicated details; which have been from the formation of society, and still are, continually accumulating, and which the

labor of a life is incompetent perfectly to acquire. But, although the fact be conceded, it is worth while to inquire into the cause of it; and whether that cause is one at all inconsistent with the position, that in law, as in other sciences, there are certain broad and fixed principles, which embody the essence of the system, and remain unchanged amidst the fluctuations of successive ages. I think it will be found, that there are such principles; that *the increase of the law* arises, not from any change *in them*, but from that infinite variety of facts and circumstances, to which the transactions of mankind give rise, leaving room for doubt in each case as it occurs, whether to that particular case the general principle is applicable; that, in the vast mass of details, there are a few comprehensive, elementary maxims, of which those details are merely the occasional modification, while the maxims themselves remain of the same general truth and applicability as before.

It should, moreover, be understood, that the countless volumes in which the law is contained, are for the most part *reports of decided cases*. The report of a case sets forth, at length, all the facts which it involves, the arguments of counsel, and the opinion, with all its reasons and illustrations, of the Court; while *the principle* recognised or decided may be concisely but clearly expressed in a few marginal lines.

2. *The obscurity* of the law is perhaps as proverbial as its *infinity*, and equally misunderstood or exaggerated by inattentive observers. That the law abounds in subtilties and nice distinctions is not denied. But to these the same remark applies, which has already been made as to the extent and accumulation of the science. They are qualifications or exceptions, in their nature limited, to general principles in their nature universal. The law also abounds with technical words and phrases. But what art or science does not? A technical expression is no less intelligible after it has been defined, than a popular one. It is believed, that no attentive reader of the

following work will find any obscurity arising from this source. Very few technical terms are used; and, where they are used, they are either defined at the time, or else a reference to the Index will show on what page a definition may be found.

Of all popular misapprehensions and prejudices not one is more unfounded, than that which regards the law as a technical and arbitrary, and therefore a mystical and unintelligible, system. With the exception of those comparatively few regulations, which are in their character positive and directory, the law of the land is, in general, but another name for the law of nature. Municipal rules are founded upon the basis of equity, reason, and right. If this be so, then obscurity no more belongs to the former than to the latter; upon which the instinct of conscience, the conclusions of the understanding, and the teachings of revelation pour their mingled light.

To the above remark there is one exception, resulting from the nature of the law regarded as a system of *general rules.* It passes human wisdom to frame a general rule, which shall not in some individual instance operate with apparent harshness. And yet a rule must be always enforced, or never; dispense with it in any case whatever, and it ceases to be one; cut it down a hair's breadth, because it seems not to fit a single temporary exigency, and it will begin to crumble away, and soon not a fragment of it will be left. Our law, however, is fortunate enough, in departing from the line of apparent equity, to carry with it its own vindication. General expediency, — public policy, — is often the highest measure of right; perhaps we should not go too far in saying, that, with regard to the rules which govern civil society, it is the only measure. The common law has no more characteristic feature, than its *strong common sense*; nor does it in any way more strikingly exemplify this quality, than by an occasional sacrifice of immediate advantage or superficial equity, to its far-reaching views of permanent and universal good. The acute *layman,* unversed only in legal lore, if any such should honor the author with his notice, will be struck, on running over the following pages, with many a rule or principle, born, for aught that appears, amid Saxon forests, whose practical shrewdness and sagacity puts to shame "the appliances and means to boot" of modern legislation. In regard to such principles, which may seem at first sight unreasonable, or at least *quaint*, it has been the author's purpose, in general, briefly to point out the grounds of *policy* upon which they rest, and which need only a suggestion to be appreciated and understood. If he has succeeded in dissipating the cloud, real or unreal, which has hung over the law; in proving that it is not, what no less a man than Burke ironically represented, and the majority of mankind have believed it, an abstruse and arbitrary system, but built upon the solid foundations of reason and utility; — one great part of his object will have been accomplished.

3. It needs no elaborate argument to prove, that a work well and faithfully executed upon the plan proposed, will be *useful* to "students, men of business, and general readers." The author does not put it forth as a new and sovereign *recipe for making lawyers*; nor lay claim to the disinterested benevolence of disclosing secrets, out of which his own craft get their living. Possibly, the publication of this work will not prevent a single lawsuit. Possibly, as that which men study in theory they learn to love in practice, it may produce a contrary effect. But aside from this very interesting and nicely balanced question; — if it be *useful* for a man to know the nature and extent of his civil rights and obligations; with what safeguards a free constitution has encompassed his liberty and estate; what claims and duties arise out of his personal relations with other men; the tenure of his property, and effect of his contracts; the remedies provided by law for redress of his wrongs, and the course of proceeding in the tribunals, in which those remedies are administered, and to which duty may call *him* not only as

party but as judge; — if these are subjects of useful knowledge, then a book which presents a summary, correct, and intelligible view of them, cannot be condemned as *useless*.

There is hardly an art or science, excepting the one treated of in the following pages, which has not been reduced to an elementary form for the purposes of *education*. In the new spirit, no less just than liberal, that now prevails, all knowledge is held to be *practical*. The narrow, unworthy theory, which limited that appellation to the science of matter, — of matter practically inert, practically insensible; and denied it to that of mind, the intelligent mover of all things, — has gone by, never we hope to be revived. And if any branch of knowledge, not mechanical or material, deserve the name; it would seem, from the considerations already advanced, that the law is above all entitled to it. Why then should this science be made a single exception to that spirit of inquiry, so honorably characteristic of the age? Why, with the human understanding, government, morals, and religion, should it not become a subject of youthful instruction? The only possible answer is, that it *has not been*; and this, in an *anti-prescriptive* age, hardly requires serious refutation.

In conclusion, the author deprecates *unfair criticism*. If the following pages contain any *positive errors*, he holds himself open to reasonable censure; but regards mere *omissions*, since from the very nature of the work they are unavoidable, as no sufficient ground of condemnation. Of such a book the necessary basis is *selection*; and judicious selection is therefore its only practicable merit. Should this merit be conceded to it, the author will have received all the approval that he hopes, and more than he dares to expect.

F. H.

Cambridge, Massachusetts,
September 1, 1835.

CONTENTS.

BOOK I.

BOOK II.

BOOK III.

RELATIVE RIGHTS OF PERSONS.

BOOK IV.

RIGHTS OF THINGS PERSONAL.

BOOK V.

RIGHTS OF THINGS REAL.

BOOK VI.

PRIVATE WRONGS.

Proposed Alterations in the Laws of Massachusetts.

ERRATA.

In a few instances, erroneous references have been made to subsequent chapters. In such cases the mistake may be corrected, by finding in the Index the subject matter of reference, together with the page where it is treated. Thus the error in note 1, p. 46, may be rectified by turning to the word "Remainder" in the Index.

Page	67,	*line*	9,	*before*	property	*insert*	real
"	82,	"	19,	*for*	six	*read*	twelve
"	105,	"	14,	"	drawer	"	drawee
"	106,	"	6,	"	or	"	on
"	173,	"	27,	"	sales	"	sale
"	319,	"	14,	"	trials	"	trial

-*Page* 324, *lines* 5 *and* 6, *dele* in New York.

ELEMENTS OF LAW.

BOOK I.

ORIGIN AND CONSTITUENTS OF AMERICAN LAW.

THE system of law which prevails in the United States is the English common law, subject to certain modifications, which will be hereafter mentioned.

The English common law is a vast and complicated collection of rules and principles, which, though sometimes called, by way of distinction from statutes or acts of the legislature, "the unwritten law," is nevertheless contained like these in printed volumes, and by no means left to the uncertainty of ancient tradition and general usage. The common law began of course at an early period, and has grown to its present extent by degrees, with the gradual advancement of society in numbers, in commercial intercourse, wealth, and refinement. Its origin is traced back even to the aboriginal Britons; among whom, however, barbarians as they were, nothing but its broadest and simplest maxims, which are common alike to all nations, can be supposed to have existed. The successive invaders of England, the Romans, Picts, Saxons, and Danes, added their several contributions to the rude collection. It remained chiefly, however, if not wholly, in the form of unwritten customs; till at length these were compiled, first by Alfred, and afterwards by Edward the Confessor, into written volumes. It was remarked by Lord Hale, that "the original of the common law is as undiscoverable as the head of the Nile;" the volumes in question being not the source, but only the expression in a connected form, of those scattered maxims and customs, which have existed "time whereof the memory of man runneth not to the contrary."

The common law, as it is now and has been for centuries, consists of a few ancient treatises, which from their antiquity and great learning have all the weight of judicial decisions, but chiefly of *cases decided* by the courts of justice, together with the modern *digests and abridgments* of those cases. The great principle which lies at the foundation of the law regarded as a system is this; that the judgment of a regular judicial tribunal, if deliberate and final, conclusively settles the law in reference to the question at issue; so that, when the same question afterwards arises in another case, instead of an examination upon considerations of reason and justice, it is deemed sufficient simply to cite the former decision. If this were not so, there could in fact be no such thing as law, the rights and obligations of individuals must be involved in absolute confusion and uncertainty, and the community perpetually distracted by the struggles of adverse claimants. It is true, that judgments of different courts, or different judgments of the same court, are more or less authoritative in proportion to the deliberation with which they were formed, the character of the judges who pronounced them, and their harmony or inconsistency with other collateral adjudications. The English and American reports are said to contain one thousand *overruled* or revoked decisions. It is to be considered, moreover, that a judgment has no binding force in cases subsequently arising, unless the facts are the same as in the original case. In the various transactions of society new combinations of circumstances perpetually occur, bearing a general but not an exact resemblance to those upon which legal decisions have been already founded. Hence arise the nice and subtile distinctions so characteristic of the law. A single and apparently trivial fact may qualify, restrain, or enlarge an established rule. Hence also arises the necessity for that perpetual activity of judicial tribunals, and for those multiplying reports of decided cases, which render the law so emphatically an *accumulating science*.

In giving judgment upon a particular case, it will depend upon circumstances whether the court *establish*, or simply *declare*, the law. In one sense a court has no *legislative power*. To make any positive and general enactment would be a flagrant departure from its legitimate function. But, upon many judicial questions, the aid of authority, of analogous decided cases, is wholly wanting. It then becomes the duty of a judge, not indeed to pass an arbitrary edict, but, taking for his guide the universal law of reason and justice, to invest that law with the sanction and the imperative force of a distinct judgment, and thereby make it the law of the land, no longer open to argument and dispute.

With these explanations, it may be said that the English common law is to be learned from judicial decisions as appearing in the Reports. In its application to this country, the common law is subject to several modifications.

1. All *English statutes*, passed before the foundation of the American colonies, and in their nature of general applicability, are to be considered as in force in the United States. The constitution of Massachusetts declares, that "all laws hitherto adopted in the colony, and practised on in the courts, shall be in force till altered by the legislature;" and the Supreme Court have inferred the adoption of an English statute from its being in the nature of "a favor from the king." These remarks apply even to statutes enacted after the settlement of this country, and embrace *à fortiori* all previous acts. So, when the constitution of New York adopted and recognised *the common law* as one entire system, it was undoubtedly the common law subject to such alterations as had been made by the English parliament before the settlement of that State. Such is presumed to be the case in all the States of the Union.

2. The common law is subject in this country to *the constitution of the United States*, and, in each State, to *the constitution of that State*. The fundamental principle of our government is *the supremacy of the constitution.* This is regarded as the act or declaration of the people themselves in forming the government; or as the original condition upon which they consented to organize themselves into a political community. The consequence is, that whatever rule or principle of law, being in force at the adoption of the constitution, was inconsistent with it, became immediately abrogated; and that any subsequent legislative act or judicial decision, which tran-

scends or violates this primary charter, is null and void. The American constitutions, however, touch rather the *political* than the *civil* rights and obligations of the citizen; not applying to the relations between man and man in the commerce of society, but restraining the power of rulers, and protecting the privileges of the governed from oppression. The *common law*, in its broadest sense, undoubtedly embraces political as well as civil relations; and to show how it has been changed by the American constitutions would involve a history of the revolution, and an analysis of our whole frame of government. This however is foreign from the object of the present work, which is designed to be strictly *legal*, and in no degree *political*.

3. The common law is modified, in the United States, by *the statutes of Congress* and *of the State legislatures*. From the nature of the general government, whose jurisdiction is almost exclusively *national*, the statutes of Congress relate chiefly to the promotion of *specific national objects*, and do not touch those *general principles*, which concern the rights and obligations of the citizen. In other words, the formation of the United States government gave rise to a system of laws peculiar to itself, and which neither confirms, contradicts, nor in any way changes the common law, but occupies or constitutes a new and independent department of jurisprudence.

With regard to *the statutes of the State legislatures*, it may be remarked, that the object and effect of them is not in general to alter or abrogate the principles of the common law. That this is done in many instances, I do not deny. But the prevailing tenor of the statute law aims at two purposes; first, to define and affirm some principle of the common law, or reënact some leading English statute, whose provisions are so reasonable or necessary that they commend themselves alike to all nations, as for instance the *statute of frauds*, or *the statute of limitations;* second, to carry into operation a newly formed government, by organizing its departments, directing the election of its officers, and regulating those innumerable details, which the exigencies of society present, in the early stages of an original political system. Accordingly, on looking into the statute-books of the several States, it will be found, that they are to a great extent occupied by enactments upon the following subjects, and a few others similar, viz. state boundaries and territorial jurisdiction; civil divisions, such as towns, counties, &c.; public officers; funds and taxes; the public instruction, health, and defence; roads and bridges; trade; incorporations, and internal police.

It should however be further remarked, that so much of the common law, as concerns *legal and judicial proceedings*, has been greatly altered in this country; that it has been altered in some States more, and in others less; and consequently that, in this point of view, there are wide diversities among the several States themselves. It will appear in the following work, that the three great divisions of the law are *rights*, *wrongs*, and *remedies*. It is in reference to the last, that American law least resembles the English, and is in itself least uniform and systematic. Among the vast variety of acts, forms, and ceremonies, falling under the head of *remedies*, which burden the common law, many have never been known in the United States, some have been adopted in one State, and others in another. This has taken place, not so much by express statute regulation, as by silent usage from the earliest periods. For instance, titles to real estate have from time immemorial been tried, in some states by the fictitious action of *ejectment*, and in others by *writs of entry* and *writs of right*. So the process of *distress for rent* has been always in use in some States, and is wholly unknown in others. It may not be an improper phraseology to say, that the deviations from the common law above referred to, and in which there is so little uniformity in different parts of our own country, pertain to *form and practice* rather than to *rules and principles*.

In the same connexion it may be observed, that many entire *subjects or titles* in the English common law are nearly or quite obsolete in American law; and of course the principles applicable to those subjects make no part of our system. Such portions of the common law are passed over in the following work with slight, or without any notice. With respect to them, the law has been rather simplified in its variety, or abridged in extent, than changed in its principles. For instance, *entailments* are nearly done away in this country. The *subject itself*, therefore, has become obsolete, — it has been struck out from the jurisprudence of the United States. Still, however, if estates in fee-tail anywhere exist, they are governed by the *rules and principles* of the common law.

There are moreover some subjects, which, even in England, have originated or risen into great importance as a department of the law, at a comparatively recent date, and since the settlement of this country. Such are *mercantile contracts* in general, and more particularly the contract of *insurance;* which reached its present imposing magnitude in the commercial world during the last and present century, and the law pertaining to which, if not *enacted,* was to a very great extent enlarged and systematized, by the genius of Lord Mansfield and other contemporary judges. Upon this class of subjects, American law, though substantially conformable to the English, does not, as in other cases, stand upon the basis of the *common law,* but consists of the decisions of our own courts.

With the abovementioned qualifications, the common law of England is that of the several States of the Union excepting Louisiana, which, on account of its French origin and population, is governed by the *civil or Roman law.* It has, moreover, been held by the Supreme Court of the United States, in the few cases brought before that tribunal, for which the constitution or laws of Congress had not provided, that the common law, though it can never be a *source of jurisdiction* to the United States courts, they deriving all their powers from United States authority, is nevertheless so far recognised and adopted, as to be the criterion for determining the *nature, extent,* and *mode of exercise* of their jurisdiction.

It is proposed in the present work to give a summary view of American law. Being designed as a cheap manual for popular use, it can only present a summary view of that great variety of topics, any one of which affords matter for a distinct and extended treatise.

BOOK II.

ABSOLUTE RIGHTS OF PERSONS.

PRIVATE rights are divided into the *rights of persons*, and the *rights of things*. The former are again divided into *absolute rights*, and *relative rights*.

By the law of nature, every man has certain *absolute personal rights*, classed by the most approved writers into *security*, *liberty*, *and property*. It so happens, however, that, in much the larger part of the world, political institutions have been and are such, as entirely to defeat the law of nature upon this point. Under those arbitrary governments, which from the earliest ages have almost universally prevailed, the rights in question have no existence, because security, liberty, and property are all at the mercy of the ruling power in the state; and that cannot in a civil sense be called a right, the violation of which is no civil wrong, and subject to no civil penalty. It is therefore only in limited or free governments, that the absolute rights of persons constitute an appropriate branch of the municipal law.

Civil liberty is coeval with the British government, forming a prominent feature in the *common law*, properly so called, in distinction from the *statute law*. In early periods, however, and while resting upon mere tradition and usage, English freedom was exceedingly vague, imperfect, and fluctuating. To define it with precision, and establish it upon sure foundations, several acts of Parliament were passed, which, though designed rather as declarations of the existing law than to set up new principles, have ever since constituted the standard and text-book of national rights. Of these the first and most important was *the Great Charter*, passed, or rather obtained as a concession from the king, in the reign of John.

It is unnecessary to enumerate the specific provisions of this interesting and sacred act. Many of them relate to subjects, now obsolete even in England, and which have never existed in this country. Its chief value is in the broad principles of freedom which it lays down; in establishing the supremacy of law over power and prerogative; in providing against *the sale, the delay, the denial* of justice between man and man; and in securing the life, liberty, and estate of every citizen from public or private interference, till sanctioned by "the judgment of his peers, or the law of the land."

Magna Charta was followed at intervals by many corroborating statutes, all tending to the same point, the liberty of the people. The principal of these were "Confirmatio Cartarum," under Edward I., the "Petition of Right" under Charles I., the "Habeas Corpus" act under Charles II., and the Bill of Rights under William and Mary.

The American colonies, at an early period of their history, by repeated resolves and declarations, claimed as an inalienable birthright all the privileges and liberties secured by the common and statute law to British subjects. The principles thus avowed, when from colonies they rose into States, became incorporated into their respective constitutions; and it is therefore upon these constitutions, that, in reference to every citizen of the United States, the security of absolute personal rights ultimately depends.

I do not propose to draw a contrast between English and American liberty; but in this connexion there is one point of comparison not undeserving of notice. The Great Charter, and all subsequent provisions designed to secure the freedom of the people, were *acts of Parliament*, and nothing more. It is true, Magna Charta was anciently regarded in a different light, as the *paramount and unalterable law;* and a statute of Edward III. declared void all future statutes which should oppose or conflict with it. This notion, however, has long been done away. The Great Charter has been in many particulars repealed; and it is now well understood and settled, that no Parliament can tie the hands, or limit the repealing authority, of its successors. Upon the theory of the British government, Magna Charta may at any time be abrogated by an act of the legislature. Nor is this all. Parliament, being absolutely omnipotent, instead of abrogating the Great Charter in relation to the whole people, may suspend its operation upon individual citizens, while it still remains the law of the land as before. It is hardly necessary to remark, that the theory of the American government is widely different from this. The constitution, with us, is the original act of the people themselves. As such, it is the supreme law; unalterable but by the power which formed it; rendering void every repugnant statute, and least of all liable to be dispensed with, upon particular occasions or in reference to particular persons, at the discretion of the legislature.

The absolute personal rights recognised and protected by our law, though usually divided into those of personal security, personal liberty, and private property, may with sufficient precision be expressed as the right of personal security, and the right of private property.

Under the head of *personal security*, may be classed those familiar, elementary principles, common alike to all the States of the Union; that no man shall be punished without previous trial; tried twice for the same offence; compelled to testify against himself; imprisoned, but by the judgment of his peers, or the law of the land; subjected to cruel or unusual punishments: that no "ex post facto" law shall be passed, making criminal an act which was innocent when committed; that the writ of "habeas corpus," by virtue of which any man imprisoned against law may be summarily discharged, shall be suspended only in case of rebellion or invasion; and many other simple but comprehensive maxims, which enter into the essence, and constitute the distinguishing glory, of a free government. Provisions of this nature are chiefly designed to guard the citizen against those arbitrary and cruel exercises of power on the part of rulers, which have been so universally exhibited in the nations of the old world.

The right of *private property* is that privilege, which every American citizen enjoys, to hold his possessions, lawfully acquired, against any unjustifiable interference either by the government or by individuals. The American constitutions are equally explicit and comprehensive upon this point, as upon that of personal security. In the spirit of the old English statutes, they prohibit *taxation* but by the people themselves, or their legal representatives; and the taking of private property *for the public use*, unless the general necessity and convenience demand it, and a fair compensation be paid to the owner. Of a similar character, is the provision for *trial by jury*, in all suits at common law except those of the very smallest magnitude. When it is considered how proverbially eager among mankind is the pursuit of gain, these constitutional restraints appear in the highest degree salutary and requisite. Wrongs are not perpetrated without motive, and that motive is in general the personal advantage of the offending party. Violations of personal security have not usually this temptation. But private property, the engrossing object of pursuit to so large a proportion of the world, must be perpetually the prey of rapacity and crime, were it not hedged about by the impregnable barrier of the constitution.

BOOK III.

RELATIVE RIGHTS OF PERSONS.

CHAPTER I.

HUSBAND AND WIFE.

THE private relations, recognised by the law, are those of husband and wife, parent and child, guardian and ward, master and servant.

Husband and wife. Under this head we shall consider, 1st, the nature of marriage, and how it may be contracted; 2dly, how dissolved; 3dly, what legal effects and consequences, rights and duties, result from it.

1. Marriage is a *civil contract*, founded in the social nature of man, and intended to regulate, chasten, and refine the intercourse between the sexes, and to multiply, preserve, and improve the species; and, from the nature of the contract, it exists during the lives of the two parties, unless dissolved for causes which defeat the object of marriage, or from relations imposing duties repugnant to matrimonial rights and obligations.

A marriage is valid or void, according to the law of the place where it is contracted, or the "lex loci contractûs," even though the parties go there to evade the law of their own State, and immediately return. But if the law of any place should authorize *an incestuous marriage*, as, for instance, between a father and daughter, it would be held void in this Commonwealth, being grossly immoral. But a marriage between a mulatto and a white person, forbidden by our law, but not naturally unlawful, if solemnized at a place where it was not prohibited, would be treated as valid here.

Marriage, being a contract, requires suitable contracting parties, and a free consent, to render it valid. The marriage of an idiot or lunatic is void. So, a marriage obtained by fraud or force. The age of lawful marriage has been variously regulated by various States. In general, males under the age of fourteen, and females under the age of twelve, cannot legally marry. But in New York, seventeen and fourteen are the ages fixed by the Revised Statutes.

A marriage between persons, who are related to each other within the fourth degree, is void. For ascertaining the degree of relationship, in general, the mode of reckoning is from one of the parties up through the common ancestor of both, and down to the other. Thus, if the individuals are an uncle and niece; — from the niece to her father is one, from him to his father are two, and from the grandfather down to the uncle are three; so that the marriage of an uncle and niece would be within the prohibited degrees, and void. Affinity, or relationship by marriage, has the same effect as consanguinity. Upon this point, also, the laws of different States are somewhat diverse. In New York, the prohibition extends only to lineal relations, and brothers and sisters.

For the sake of public order and morality, the laws of all the States prescribe certain formalities to be observed in the celebration of marriage. Preliminary public notice, and, in case of minors, consent of parents or guardians, are usually required, and certain responsible officers designated to perform the ceremony. A neglect to give such notice, or a want of such consent, does not avoid the marriage; but a marriage celebrated without the presence and coöperation of the prescribed officer is in general invalid.

A second marriage, while the former husband or wife is living, and the first marriage remains undissolved, is illegal and void. It is usual, by statute, to except from the penalties of such an act, termed *bigamy* or *polygamy*, those cases where the first husband or wife has been for a long time absent or unheard of; but the second marriage is nevertheless even under such circumstances wholly void.

It has been held, that a wife, who had been absent from her husband for a series of years, or whose husband had driven her away by cruelty in another State or country, and who had provided her own support, might be treated in Massachusetts as a *feme sole* for some purposes. Some distinction has been taken in this respect between the wives of foreigners and of our own citizens. In New York, after five years' absence of the husband, though living, the children of a second marriage may be legitimate.

Impotence in either of the parties, also renders a marriage void.

2. A marriage *may be dissolved* by the death of either of the parties, or by divorce.

Under this head it may be remarked, that some of the abovementioned disabilities and impediments are termed *civil*, and others *canonical*. Of the former class, are prior marriage, want of age, ability, or will; and probably a neglect of the particular mode of celebration prescribed by law. Of the latter, are consanguinity, affinity, and corporeal infirmity. *Civil disabilities* render the contract *void* "ab initio," and the union meretricious: *canonical disabilities* render it only *voidable;* and, unless avoided in the parties' lifetime by divorce, it is valid for all civil purposes. In New York, children are not in all cases illegitimate by reason of civil impediments to the marriage, and on the other hand are sometimes rendered so by divorce for adultery of the wife.

Divorce is of two kinds; "a vinculo matrimonii," from the bond of marriage, and "a mensâ et thoro," from bed and board. The former is founded, by the common law, only upon canonical disabilities existing before marriage. But with us, adultery also; in some States, ill usage or desertion; and in New York, imprisonment for life, are grounds of divorce "a vinculo"; though, if obtained for these causes, it does not, as in other cases, render the offspring illegitimate. In a divorce "a vinculo," the marriage is declared null, as having been absolutely unlawful from the beginning, and the parties may in general lawfully marry a second time.

Divorce "a mensa et thoro" is rather a separation of the parties by act of law, than a dissolution of the marriage. It does not affect the legitimacy of children, nor authorize a second marriage. It is granted for the cause of extreme cruelty or desertion of the wife by the husband. The cruelty must consist either in violence or threats; mere insult, irritation, or unkindness is no sufficient ground. After such divorce the wife may sue alone.

Divorces are granted in some of the States only by the legislature; but usually by the courts of justice.

3

In New York the Court of Chancery, which has jurisdiction of this subject, may declare a marriage void for civil impediments existing at the time of marriage.

Except in cases where there could be no collusion, a party's own admission of adultery is held insufficient evidence for a divorce.

An agreement between a husband and wife, and a *third person* as trustee for her, to live apart, usually termed an agreement for *separate maintenance*, is valid, and may be enforced by action. And if it provide for her support, which is accordingly furnished, the husband is not liable for any debts to one who had notice of the agreement.

3. The *legal consequences* of marriage, or the rights and duties of husband and wife, as they relate in some measure to property, and are not strictly personal, will be in part considered in a subsequent portion of this work. A few of them only will now be mentioned.

By marriage, the husband and wife become one person in law; that is, the very being or legal existence of the woman is suspended, or at least is incorporated and consolidated into that of the husband, under whose wing, protection, and *cover* she performs every thing; and is therefore called a *feme covert*, in distinction from a *feme sole*. Upon this principle depend almost all their respective rights, duties, and disabilities.

A man cannot convey to or covenant with his wife, except by the intervention of a third person; and, in general, a covenant made between them before marriage becomes void by that event, unless it is to be performed after her death. It is otherwise with a bequest by will, which cannot take effect till after his death. A woman cannot sue or be sued without joining her husband. But she is liable alone for crimes, unless they are of an inferior class, and committed in presence and by coercion of the husband. He is bound to support her, and, if he does not, to pay any debt contracted by her for necessaries, even though she is not his lawful wife, but only by cohabitation, and though he is a minor. So, if by ill treatment she is compelled to desert him; but not, if she voluntarily leaves his house, or he turns her away for the cause of adultery.

The husband is liable for his wife's debts, contracted before marriage. But he is not thus liable after her death.[1]

Husband and wife cannot be *witnesses* for or against each other; the law taking care, on the one hand, to avoid the temptation to falsehood arising from affection and partiality, and not to destroy domestic harmony on the other. So in any case, where from interest one is incapacitated to testify, the other is so likewise, though neither is a party to the trial. There are one or two exceptions to this rule, arising from necessity. Thus the wife may *swear the peace*, as it is called, against her husband, in case of personal violence. And her dying declarations are evidence against him on a trial for murder. So a wife may be the agent of her husband, and her admissions will then bind him.

The wife, during coverture, may be taken in execution without her husband for a debt contracted,

---

[1] But, in New York, the husband is liable for her debts after her death, unless he administer upon her estate.

or an injury committed, before marriage; unless it is done by collusion between him and the creditor. But a wife cannot be held to bail.

Although, at common law, the wife cannot hold property separately from her husband, yet a court of equity or chancery, through the medium of a trustee, may treat her as having interests and obligations distinct from his. Upon this ground, *marriage settlements*, made before or after marriage for the exclusive benefit of the wife, are sustained, being designed to secure to the wife a certain support in case of misfortune. But an ante-nuptial contract, by which the wife is to hold her own earnings to her separate use, is void as against previous or subsequent creditors of the husband. Courts of chancery will hold the wife's separate property liable to pay debts incurred by her.

In real estate belonging to the wife, the husband acquires a life-interest by the marriage. The fee-simple or absolute property may be conveyed by a deed executed by them jointly. In some of the States, however, to guard the rights of married women, some peculiar forms are required before such a conveyance can be valid. And a deed made by the wife alone is void. A joint deed has merely the effect to pass her estate; but does not bind her by the covenants contained in it.

CHAPTER II.

PARENT AND CHILD.

Children are either legitimate or illegitimate.

1. *Legitimate* children are those begotten or born in lawful wedlock. By the law of Massachusetts, subsequent marriage of parents does not legitimatize children born before marriage.[1] The Parliament of England anciently replied to a solicitation of the ecclesiastics that they would adopt the canonical law on this point, with great spirit, "We will not change the laws of England." In eleven of the United States, however, the canonical rule prevails.

In connexion with legitimate children, we may properly consider the duties and the rights of parents.

The father is bound to support his children *during minority*, that is, by our law, till they are twenty-one years of age. And he is not excused from this obligation, if he have the ability to support them, even by their ability to support themselves. It is otherwise with the mother. If the father be not of sufficient ability, he will be entitled to a reasonable compensation for their support out of their own property. Generally, as an equivalent for the duty abovementioned, the father, and in case of his death the mother, are entitled to the *earnings* of their minor children. But not where the duty has been disclaimed by the parent. In such case, the law im-

---

[1] By St. 1832, ch. 147, children born before marriage may inherit to other children of the same parents born after marriage, if recognised by the father.

plies an *emancipation,* and entitles the child to his own earnings. The parental obligation of support applies to the children of a man's wife, if domesticated in his family.

The parental obligation does not continue beyond the parent's lifetime; nor does our law, like the *civil or Roman law,* prohibit him from totally disinheriting his children without assigning a valid reason. It only requires, that the testament which produces this effect should in some way show, that they were not forgotten by him at the time of making it.

In general, by statute provision, children are required to support their lineal relations in the ascending line, if unable to support themselves. In New York, the obligation does not extend beyond *parents.*

The father has no power over the child's property, except as *guardian.* He may delegate his authority to the *tutor* or *schoolmaster* of the child, who is then "in loco parentis," and has a right to exercise all necessary restraint and correction.

The father may obtain custody of his children by the writ of *habeas corpus,* when they are improperly detained from him; except under very special circumstances, and even against the will of the children. In one case a child at the breast was thus restored to the father. In New York, special provision is made for releasing a child from confinement among the sect of *Shakers*; but recently in Massachusetts, the court refused to interfere by *habeas corpus* for such purpose.

2. *Illegitimate* children are, either the offspring of parties who have never intermarried; or else those born so long after the death of a husband, that by the usual course of gestation they could not have been

begotten by him, or during his long and continued absence, so that no access to the mother can be presumed. These last are questions of presumption, to be tried by a jury in each particular case, with the distinction, however, that where the parties separate by act of law, the presumption is against, and where by voluntary consent, in favor of the legitimacy. The mother of an illegitimate child, as natural guardian, is entitled to his custody, and bound to support him; and the statute law, in most of the States, provides a process for compelling the putative father to discharge this duty.

The only rights of an illegitimate child are such as he may *acquire;* for he can inherit nothing, being looked upon as the son of nobody; nor will he come under the general term "children" in a will. Neither can he have heirs, but of his own body, as he has no ancestor from whom any inheritable blood can be derived. But if an estate be given to him *and his heirs,* he will take an interest in fee-simple; and, in several of the United States, the rigor of the English law has been relaxed, and natural children can inherit to their mother; and in Connecticut, if by the same mother, to each other. In Massachusetts, the mother cannot inherit to her illegitimate child; but she or her relations may in New York. The rule of "nullius filius" applies only to inheritances. Thus, a natural child cannot lawfully marry within the Levitical degrees, and is within the act requiring consent of parents to his marriage. In Louisiana, little distinction is made between the rights of illegitimate children and others.

CHAPTER III.

GUARDIAN AND WARD.

A GUARDIAN has been called "a temporary parent," that is, for so long time as the ward is an infant or under age; and has the same power as a parent over his child. Guardians, in relation to property, are *the mere agents* of their wards, having an *authority* not coupled with an *interest.*

The father, during his life and his children's minority, is their guardian *by nature.* Upon his death, the same office devolves upon the mother, unless superseded by other modes of guardianship, hereafter to be mentioned. The guardian by nature has simply the custody of his ward's person, and neither of personal nor real estate, except perhaps that he may receive the profits, to be accounted for on the ward's coming of age.

A father has the power *by deed or will* of appointing a guardian to his minor children, in either case called "testamentary," a deed made for this purpose being, like a will, *revocable.* A mother has no such power. Such guardianship supersedes every other, extends to the person and personal and real estate, and continues till twenty-one. The English statute which introduced this kind of guardianship has probably been adopted throughout the United States.

Upon the death of the father, however, the care of his minor children is now almost universally committed to a guardian appointed by some judicial tribunal, either a court of chancery or of probate.

In Massachusetts, if over fourteen, the minor chooses for himself; and he may take this course against the will of his mother, who would otherwise be his guardian by nature. If under fourteen, the court chooses for him. The same court has authority to appoint guardians for spendthrifts, idiots, and insane persons.[1] The powers of a guardian thus appointed, are understood to be substantially the same, as those of the testamentary guardian already mentioned.

In addition to these general guardians, every court has the incidental power to appoint a guardian "ad litem," for the purpose of defending a suit brought against an infant, *non compos*, &c.

The guardian's trust is one of obligation and duty, and not of speculation and profit. He cannot reap any benefit from the use of the ward's money, but the advantage accrues entirely to the latter; and, upon the infant's coming of age, he shall be held to a strict account of his doings as guardian. Courts of chancery will compel an account during the ward's minority. All reasonable expenses will be allowed in the settlement.

No action lies against a guardian upon a contract made by the ward; but only against the latter, who may defend by guardian.

It is said, that a guardian ought to sell all moveables of the ward not required for immediate use, and convert them into land or money. He shall pay interest for money in his hands, which might have been put out at interest. When any proposed act is of

---

[1] In New York, these are under the charge of the chancellor.

doubtful propriety, a guardian may refer it to the judgment of a court of chancery, and thereby exempt himself from responsibility.

CHAPTER IV.

INFANTS.

In immediate connexion with the titles of parent and child, and of guardian and ward, may properly be considered the subject of *infancy and infants.*

Infants have various privileges and various disabilities. Even their disabilities, however, are designed to guard them from the effects of youthful improvidence.

An infant, as has been seen, must defend a suit by *guardian.* And he can commence one, only in the name of his guardian, or else of his *prochein ami*, or next friend. But he will be allowed to amend the writ by inserting the name of such a party.

In general, an infant shall lose no right or estate by neglecting to claim it during his infancy, or, in other words, no *laches* or neglect shall be imputed to him. The statutes of limitation, by special exception, are made inapplicable to infants.

An infant is not, in general, liable upon his contracts. These however are not *void*, but *voidable* at his election. Consequently the promise of an infant is a good consideration for that of the other contracting party. If it were absolutely void, the promise on the other side would be void also, being purely gratuitous. On the same principle, it is said that infancy is a *personal privilege*, of which no third person can take advantage. For instance, if a note made to an infant be indorsed by him, and sued by the indorsee, the maker cannot object that the indorsement was void. The personal representatives of an infant may of course make the same exception that he might himself. Thus his executors may defend against a suit, or his heirs avoid a deed made by him.

An infant must use his privilege "as a shield, not as a sword;" that is, to protect himself, and not to defraud others. Hence if he buy and pay for goods, he cannot recover the money without restoring the goods. So, if he should mortgage his land for money borrowed, he could not both keep the money and reclaim the land.

For the benefit of infants themselves, their contracts for *necessaries* are binding; and the question, what are necessaries, must be determined by the age, fortune, condition, and rank of the individual. Food, clothing, habitation, education, &c., are *in themselves* necessaries, whether provided for the infant himself, or for his family; and other things may be considered as such, according to circumstances. It seems, that an infant, supported by his father, is not liable for any thing furnished him. Nor can an infant bind himself by *a negotiable instrument*, even for necessaries; because, in the hands of an indorsee, the consideration could not be inquired into. The trading contract of an infant is not binding, he being supposed incapable to do business.

Infancy is no defence to an action for *tort* or *wrong*, for instance, slander or trespass.

But where the substantial cause of complaint against an infant is founded upon a contract, no action is maintainable as for a *tort*, though the contract be accompanied or followed by some wrongful act or neglect. For instance, an infant cannot be sued for the immoderate or negligent use of a horse hired; nor for a false warranty; nor, as innkeeper, for goods lost in his house. Whether he shall be chargeable at law for a false representation concerning his age, seems to be unsettled. In a court of equity he would be.

A promise by an adult, to pay a debt incurred in his infancy, is binding. A mere acknowledgment is not; as it would be in case of a debt barred by the statute of limitations. And a contract may be affirmed by a mere act or omission, as well as by a declaration. For instance, if an infant lessee retain the premises a reasonable time after coming of age, he thereby affirms the lease. The acceptance of rent by an infant lessor, after coming of age, has the same effect.

One who contracts jointly with an infant is bound, and may be sued alone.

CHAPTER V.

MASTER AND SERVANT.

THE several kinds of persons who come within the description of *servants*, may be divided into *slaves, hired servants,* and *apprentices.*

1. *Slavery* has been defined, as that kind of subjection or service, which gives the master an absolute and unlimited power over the life and fortune

of the slave. It may be doubted, however, whether in any civilized state this definition is fully applicable; with regard to the power over life, it certainly is not.

Domestic slavery existed throughout the United States when they were colonies of Great Britain. It exists to this day in all the southern, and some of the western States, but has become entirely extinct in New York, and New England, and is in a course of abatement in other parts of the Union. In Massachusetts, it was abolished by virtue of the first article of the bill of rights, "All men are born free and equal." The children of slaves born afterwards were born free; for (as it is said), in a free country, slavery cannot be transmitted by parents to their children. Still, however, a slave bought in one State, acquires no rights as a freeman by being brought into another. No contract made with him would be binding on the master. Upon the same principle, if a slave escape into one State from another, the master may seize and remove him without any warrant for the purpose. In New York, the master may regain possession of such slave by *habeas corpus*; but the slave may afterwards have a writ "de homine replegiando," for further examination of his rights.

The history, justice, expediency, and prospects of slavery, though topics of deep interest and importance, are foreign from the objects of the present work.

2. *Hired Servants.* This relation rests altogether upon contract. The one is bound to render the service, and the other to pay the stipulated consideration. By the law of England, a menial servant or domestic was formerly understood, if no time were specified, to be hired for a year, upon a principle of

natural equity, that the servant shall serve, and the master maintain him, through all the revolutions of the respective seasons. It may be doubted whether this principle has been adopted with us. Probably it was never applicable to any but agricultural servants.

A master is in general answerable for any injury suffered through the act or negligence of his servant, while he is employed about the master's business. He is not, however, understood to be thus employed, and the master is not liable, where he commits a wilful and malicious wrong; as by intentionally driving the master's carriage against another.[1] For any *fraud* of the servant the master is liable.

For injuries from *neglect*, the servant himself is not generally liable; nor for the neglect of a *sub-agent.* The master alone is responsible.

A master is bound by the *contract* of his servant, if within the scope of his authority. A *special* servant is one authorized to act only in some particular way, and cannot bind the master in any other. A *general* servant is one authorized to transact the master's business generally, or all of a certain kind; and may bind the latter even against his consent, for any thing within the regular dealings of his agency. For instance, one employed merely to keep a horse, cannot sell him, so as to bind the owner. But one employed to sell a horse, may bind the master by a warranty, though expressly forbidden to warrant.

A master may maintain an action upon any contract made by the servant for his benefit, though his name were not mentioned. If the contract were made in the master's name, the servant cannot him-

---

[1] Provided otherwise in New York, in regard to *public carriages.*

self sue upon it, unless he is interested, by way of commissions or otherwise, in the proceeds. A servant is not bound by a contract, if he discloses the master's name, unless the instrument be under seal; nor even then, if he be a *public* agent. If he has received money on a contract, which for any cause is void, he is not liable after paying it over to the master.

A servant, having the mere custody of goods, cannot sue for an injury to them; — for instance, the keeper of goods attached by a sheriff.

3. *Apprentices.* These are servants, bound to service for a term of years, to learn some profession or trade. The temptations to imposition and abuse, to which this contract is liable, have rendered legislative regulations particularly necessary. The English statute law has probably been very generally adopted in this country, with considerable local variations. The purport and object of it is, in general, a summary provision, for protection and instruction on the one hand, and discipline on the other. Whether, independently of the statutes, a parent has authority at common law to bind out his minor child, is a point that has been variously determined in different States. In Massachusetts, he has such power, all contracts of service legal at common law remaining legal since the statute; in New York and Pennsylvania he has not. The statute of Massachusetts provides, that all considerations, allowed by the master, shall be secured to the sole use of the minor; and that, if over fourteen, the minor's consent shall be expressed in the deed. A guardian has the same rights on this subject as a parent.

A master is entitled to the wages and emoluments of the apprentice, while the relation continues. He may correct him moderately for misbehaviour. The master has a mere personal trust, which he cannot legally assign to another. Neither can he transport the apprentice beyond the jurisdiction within which the contract was entered into, and with reference to the laws of which the parties contracted.

CHAPTER VI.

CORPORATIONS.

A CORPORATION is a franchise or privilege, possessed usually by many combined individuals, under a special name, for the purpose of enabling them to act by one united will, and to continue their joint powers and property in the same body, undisturbed by the change of members. The word *corporation* is usually applied to the society itself.

1. *Kinds of Corporations.* — Corporations are divided into *sole* and *aggregate.* The former consist of a single person, who is made a body corporate, in order chiefly to give him the character of perpetuity. Thus a minister, seised of parsonage lands in the right of a town or parish, is a *sole corporation* for that purpose, and holds them to himself and his successors in office.

An *aggregate corporation* is the union of two or more individuals in one body politic, with a capacity of succession and perpetuity. Besides the *proper* aggregate corporations, the inhabitants of any *district,* as counties or towns, instituted with particular jurisdiction, are sometimes called *quasi corporations.*

Such bodies, it seems, possess all the authority, by necessary implication, which is requisite to execute the purposes of their creation. It is questionable whether they can contract by deed; for, though they are corporations for some purposes, they have not the distinguishing trait of corporations, *a common seal;* but must act by vote at regular meetings. They may, however, take and hold property in trust for the general use of the inhabitants. No private action lies against a *quasi* corporation, unless given by statute. In such case, having no corporate fund, each inhabitant is liable to satisfy the judgment, and shall have his remedy over against the rest. In New York, a large number of *quasi* corporations are by statute enabled to sue and be sued.

A county is the civil division particularly noticed in *judicial proceedings;* for defraying the expenses of which, *county-taxes* are in a great measure imposed. Thus *jurors* are always summoned from the county where the court is held; *Sheriffs and Justices of the Peace* can exercise their respective offices anywhere within their county; and, in many States, inferior tribunals are established with this limit to their jurisdiction. Counties have also jurisdiction in general, through their officers, of *high ways.*

Towns are smaller corporations, with more numerous powers. They are, in general, specially charged with the support of *roads,* of the *poor,* and of *schools,* where these are required by law. Towns may also raise money for other purposes of public convenience and necessity, such as a burying-ground, a market-house, or a town-clock. A town can make *by-laws,* and impose penalties for breach of them, which may be incurred by strangers as well as inhabitants.

For every object within its legal jurisdiction, a *quasi* corporation may impose a tax upon the inhabitants; but for no others.

Corporations are further divided into *ecclesiastical* and *lay*. The former are those whose object is *spiritual* or *religious*. A Christian church has been held in Massachusetts not entitled, as such, to the privileges of a corporation, and not to exist for any legal purposes, except as connected with a parish or incorporated society. A conveyance of land to a church is construed as a trust for the use of the parish; and a minority of the church, adhering to a majority of the parish, in case of separation, will hold the property.

In Virginia, while a colony, the religious establishment of England was adopted with some modification; and also to a certain extent in New Hampshire and some other States. A grant to *a church* of this order has been held to vest the estate in the parson and his successors. Church lands can be conveyed only by the parson and vestry jointly.

A congregational minister, regularly ordained over a parish, is understood in law to be settled for life. But various causes will justify a dissolution of the contract. Any immoral or unchristian conduct on his part will authorize an immediate separation from him; and, in case of serious disagreement with the parish, the law provides for an *ecclesiastical council*, whose decision or *result* will be binding upon both parties.

Lay corporations are again divided into *eleemosynary* and *civil*. An *eleemosynary* corporation is a private charity, constituted for the perpetual distribution of the alms and bounty of the founder; as, for example, hospitals, colleges, and academies. *Civil* corporations are established for a great variety of purposes, which need not be particularly enumerated. They are either *public* and *political,* as cities, towns, &c.; or *private,* as banks, canal and insurance companies, the stock of which, though their objects and operations partake of a public nature, is owned in part by private persons.

2. *How Created.* — Corporations are created by prescription and custom, and by acts of the legislature. There are also several corporations in this country, which owe their origin to the crown under the colony administration. Of such the charters are protected, either by express constitutional provisions, or by general principles of law. The clause of the constitution of the United States against *impairing the obligation of contracts* received from the Supreme Court its fullest and most satisfactory exposition in sustaining the charter of Dartmouth College, granted in 1769 by the British crown, free from legislative interference and assumption.

3. *Nature, Powers, Duties, &c.* — When a corporation is erected, a *name* must be given to it. This has been called the *knot of its combination.* If none has been expressly given, it may assume one; and it may be known by several names.

The ordinary incidents to a corporation are, first, to have perpetual succession, and of course the power of electing new members; second, to sue and be sued, to grant and receive property; third, to have a common seal; fourth, to make by-laws; fifth, to remove members and officers. Numerous instances, however, may be found, of persons having corporate powers "sub modo," to a limited extent, and therefore wanting in a part of the above-mentioned incidents.

An aggregate corporation may take donations and bequests in trust for pious or charitable uses, if not clearly foreign from the purposes of its institution. The English statutes of *mortmain*, by which corporations are incapacitated to hold real estate without special license, have, it seems, been adopted in this country, only in Pennsylvania. In New York they cannot take by devise.

If a corporation be created with a limited fund, it cannot enlarge or diminish that fund, but by license from the legislature ; nor can it change the number of shares into which the capital stock is divided, nor make an assessment for any thing beyond the preliminary expenses of the incorporation, until all the shares have been subscribed for, unless specially authorized by the act. If privileges be granted to a corporation upon certain conditions, a non-performance of them may furnish ground of forfeiture, but cannot be taken advantage of by a stranger. The charter is valid for all purposes, till revoked. So is a charter, which has been obtained by false and fraudulent representations. A corporation is liable for the acts of its agents or officers, while acting within the authority conferred upon them by statute or by the corporation. A contract by a corporation need not always be made and proved by express vote, nor by the corporate seal ; but may, under some circumstances, be implied from corporate acts. But the doings and declarations of individual members are not binding upon the corporation.

The acts of a majority of the members present at a regular meeting, unless the charter provide otherwise, bind the corporation. When the mode of electing officers is not regulated by charter or prescription, the corporation may make by-laws for the purpose, provided they be not repugnant to any chartered right or privilege, nor to the law of the land. A by-law cannot exclude an integral part of the electors, nor impose upon them a new and independent qualification for voting. Though the charter require an annual election of officers, yet, it seems, if the regular time pass by, the old officers continue till new ones are chosen. Where a corporation makes a by-law, that all transfers of shares shall be made in the treasurer's book, a transfer by deed and delivery of certificates will still pass the property. The power of making by-laws may be delegated to a committee. A by-law must be *reasonable.*

Every corporation has the power to remove its members. But it can be exercised only for good cause, and for some offence that relates immediately to the duties of the party as a corporator.

The general rule is, that a corporation has only such *powers,* as are either specifically granted, or are necessary for the purpose of carrying into effect those which are granted.

4. *The Visitation of Corporations.* — This is a power applicable peculiarly to eleemosynary corporations. It belongs to the *founder* or his heirs, or to some person or body to whom it is given by him. *Visitors* have the right of inspecting the affairs and superintending the officers of the corporation, according to such regulations and restrictions, as are prescribed by the founder in the statutes which he ordains, without any control or revision except that of the judicial tribunals, by which they may be kept within the powers granted to them, and the constitution and

general laws of the land. But such visitors cannot deprive a person of his office, without a hearing upon a written complaint; in which his offence, or the ground of removal, is fully and plainly, substantially and formally, described to him. The trial, however, need not be public.

Civil corporations, whether public or private, are not subject to this species of visitation; but are merely amenable to the judicial tribunals for the exercise and the abuse of their powers.

5. *The Dissolution of Corporations.* — Every incorporation is a *contract* between the legislature and the company, which, by the constitution of the United States, cannot be affected by subsequent legislation, unless a power has been expressly reserved to that effect. This does not apply, however, to corporations which are created merely for public purposes, as counties, towns, &c. It has become usual for the legislature to reserve a power to alter, modify, or repeal the charter of a private company at pleasure; and, in Massachusetts, there is a general act, authorizing them to exercise absolute control over any manufacturing corporation, after giving notice of their intention. The same act, however, declares manufacturing to be *public* corporations. In New York, the constitution of the State requires the assent of two-thirds of the members elected to each branch of the legislature, to every bill altering any body politic or corporate.

A corporation may be *dissolved*, by a voluntary and solemn surrender of its franchises into the hands of the government, and an acceptance by the government; or by neglecting to use or a misuse of them, and a judgment of law founded thereon. The officers of a corporation, however, cannot in general dissolve it without the assent of the society. There are two modes of proceeding judicially, to ascertain and enforce the forfeiture of a charter. The one is by "scire facias," where there is a legal existing body, capable of acting, but who have abused their power. The other mode is by information, in the nature of a "quo warranto," where there is a body corporate "de facto" only who take it upon themselves to act, though, from some defect in their constitution, they cannot legally exercise their powers. Both these modes of proceeding are in the name and on behalf of the government. A process for dissolution may also be brought in Chancery by the corporation itself.

Upon the dissolution or civil death of a corporation, all its real estate reverts back to the original grantor and his heirs; the personal estate vests in the public; and the debts due to and from the corporation are extinguished. But it is the universal practice, by special provision, to authorize a continuance of the corporation after a general dissolution, for the purpose of disposing of its property and collecting and paying debts; and also a division among the members of any remaining surplus.

BOOK IV.

RIGHTS OF THINGS PERSONAL.

CHAPTER I.

THINGS PERSONAL.

HAVING treated of the absolute and relative *rights of persons*, or "jura personarum"; the objects of enquiry will now be "jura rerum," or those rights which a man may acquire in and to such external things as are unconnected with his person. These are usually termed the *rights of property*.

Things are by our law distributed into two kinds, — things *real* and things *personal*. The former are such, in general, as are permanent, and immoveable; the latter are goods, money, and all other moveables, which may attend the owner's person. This is a general definition, and subject to some qualifications.

It will be seen, that the thing which is the subject of ownership, though in its nature *real*, may be owned in such a way as to constitute a *chattel interest* or *personal estate*. Thus *an estate for years* in land is personal property. So is every other estate less than freehold. The terms *real estate* and *personal estate*, therefore, denote sometimes the nature of the property, and sometimes the particular interest in that property. The former is the popular, and the latter the technical, use of the expression. In England, *real estate* descends to the heir, and *personal estate* passes to the executor; but this distinction has become nearly nominal in the United States, *the whole property* of a deceased person passing directly or indirectly to his heirs.

We shall begin with the law of *personal* property; as most naturally connected with the subjects already discussed, and as more simple and intelligible than that of real estate.

Things personal, or *chattels*,[1] are distributed by the law into two kinds, — *chattels real*, and *chattels personal*.

1. *Chattels real* concern the realty, as a lease for years of land. They are so called, as being interests issuing out of, or annexed to, real estates, of which they have one quality, viz. *immobility*, which denominates them real; but want the other, viz. *an indeterminate duration*, and this want it is that constitutes them chattels. The nature of this species of property, however, will be better understood, when we come to speak of *real estate*, technically so called.[2]

2. *Chattels personal* are, properly and strictly speaking, things *movable*. There are however some chattels, which, though of a movable nature, yet being necessarily attached to the land, and contributing to its value and enjoyment, go along with it as real estate. This is the case with the deeds and other papers, which constitute the proofs, or *muniments* of title; and also with shelves, iron stoves,

---

[1] The word *chattels* (*catalla*) applies to animate as well as other property. *Goods* only to inanimate things.

[2] See B. 5, ch. 10.

and other fixtures, in a house, which cannot be dismembered without injury. In modern times, for the encouragement of trade and manufactures, and as between landlord and tenant, the ancient rule has been relaxed, and many things are treated as personal property, which seem to be attached to the freehold. Thus the vats and coppers of a soap-boiler, machines for carding wool, chimney-pieces, and, in general, all such improvements, erected or placed by a tenant, as may be removed without injuring the premises, may at the expiration of his estate be taken away by him. So, if a building be erected upon the land of another by his permission, it is liable to be sold on execution as the property of him who erected it, and the purchaser may remove it from the land without being a trespasser.

CHAPTER II.

PROPERTY IN THINGS PERSONAL.

PROPERTY in chattels personal is either absolute or qualified.

Absolute property, is a full and complete title and dominion, which the owner cannot lose, without his own act or default. Of this kind of property, all *inanimate* things may be the subject. With regard to *animals*, the law makes a great difference, in this particular, between their several classes. In such as are of a nature *tame and domestic* (as horses, kine, sheep, poultry, &c.), a man may have an absolute property. They continue perpetually in his occupation, unless carried or enticed away, and are of intrinsic value, serving for the food of man, or else for the uses of husbandry. The question whether an animal be wild or tame, is referred, not to its original constitution, but to our knowledge of its existing habits, derived from fact and experience.

Of all tame and domestic animals, the *brood* belong to the owner of the dam or mother.

A *qualified* property, is such as is not in its nature permanent, but may sometimes subsist, and at other times not subsist.

While it continues, it is as much under the protection of the law as any other, and any invasion of it is redressed in the same manner. This kind of property may arise from the *nature* of the thing possessed. Wild animals, such as deer, rabbits, doves, &c., so long as they are reclaimed by the art and power of man, are the subject of a qualified property; but when they go back to their natural liberty and ferocity, without the will to return, *animus revertendi*, the property in them ceases. To give a property in a wild animal, he must have been brought within the power of his pursuer. Mere *pursuit* is not sufficient, nor is actual *capture* necessary, to produce this effect.

A qualified property may subsist in *the elements* of light, air, and water. In these a man can have no absolute, permanent property. They admit of an ownership only while they are in actual use and occupation. If one man disturbs another, and deprives him of the lawful enjoyment of them, as by obstructing ancient windows, corrupting the air of his house, or fouling his water,[1] the law will give redress; but so soon as they are out of possession, they become again common, and every one has an equal right to appropriate them to his own use.

Property may also be of a qualified nature, on account of the peculiar situation, at the time, of the thing to which it pertains; as where goods are bailed,[2] pledged,[3] distrained,[4] or attached.[5] In these cases, the *right of property* and the *possession* are separated, or rather there is no unqualified property in any one, — the ultimate owner having only the right, and not the immediate possession; and the occupant having the possession, but only a temporary right.

Chattels may also be divided into *things in possession* and *things in action*, — usually called *choses in action*. The latter are personal rights not reduced to possession, but recoverable by suit at law. Thus money due on a bond, or damages for any wrong or injury, for which the law always gives some remedy, are, while the party has only the right and not the occupation, *choses in action*.

One distinction of a *chose in action* is, that it cannot in law be *assigned*.[6] "No man can *buy* a quarrel or law-suit." This rule, however, does not prohibit an equitable transfer, for valuable consideration, of any contract whatsoever; which will authorize the assignee, in the original creditor's name,

---

[1] See B. 6, ch. 7, (2.) [2] B. 4, ch. 8. [3] Ib. [4] B. 6, ch. 1, (1.)
[5] B. 6, ch. 8.

[6] In several of the States, *bonds* are made by statute *negotiable instruments*; and *bail-bonds*, though given to the sheriff, are universally sued in the name of the creditor. *Bills of exchange* and *promissory notes*, and also *bills of lading*, are exceptions to the general rule.

to enforce payment to himself, and, after notice to the debtor, prevent a valid release from the assignor. Such assignment cannot interfere with any equitable claims, allowances, and off-sets, in favor of the debtor, against the assignor, incurred before notice. The assignment of an instrument must be of as high a nature as the instrument itself. A deed can be assigned only by deed. But in general, any unsealed instrument, by mere delivery. In New York, no *chose* can be assigned without writing. The right of an assignee is not defeated by the assignor's death; but he may sue in the name of his executor or administrator.

Personal property may be held by two or more persons in *joint tenancy* or *in common*. The nature of such ownership will be hereafter more fully explained in treating of real estate.[1] The same principles apply to lands and to chattels; excepting that, for the encouragement of husbandry and trade, stock on a farm, and also stock used in a joint undertaking, shall always be considered as *common*, and not as *joint* property, and there shall be no survivorship therein. With these exceptions, a gift of a chattel to two or more creates a joint tenancy, and either may dispose of the whole. Copartners in trade[2] may do the same.

If chattels be conveyed to two persons jointly, in payment of, or as security for, their several demands against the owner, they will become jointly interested in them in proportion to their respective claims. If two persons agree to build a ship together, to be paid for and owned by them in certain proportions,

---

[1] B. 5, ch. 15. [2] B. 4, ch. 10.

they will become tenants in common of the ship so built; but, in general, the joint builders of a ship, unless there be an agreement to the contrary, will be presumed to own equal shares.

Chattels may be limited over by way of *remainder*,[1] after a life interest. The ancient common law did not in general allow this; making a distinction in this respect between land and goods, on account of the transitory and perishable nature of the latter. But now that distinction is at an end. Nothing, however, can be given in remainder, of which the use is inseparable from the consumption, — as, for instance, fruits. Nor can there be an estate in tail[2] of a chattel; but words of entailment give the absolute title.

CHAPTER III.

TITLE TO PERSONAL PROPERTY BY ORIGINAL ACQUISITION.

1. By *occupancy*. Goods taken by *capture* in war, at common law, belonged to the captor. But now they vest primarily in the sovereign, and belong to the captor only to such extent and under such regulations, as positive laws may prescribe. By the general practice of the law of nations, *condemnation*, as well as capture, is required to vest a ship in the captor.

---

[1] B. 5, ch. 13. [2] B. 5, ch. 9, (2.)

Goods *casually lost*, and unreclaimed or designedly abandoned by the owner, if found upon the surface of the earth or sea, belong to the finder. If hidden beneath the ground, they fall under the denomination of *treasure-trove*, belong in England to the King, and in strictness perhaps, with us, to the State, although the right has rarely, if ever, been enforced, unless on behalf of the original owner.

Substantially the same observations will apply to what the law calls *waifs*, that is, goods waived or scattered by a thief in his flight; estrays, or cattle whose owner is unknown; and wrecks. By a statute of Massachusetts, the proceeds of all goods found as above-mentioned, and unreclaimed for a year, are given one half to the finder, and the other to the poor of the town. In New Hampshire, after the expenses are paid, they go wholly to the town. It is suggested by Mr. Dane, in his "Abridgment of American Law," that in this country, unless special statutes provide otherwise, estrays, treasure-trove, and waifs belong to the *finder*.

2. By *accession*. This is the right to all which is produced by, or becomes either naturally or artificially united with, one's real or personal property; as for instance fruits, the young of animals, and new articles manufactured from old materials. If an animal be hired for a time, its increase belongs to the hirer. But it is otherwise with the children of slaves. Upon the principle of accession, whatever is built upon one's land, becomes his property, though the materials belonged to the builder. If a ship-builder, after having laid the keel, and raised the stem and stern-posts, sell the ship in its unfinished state, and afterwards complete it, the ship when completed be-

longs to the purchaser. The same principle would apply to the frame of a house sold and subsequently finished. So a tree, planted by one person in another's ground, so soon as it shall have taken root, becomes the property of the latter. If, however, one man build upon another's land by mutual consent, the owner of the soil does not become owner of what is affixed to it, but the builder may enter and remove it, subject perhaps to nominal damages for entry upon the land. Nor can one man gain a title to the property of another upon the principle of accession, if he took it wilfully as a trespasser, and not through ignorance or mistake; but whatever alteration of form the property may have undergone, the owner may seize it, if he can prove the identity of the materials. Another distinction seems to be, that a person can acquire no title by accession, founded on his own act, unless the materials are incapable of being restored to their original form. The right of *alluvion* may be referred to this head; — by which every addition to the shores of rivers, whether happening from natural causes, or from a union of natural and artificial causes, belongs to the owners of the shores.

In case of *confusion* of goods, if by consent, the owners become tenants in common; if otherwise, the whole belongs to the innocent owner. Where the goods, however, can be easily distinguished and separated, as furniture, no change of property takes place. So, if corn or flour mixed together be of equal value, the owners share equally. If an officer, having attached goods on a writ, suffer them to remain mingled with other goods of the debtor, and refuse to designate what he has attached, another officer may take the whole.

3. By *intellectual labor.* This title includes the property of a person in his original *literary compositions*, or *mechanical inventions.* Whether, at common law, this property subsists after the subject of it has once passed from the original owner's hands, has been made a grave question, on which very learned judges have held opposite opinions. The statute law, however, both of England and the United States, (the latter being invested by the constitution with jurisdiction of the subject,) has secured to authors and inventors, for a limited time, the exclusive use and profit of their productions and discoveries; and this has been held to supersede any right at common law.

Only a very concise view of our law of patents and copy-rights will here be given. The time for which an exclusive patent right is allowed is fourteen years. The applicant must swear that he is the inventor or improver according to his belief, and give a written description, with a drawing or model, of the invention, showing how it may be used. His legal representatives, if he be dead, may procure a patent. A mere change of form or proportions is not a discovery; it must be in the principle. If there be any misrepresentation in the specification, the patent is void. If there be two inventors, the one who first reduces the invention to practice has priority of the other, though the latter obtain the first patent. If the invention has been suffered to go into use, no patent can be afterwards obtained. The invention must be *useful*, that is, not injurious, frivolous, or insignificant; and it must be substantially *new* in its structure and mode of operation. If it be new, only in the production of a single effect, added to an old machine, the inventor shall have a patent for no more than the improvement; — otherwise the whole will be void.

Copy-rights of maps, charts, books, and engravings, may be taken out for twenty-eight years; and, if the author be then alive, or, being dead, have left a widow or children, for the additional term of fourteen years, — on compliance with certain prescribed formalities. The statute upon this subject does not in any way affect the right to republish foreign works. *Musical compositions* are protected under the general name of *works*. A representation of a *dramatic composition* on the stage is no breach of the copy-right. It is however a breach, to take down a play in short-hand before it is published, and publish it. An abridgment of, and notes to, an old work are protected. So a translation. A court of equity, in England, may grant *an injunction* to restrain the publication of unpublished manuscripts; and the courts of the United States, having equity jurisdiction, undoubtedly possess the same power.

It has been very recently determined by the Supreme Court of the United States, that a *reporter of decisions* can have no copy-right in the opinions of the court. A similar doctrine has been held in regard to a work containing *forms of indictments*.

CHAPTER IV.

TITLE TO PERSONAL PROPERTY BY TRANSFER BY ACT OF LAW.

I. By *Forfeiture.* The title of government to goods by forfeiture, as a punishment for crimes, so far as it exists in this country, depends mostly upon local statute law. In relation to the United States, and by several of the State governments, it has been expressly abolished; in other States, limited to the life of the offending party; in one, to the crimes of treason and murder; and in New York, to treason alone.

II. By *Judgment.* A *judgment*, rendered in some suit or action in a court of justice, may vest the property of chattels in the prevailing party. Thus where a *penalty* is given by statute, to be recovered by him that will sue for it; whoever brings his action first, and can "bonâ fide" obtain judgment, will secure a title to it in exclusion of every body else. So, in case of *damages awarded by a jury*, as a compensation for some injury sustained; a judgment therefor gives the injured party a right to that specific sum. On the other hand, a recovery by law of the value of a specific chattel, the possession of which has been acquired or retained by wrong, alters the title and transfers it to the defendant, the damages recovered being regarded as the price of the chattel. For instance, if one man sues another for taking his horse, the damages will be *the price* of the horse. It seems, however, that this change does not take place, till actual *satisfaction* of the judgment. To this head also may be referred all title to *costs and expenses of suit*, awarded to the prevailing party.

A claim founded upon a judgment is termed *a debt of record;* as it appears to be due by the evidence of a *court of record.* This, though not strictly *a contract*, like most other debts, being "in invitum" or without the debtor's consent, has nevertheless *the effect* of a contract of the highest nature. A judgment is in all cases, until avoided or reversed, conclusive evidence of the existence and justice of the claim upon which it is founded, and the latter can never again be drawn in question. This point will be hereafter more fully explained under the head of *Evidence.*[1]

Another debt of record is that by *recognizance*; where a sum of money is *recognised* or acknowledged to be due to the State or an individual, in the presence of some court or magistrate, *with a condition* that such acknowledgment shall be *void* on the *party's appearance, good behaviour*, or the like. On breach of the condition, the penalty becomes *forfeited* at common law; though, by statute provision in some of the States, the court has authority to relieve against it as in case of a bond.[2]

III. By *Succession.* This title applies to *corporations;* and is that whereby they hold their property *in perpetuity*; upon the maxim, that *a corporation never dies*, whatever change may take place in the individual members. One aggregate corporation, however, cannot be successor to another. For instance, a parish cannot *succeed* to a town.

---

[1] See *Judgment.* [2] See *Bond.*

IV. By *Insolvency*. The constitution of the United States gives to Congress the power of establishing uniform laws on the subject of *bankruptcy*. A State has the same power within its own limits; but no State law can be permitted to impair the obligation of previous contracts, to conflict with any existing act of Congress, or to act upon the rights of the citizens of other States. Even if a discharge, by virtue of an insolvent law, has any effect upon creditors out of the State, it is no bar to an arrest, or an execution running against the body; but the insolvent must resort to his action for damages. Nor does the circumstance, that the contract was made in the State where the law was passed, make any difference.

At present, there is no general bankrupt law; but many of the States have insolvent laws of their own, the varying details of which it is unnecessary to enumerate. They are all intended to provide relief for debtors, in case of inevitable misfortune, by securing the application of their effects to the payment of debts, and discharging them from subsequent liability, or their persons from arrest.

An assignment by commissioners of bankruptcy, in a foreign country, will not operate to transfer the bankrupt's property situated here, so as to prevent its being taken by legal process by our own citizens. And the same principle has been settled in Massachusetts, with regard to a voluntary assignment, for benefit of creditors, even in another of our own States; a subsequent attachment being allowed precedence of a prior assignment.

V. By *Marriage*. Marriage is an absolute gift to the husband, of all the wife's personal chattels in possession, and also of choses in action, if he reduce them to possession, by receiving them, or recovering them at law. But the latter, if not reduced to possession during the coverture, remain her property on dissolution of the marriage, either by his death, or a divorce "a vinculo." A note given to her, though it be for a debt due to her while *sole*, is legally payable to the husband, and the property vests absolutely in him, and will not go to the wife on dissolution of the marriage. But a security, given to husband and wife jointly, will belong to the wife, if she survive him, and not to his executor or administrator, provided there be property enough without it for payment of his debts; and if the consideration of such security be a conveyance of land which belonged to the wife, she will have a right to it by survivorship, though the husband's estate be insolvent. The husband, by marriage, becomes possessed also of the chattels real of his wife, as a lease for years; may dispose of them in his life-time; and, if he survive the wife, takes them absolutely by survivorship. But if he do not dispose of them, they become the wife's upon his death. By a statute of Massachusetts, all personal property of a married woman deceased, after payment of debts and funeral charges, goes to the husband; and in New York, whatever is not otherwise taken by him, he takes to his own use as her administrator. A divorce "a mensâ" does not extinguish the power of the husband over his wife's choses in action.

The rents of the wife's lands, which become due before the husband's death, are absolutely his, and do not survive to her.

If a husband bring a suit in chancery, to recover a

legacy or distributive share due to the wife; she must be made a party with him, and then the court will require the husband to make a suitable provision for her out of the property.

Money in the hands of a wife at her husband's decease, either earned by her before marriage, or given to her by her husband, passes to his administrator.

VI. By *Testament and Administration.* Under this head, will be considered the nature and effects of a *will of personal property,* and the rights and duties of *executors and administrators.*

1. *Who may make a will.*

Every person may make a will, unless there be some special reason to the contrary. A male infant of fourteen years of age, and a female of twelve,[1] are in general legally competent thus to dispose of their personal estate; though the question of actual discretion and ability is still open, to be judged of by the nature of the disposition and other circumstances, and the will to be rejected or approved accordingly. A married woman, with the assent of her husband, may dispose of money or other chattels by will.[2] All persons laboring under any mental disability are incompetent to make a will; as idiots, madmen, or persons besotted with drunkenness, or bereft of their faculties by old age. But if one who has been placed under guardianship, as *non compos mentis,* be restored to his reason; he is capable of making a will, though the letters of guardianship remain unrevoked. If a testator, at the time of dictating his will, have sufficient discretion for that pur-

---

1 In New York, the ages are eighteen and sixteen.

2 In New York, otherwise.

pose, and be able to recollect, at the time of executing it, the particulars he has dictated, it will be evidence of a sound and disposing mind and memory. But a will is invalid, unless it appear that the testator knew it, at the time of execution, to be his will. A will is also invalid, if not made freely, but by undue influence, compulsion, or duress. The subscribing witnesses of a will may testify to *their opinion* of the testator's mind at the time of executing it; but other witnesses, only to his appearance, and to particular facts, from which the state of his mind may be inferred. When a will is questioned on the ground of insanity, the burden of proof in the first instance is on those who present it for approval; after they have proved sanity by the subscribing witnesses, the burden will be shifted upon the other party to prove insanity; and if any doubt remains, the law will presume sanity. The committing of suicide by the testator is not conclusive evidence of insanity.

2. *What is a will.*

A testament is defined, as "the legal declaration of a man's intentions, which he wills to be performed after his death;" or "a disposition of real and personal property, to take effect after the death of the testator." Testaments may be *verbal* or *nuncupative,* and *written.* The former are now become very unusual, and, being liable to great impositions, have been by special statutes laid under many restrictions, relating to the manner, place, occasion, and proof of making them, which it is needless to enumerate.[1] A testament of chattels, written in the testator's own

---

1 In New York, this kind of will can be made only by soldiers in service, or mariners at sea.

hand, or in another man's hand, if by his direction, though it has neither his name nor seal to it, nor witnesses present at its publication, is in general good. But in New York witnesses are required. And in Massachusetts, a will which purports to dispose of both real and personal property, and is not so executed and attested as to pass the former, will be invalid also as to the latter; because it is reasonable to suppose, that in the testator's mind every part of the will was connected with every other part, and that he would not have altered one provision without altering the whole. If, however, the will be sufficient *in form* to pass real estate, but that part of the disposition be void, by reason of *some incompetency* in the testator; the will may still be allowed as a testament of personal property. So, it will be good to that extent, though imperfectly executed, if the whole be given to one person; the reason, that one bequest is a condition of the others, not in such case applying.

A *codicil* is a supplement to a will, made for the purpose of altering, explaining, or enlarging it; and in law regarded as annexed to, and making part of, the will.

3. *Revocation of wills.* — A will is always *revocable* during the life of the testator. This results from the nature of the instrument, it being of no effect till after the testator's death. Hence, though a will be made irrevocable in the strongest words, it may still be revoked. The revocation, to prevent the admission of loose and uncertain testimony, is required to be made by another instrument in writing; or else by burning, cancelling, or tearing. The mere act of cancelling, however, amounts to nothing, unless it be

done "animo revocandi," with the intent to revoke. It is *primâ facie* evidence of revocation; but may be rebutted by contrary proof. An obliteration of part of a will is a revocation only of that part.

There may be an *implied* revocation, arising from a change in the circumstances of the testator. Thus *marriage* and the *birth of a child*, subsequent to the execution of the will, are a revocation in law, provided the wife and child were wholly unprovided for. But one of these events, without the other, is not in general, sufficient. The will of *a woman* is revoked by her *subsequent marriage*; and, it seems, is not revived by the death of her husband. A second will is a revocation of a former one, provided it contain express words of revocation, or make a different and incompatible disposition of the property. If the first will be not actually cancelled or destroyed, or expressly revoked, on making a second, and the second be afterwards cancelled, the first is thereby revived. It is otherwise in New York, unless such is the avowed intention.

An instrument, intended for a will, but inoperative as such on account of some defect, although it contain an express clause of revocation, is ineffectual for that purpose; nor can any will be used for a revocation, without *probate.* But a second will, inoperative from some extrinsic cause, as for instance the incapacity of a devisee to take the devise, is still good as a revocation.

4. *Construction of wills.*—In *the construction* of wills, it is the general rule, that the *intention of the testator*, where it can be satisfactorily discovered, being collected from the whole will and not from detached passages, shall be carried into ef-

fect, if it can be done consistently with the rules of law. If any word or expression in a will have no intelligible meaning, or be absurd, or repugnant to the clear intention of the testator, as manifested in other parts of the will; it may be rejected as superfluous, and shall not defeat a legacy or bequest. A will must be construed by itself, and not by the aid of other evidence.[1] Thus the verbal declaration of the testator cannot be used to control the import of the will. Extrinsic evidence however is admissible, where there is an ambiguity as to the person who shall take, — as where there are two of one name; or as to the subject matter of the bequest; or (if the construction be doubtful) in relation to facts which were known to the testator, and may reasonably be presumed to have influenced him in the disposition of his property. Where a testator bequeathed to his wife *all rents in arrear* on certain real estate belonging to her; memoranda of the testator were admitted to show, that by the terms "rents in arrear" he meant to include, not merely rents unpaid by the tenants, but all the money he had ever received for rent, or otherwise, belonging to his wife, with interest.

5. *Probate of wills.* — The laws of probably all the States require that a will should be *approved* and *allowed*, by a court specially instituted for this purpose, before it can be held effectual for any use whatever. Probate cannot be dispensed with, even where it can be shown that the will has been fraudulently destroyed. The probate of a will, by a court of competent jurisdiction, is conclusive upon all persons who have notice; and its validity can never afterwards be dis-

---

[1] See *Parol Evidence.*

puted.[1] Whoever has a right to offer a will in evidence, or to make title under it, may insist on having it proved; and the court, upon application, will summon any person having the custody of it, to exhibit it for probate. A statute of Massachusetts gives full effect to a will approved in another State, on the filing of a copy in our Probate Court. Other States have a similar provision. In Kentucky, the will is admissible, though not conclusive, evidence. In Tennessee, it is not received in relation to lands.

The subject of Executors and Administrators will be considered in the next chapter.

CHAPTER V.

EXECUTORS AND ADMINISTRATORS.

An *executor* is he to whom another man commits by will the *execution* of that will. All persons may be executors, that are capable of making wills, and many others besides, as *feme-coverts* and infants. But, in general, no infant can act as such till the age of seventeen years, till which time administration must be granted to some other, "durante minore ætate," during minority.[2] If the will names no executors, or incapable persons, or if those named re-

---

1 See *Judgment* "*in rem.*"

2 In New York, additional disabilities exist. And executors cannot act, without letters testamentary from the *surrogate*, who, on application of creditors, may require bonds, or, if necessary, remove them from office. In case of any difficulty with regard to the administration, a temporary *collector* is appointed.

fuse to act, the court will grant administration "with the will annexed" to some suitable person.

An *administrator*, is one appointed by the Probate Court, or other similar tribunal, to administer the estate of *an intestate*, that is, of a deceased person who has left no will. The *widow*, or the *next of kin*, of an intestate, in Massachusetts and probably all the other States, is entitled to be administrator, or take out *letters of administration*, upon his estate. In default of these, *a creditor* has the right of administering, for the purpose of obtaining payment of his own debt. In New York, *public administrators* take charge of the property, in certain cases, till regular administration can be taken out.

Administration is required to be granted within a certain period after the intestate's death, — in Massachusetts twenty years; — and if granted later than that, is wholly void. Letters of administration are revocable; and they may be granted upon condition, or for a limited time, or a special purpose. Thus when an executor dies, not having completed his trust, some person is appointed administrator "de bonis non"; that is, of the goods not administered by the executor.

The rights and duties of executors and administrators are very much the same. They are substantially as follows: to prove the will, if there is one, and give bond for the due performance of their trust, called a *Probate bond*; make an inventory of the estate of the deceased; collect all the goods and chattels so inventoried; pay the debts and legacies; and deliver over the residue, if any, to the *residuary legatee* or *next of kin*.

1. *Collecting of goods.* — For the purpose of collect-

ing the goods and chattels inventoried, an executor or administrator has very large powers and interests conferred on him by law; being the representative of the deceased, and having the same property in his goods as the principal had when living, and the same remedies to recover them. Whatever is so recovered, that is of a salable nature, and may be converted into ready money, is called *assets* in his hands, that is, *sufficient* or *enough* (from the French "assez") to make him chargeable to a creditor or legatee, so far as it extends.[1] At common law, *lands* were not *assets*; but, by the statute law of most of the States, the real property of a deceased person is made liable to the payment of debts, if the personal estate is insufficient, or before the personal estate, if the will so direct. A license of Court however is usually required, before the executor can intermeddle with the real estate, unless by the will he be authorized to sell it.

A creditor, who recovers judgment against the executor, may in general take the real estate of the deceased to satisfy his execution, even though it be devised. In such case, the devisee may recover damages from the executor for not paying the debt, provided the personal effects were sufficient for that purpose. Or he may sue other devisees to obtain a contribution of their share. In New York, lands cannot be thus taken on execution. But in some cases, when the assets prove insufficient, an action

---

1 In New York, Massachusetts, and other States, the first appropriation is of certain necessary articles for the widow and minor children. These are not "assets" for payment of debts. This allowance, however, cannot exceed the means of an immediate and temporary support, nor will an administrator be allowed in his account any expenditure for such purpose.

may be brought against an heir, devisee, legatee, or next of kin, to recover the amount which has been paid him.

If a foreigner or a citizen of any other of the United States die, leaving debts and effects in Massachusetts, these can never be collected by an administrator, appointed in the place of his domicil; but administration must be granted for that purpose to some person here, which will be considered as merely *ancillary* to the principal administration. If the estate is insolvent, the creditor here cannot be paid in full, though the assets here exceed his debt.

If an administrator release a debt due the deceased, he is liable for the amount. If he compound a debt due from the deceased for less than is due, the profit shall go not to him but to the estate. The property of the goods of a deceased person will be considered as vested absolutely in the administrator, after an administration to the full amount and value.

2. *Payment of debts.*— In the appropriation of the assets to the several debts due from the deceased, different rules prevail in different States. In nearly all, *expenses of last sickness*, and *funeral* and *probate charges*, have the first claim; generally *debts due to the State* are next preferred; and then all other debts are placed on an equality, and paid ratably in case of a deficiency of assets.[1]

Where such deficiency is supposed to exist, the administrator is allowed time to ascertain the fact, by comparing the debts with the property. If he

---

[1] In New York, the only specified classes of debts, are 1. Those preferred by United States laws; 2. Taxes; 3. Judgments and decrees.

then believe the estate to be insolvent, he will represent the facts to the Probate Court, who may thereupon award a *commission of insolvency* for the purpose of examining the claims, and equally apportioning the effects among them. Such proceeding will be a protection to the administrator against any compulsory process by a creditor for the recovery of his entire debt. And if, believing the estate to be solvent, he pay debts in full, and afterwards new claims come in and render it insolvent, and he proceed accordingly; he may have an action to recover back the excess of what he has paid over the creditors' equal proportion.[1]

It is the duty of an executor or administrator to object to claims against the estate, which cannot be recovered by law.

An administrator has no power of charging the effects in his hands to be administered, by any contract originating with himself; but his contracts in the course of his administration, or for the debts of the deceased, render him liable personally, though made expressly in his official capacity. For instance, he is personally liable upon the covenants in a deed of conveyance, though he execute it as administrator.[2] But a note by an administrator, as such, "for value received by the intestate and his heirs," is void for want of consideration.

3. *Legacies.* — After payment of debts, *legacies* are

---

1 Similar proceedings to the above prevail in New York and other States. In New York, a legatee may be required to give bond for refunding what he has received, if necessary to pay creditors or other legatees.

2 Held otherwise in the United States Court, where one covenants "as administrator and not otherwise."

to be paid, so far as the assets will extend. A *legacy* is a bequest or gift of goods and chattels by testament; and is either *general*, of so much money; or *specific*, of some certain thing. This bequest transfers an imperfect or *inchoate* property to the legatee; but the legacy is not perfect without the consent of the executor. If, however, a specific legacy be in the possession of the legatee at the death of the testator, the executor's acquiescence will be sufficient, without any formal consent, provided the estate be solvent; and consent of the executor will be presumptive evidence of *assets*. At common law, no action lies to recover a legacy; but, in Massachusetts and other States, this defect has been supplied by special statute.[1] In case of a deficiency of assets, all *general* legacies must abate proportionably, in order to pay the debts; but a *specific* legacy will not, until the former are exhausted. Lands devised cannot be sold to pay specific legacies. If the legacies have been paid, the legatees shall refund a ratable part, in case debts come in more than sufficient to exhaust the *assets*.

If the legatee dies before the testator, the legacy becomes lost or *lapsed*. So if the legacy be contingent;—as *when* one attains, or *if* he attains, the age of twenty-one, and he dies before that time;—it is a *lapsed* legacy. Otherwise, if it is merely *to be paid* at a future time. If a specific legacy be alienated by the testator before his death, the law presumes an intention to revoke or *adeem* it, and (unless circumstances repel the presumption) the legatee shall have no compensation from the estate,

[1] In several States, the suit is *in Chancery*.

or equivalent sum of money. Thus, if the testator bequeath a certain amount of stock in a particular bank, being the owner at the time of that precise amount; a sale before his death will make *an ademption* of the legacy. A legacy does not in general carry *interest*, but from the time when it is payable; unless the legatee is *a minor*, whom the testator is under a moral obligation to support, and for whom no support is provided until the legacy is payable. A legacy will not be considered as *a satisfaction of a debt*, due from the testator to the legatee, unless such evidently appear to be the testator's intention. Thus it will not, if it be less than the debt, specific in its nature, or if the testator make provision, and leave sufficient property, for payment of debts as well as legacies. A legacy cannot be charged upon real estate, unless the will be duly executed to pass lands. When so executed, the legacy may be recovered by an action against purchasers of the estate, if the legatee choose to adopt that remedy. The usual remedy is upon *the probate bond*, by an action brought in the name of the judge.

A residuary legatee, is one to whom the will bequeaths what shall remain, after payment of other legacies.

4. *Distribution.*—After payment of debts and legacies, the surplus property shall be distributed by the executor or administrator, to *the next of kin.*[1] This is the general rule; but the statute laws of the several States have given rise to various deviations from it. These apply chiefly however to the more re-

---

[1] For the mode of calculating the degrees of kindred, see page 15.

mote relations. Probably, in all the States, children, or, if dead, their representatives, take in the first instance, and representation continues in the descending line "ad infinitum." In general, the father claims next, and then the mother and brothers and sisters in equal shares. This however is by no means a universal rule. In some of the States, there is a preference given to the whole blood over the half blood. In New York, the property of *a child* goes to that parent, or the relations of that parent, from whom it came. The right of *representation*, that is, the right of lineal descendants to take what the ancestor would have taken, does not usually extend beyond the second degree of relationship, or beyond the children of brothers and sisters. Thus, if there are children of a brother of the intestate, and one is dead, and has left children, these last cannot take either as next of kin or by representation. The surviving children of the brother take the whole, as next of kin. When several claimants are all in the same degree of kindred, they take, as next of kin, each an equal share, or *per capita*; but when one or more of them are more remote than others, they take by representation, *per stirpes*, each class of children, whether more or fewer in number, the same which their own parent would have taken.[1] *Affinity* furnishes no title to a distributive share. Thus the husband of a deceased sister cannot take. Neither can an illegitimate child. *The wife* can never come under the denomination *next of kin*;—but, in general, a certain share of the property is allotted to her by statute. In Massachusetts, where there are two collateral relations of

1 In North and South Carolina, they always take in this mode.

the same degree, that one is preferred, who claims through an ancestor the more nearly related to the deceased. Thus a nephew is preferred to an uncle; the former claiming through the father of the deceased, the latter through the grandfather.

Distribution is always made conformably to the law of the State to which the deceased at his death was subject.

Posthumous children inherit, in all cases, like others.

Where a child has received from his parent, while living, property to any amount, termed *an advancement*; it is usually held, wholly or "pro tanto," a satisfaction of his distributive share. In Massachusetts, certain written evidence is required of the parent's intention to that effect. But an acknowledgment of full satisfaction, and a release of all claim, by the child, will have the same operation. An advancement made to a child, who dies before the parent, will be allowed against the grandchildren. A debt due from a child is not an advancement, though charged in the form of a book debt, unless the parent by his will so direct.

5. *General liabilities of an executor, &c.* — The general rule of the common law is, that an executor or administrator *can be sued* only for the *debts*, and not for the *torts* or wrongs, of the deceased. In many of the States, however, he is now liable, or in the usual phrase *an action survives*, for injuries *to real or personal property*, but not for mere *personal wrongs*, such as assault or libel. Actions against executors &c. are limited by statute to a certain period, — usually much shorter than that of ordinary cases, — from the death of the deceased. The limitation does not apply to a claim for property held *in trust*, but only to debts.

Executors and administrators are not subject to arrest or commitment, or to executions against their own estate, except in actions brought for wasting the property of which they have charge, by some party interested. And in New York, after judgment against them, execution does not issue, till application to the *surrogate* or Probate Court. In some cases, they are by statute made personally liable; particularly for *costs of suit.*

Executors are not liable to pay *interest,* unless they have been guilty of negligence, or used the funds in their hands.

Any person, who wrongfully intermeddles with the effects of a deceased person, thereby becomes *an executor de son tort,* or in his own wrong, — liable to creditors, at their election, to the extent of the property which he takes. In New York, this kind of executorship has been expressly abolished. In Georgia, lawful executors and administrators, neglecting their duty, become responsible as executors "de son tort."

CHAPTER VI.

TITLE TO PERSONAL PROPERTY BY TRANSFER BY ACT OF PARTY.

A *GIFT* of personal property is the act whereby one man renounces, and another immediately acquires, without price or *consideration,* all title and interest therein. *Delivery* is essential to a gift. A mere intention or promise to give, is not a gift, and is in law wholly invalid. The delivery must be according to the nature of the thing. If not susceptible of actual delivery, there must be some act equivalent to it. The donor must part not only with the possession, but with the dominion, of the property. If the thing given be a *chose in action,* the law requires an assignment or some equivalent instrument, and the transfer must be actually executed. In Virginia, it seems, a verbal gift of *a slave* is void. Money, paid to one person for the benefit of another, is countermandable, while it remains in the hands of the former, but not afterwards. When the gift is perfect, it is then irrevocable, unless it be prejudicial to the creditors of the donor,[1] or he was under a legal incapacity, or was circumvented by fraud.

A gift "causâ mortis" is one made by a person *in his last sickness,* and in contemplation and expectation of death. Such a gift is revocable and conditional, becoming void if the donor recover. It is invalid without delivery; but the delivery may be made to one person for the benefit of another. Whether a mere security for money can pass in this way, unless payable to bearer, has been made a serious question.

CHAPTER VII.

CONTRACTS.

A CONTRACT is "an agreement, upon sufficient consideration, to do or not to do a particular thing." This title, it will be at once perceived, is one of the

---

1 B. 4, ch. 8, (2.)

most copious and comprehensive known in the law; and of course nothing more will be here attempted, than a general outline of the subject to which it applies.

I. *Nature and effect of contracts.* — A contract is an *agreement*; which word implies, that there must be at least two parties to constitute it, namely, one to make, and the other to receive, the promise.

A contract is either *under seal,* or *not under seal*; the former called *a specialty,* the latter, whether written or verbal, an *agreement by parol,* or *simple contract.*

Of the former class, the most usual form is *a bond. A bond* is an instrument, whereby one man obliges himself to pay a certain sum to another, at a day appointed. If this be all, the bond is called a *single* one; but there is generally *a condition* added, that if the obligor does some particular act, the obligation shall be void. In this case, the obligatory part of the instrument is called *the penalty,* which is usually twice the amount of the debt due. In case the condition is not strictly performed, the bond becomes at law *forfeited*; but by a special statute in England, which has probably been either adopted or copied in every State of the Union, the obligor shall be discharged on payment of the amount really due under the condition. Payment made before an action is brought, though not at the day appointed, will save the condition of the bond. If no interest be reserved, such payment of the principal sum will discharge the bond; but not without interest, if that be agreed for. Interest beyond the penalty may be recovered at law as *damages.* If the condition of a bond be *impossible* at the time of making it; or to do a thing *contrary to some rule of law, that is merely positive*, as, for instance, an embargo law; or if it be *uncertain* or *insensible*; the condition alone is void, and the bond shall stand single and unconditional. If it be to do a thing that is "malum in se," morally wrong, the obligation itself is void. So if founded upon *an immoral consideration.* So if the condition become impossible by *act of God*, or *the law*, or *the obligee himself.*

The obligatory clause of a bond is sometimes construed as an agreement for *liquidated damages*; that is, as a definite price or valuation fixed by the parties upon a breach of the condition. In such case, the amount specified shall be recovered in full, without inquiry into the actual damages. Whether this construction shall be given in any particular case, is to be determined by the instrument itself, and by extraneous circumstances connected with the contract. In a case of liquidated damages, a Court of Chancery will not interfere for relief.

Debts by specialty are created also by *deeds*, relating to the conveyance of real estate, which will be more properly considered in a future part of this work.

Simple contracts are of various kinds, the most important of which will be hereafter treated in distinct chapters.

A contract conveys an interest, either *in possession* or *in action.* If, for instance, one person sells and delivers goods to another, for a price paid, the agreement is *executed*; but if he agree to sell and deliver at a future time, it is *executory*, and rests *in action* merely. It is to bargains of the latter description that the term "contract" is for the most part applied. In Chancery, executory contracts sometimes have the effect of actual conveyances; upon the maxim that "what is agreed to be done, shall be considered as done." For instance, if a man bargain for real estate, and die before a conveyance, the money which he was to pay for it will sometimes be treated as land, in the disposition of his property among heirs and next of kin.[1]

Contracts are moreover either *express* or *implied.* An *express contract* is one whose terms are openly uttered at the time of the making, — as, to deliver certain goods for a certain price. An *implied contract* is one which reason and conscience dictate, and the law therefore presumes that every man undertakes to perform. As, for instance, if I employ one to work for me, I tacitly agree to pay him what he deserves to have for it. Where work is done by one for another's benefit, especially if under his eye, an implied contract arises to pay for it; unless it can be shown that there was an express contract, or that the work was done on the credit of a third person. But the law will never imply a promise against a party's express declaration at the time.

A promise, by simple contract, to do a certain act, without expressing to whom the promise is made; or a promise, given to one, to do some act for the benefit of another, is substantially made to the person beneficially interested, and he may sue upon it. But if a contract be under seal, no one can legally enforce it, who is not a party to the instrument. For instance, if A promise B to pay C a certain sum; C may sue for it, unless the promise was made by a

---

1 Upon a similar principle, the statutes of several States empower executors, &c. to convey lands which the deceased had *contracted to convey*, without having actually granted.

sealed instrument. In the latter case, B alone can maintain an action.

II. *Validity of contracts.*

All contracts, fairly made, by persons of suitable capacity, upon a valuable consideration, which infringe no law, and are not repugnant to the general policy of the laws or to good morals, — are valid, and may be enforced by legal process. From this general principle, it may be seen summarily, what circumstances have the effect of rendering a contract *void.* These may be more particularly considered under distinct divisions.

1. *Incapacity* or *disability* of the contracting party — as in the case of infants, *femes-covert,* &c. — avoids a contract. It was the doctrine of the old common law, that a man could not avoid his contract, upon the ground of *insanity* or want of reason ; or, in legal phraseology, *stultify himself.* It is now held otherwise. But no degree of physical or mental imbecility, which does not deprive one of legal competency to act, will *of itself* avoid his contract. Thus the contract of a deaf and dumb person may be valid.

2. Any *deceit* or *duress,* practised upon a party to the contract, renders it void. In general, however, deception must amount to actual fraud or misrepresentation, to have this effect; mere *concealment* is not sufficient.[1] A contract is also avoided by *deceit upon third persons,* operating as a public mischief.

---

[1] To this rule the contract of *insurance* is an exception. (See B. 4, ch. 12, (3, 3.) Also any contract made by *an agent or trustee,* for his own benefit, in relation to the property entrusted to him. In such case, *mere concealment* will be *fraud,* and avoid the bargain. But if the matter is of long standing and complicated nature, the trustee will only be bound to put the party upon inquiry, and communicate such facts as are within his recollection.[2]

[2] See B. 5, ch. 14.

Upon this ground, a bargain to procure marriage between two persons, called "a marriage brokage bond"; a bargain to procure any *public office*; and a secret contract by *an heir*, to convey on the death of his ancestor a certain part of what he shall inherit; are held to be void. The latter contract will be good, if made fairly, and *with the ancestor's consent.*

3. An *unconscionable* contract may be held invalid in part, and only reasonable damages allowed for breach of it. This exception, however, can in general be taken, only where there is a stipulation in the nature of *a penalty*, or a contract of *letting and hiring*, which, though not technically usurious, is of a *usurious* tendency. But a contract can never be avoided as *unconscionable*, merely because it is disadvantageous, unless there have been an attempt to mislead, or the consideration be so grossly inadequate as to prove fraud and imposition. Mere *inadequacy of price* will not vacate a contract, even in Chancery; but this tribunal will enforce performance, unless the hardship and absurdity of the case be such, as to afford judicial proof, that the party did not mean what is expressed, or was overcome by undue means. Of this description, was a contract to pay for a horse a barley-corn for every nail in his shoes and double every nail, which came to five hundred quarters of barley.

A contract by *seamen*, to pay for medicines during the voyage, has been held *unconscionable* and void.

4. A contract must be founded on sufficient *consideration.* There must be something given in exchange,—a "quid pro quo"; something that is mutual or reciprocal, and operating as the price or motive of the contract; otherwise it is "nudum pactum," and void.

A consideration is either *good* or *valuable.* The former is that of *blood* or *natural affection* between near relations. This however is not sufficient to support a *parol executory contract.*

A *valuable* consideration is either a *benefit to the party promising*, or *some trouble or prejudice to the party receiving the promise.* A *mutual* promise amounts to a valuable consideration; that is, one part is a consideration for the other. If the promise, however, on one side, is *void* from some personal incapacity, the promise on the other is not binding, for want of consideration, — as in case of a contract with a *feme-covert*; but if one promise be only *voidable* at the election of the promisor, like that of an *infant*, it is consideration enough, and the other party is bound.[1]

The mutual promise of a man and woman to *marry* each other is valid, and either may sustain an action against the other for a breach of it. In such action, no express promise need be proved, but it may be inferred from the circumstances which usually accompany a matrimonial engagement. If *seduction* have been practised under color of the promise, it will aggravate the damages. The bad character of a party will be sufficient ground for breaking the engagement.

If the consideration of a promise be wholly *past and executed* before the promise is made, it is not sufficient, unless it arose at the request of the promisor express or implied. For instance, a promise by one who has *received a gift*, after receiving to pay for it, is void.

Any degree of reciprocity, however slight, will

---

[1] See B. 5, ch. 18, (6.)

amount to a consideration; because the law will not judge for a party as to the value of the inducement upon which he acts. A consideration proceeding from one person will support a promise made to another. A *moral obligation* is sufficient to support an express promise, where there has been an antecedent valuable consideration; as, for example, a promise to pay a just debt, barred by the Statute of Limitations, or a discharge under the bankrupt law; or, by a widow, to pay a debt contracted during her marriage. The assumption of a supposed, but unreal, danger or liability, is not sufficient consideration for a promise. Upon this ground, a *premium* of *insurance* may be recovered back, where the risk never attached.[1]

The consideration of a written contract need not be expressed in the contract itself.

These principles equally apply, whether the contract be verbal or in writing, unless the written agreement be *under seal.* A *promissory note,* for instance, in the hands of the original holder, if made without consideration, is void. But *specialties* or *sealed instruments,* from their solemnity, *imply a consideration,* and can never be impeached for the want of it.[2]

5. A contract is void, if it be *repugnant to law, sound policy, or good morals.* "Ex turpi contractu actio non oritur;" no person can stipulate for iniquity. For instance, a contract for the sale of blasphemous or obscene books is void. This objection may be made even by a guilty party himself, if the other party be also in fault, "in pari delicto."

---

1 See *Return of Premium.*

2 In New York, specialties are placed on the same footing in this respect with parol contracts.

The general rule is, where both sides are in fault; "Potior est conditio defendentis," the condition of the defendant is the best; and no action can be sustained. Yet, in some instances, where the law regards one as the less guilty, and oppressed by the other, as in case of usury, money wrongfully paid may be recovered back.

Illegality or turpitude, unlike the want of consideration, avoids all agreements, whether sealed or parol. If a promise be made on two considerations, one of which is fraudulent, unlawful, or immoral, and the other good; the promise is void.

Where the consideration of a contract, or the act undertaken to be performed, though not *morally wrong*, is in violation of a statute or any principle of the common law; the contract is void. Thus an obligation given for the settlement or *compounding* of a crime. So a contract, founded on the sale of a *dormant title* to lands by a person not seized to one who knows of the adverse title, cannot be enforced; the transaction amounting to a punishable offence.[1] But where an act of incorporation prohibits the company from taking notes from its members for their shares; the notes, if taken, are still valid, and the only consequence is a liability to forfeit the charter. A contract, made in violation of an existing statute, is not rendered valid by a subsequent repeal of the statute.

Contracts *in restraint of trade* and business, are in general void, as *against the policy of the law.* But a contract, for valuable consideration, not to engage in *a particular trade*, limited in its nature, or confined to a certain place, is valid; as it may be beneficial to the public as well as the parties. Thus an agree-

---

[1] See *Maintenance.*

ment, not to be interested in any voyage to the North West Coast for a certain number of years; or not to run a stage on a particular road; or with a tradesman, to give him all the promisor's custom, is good.

In Massachusetts and some other States, all *bets* or *wagers* are held void, as being *against public policy*. In New York, a wager is not *in itself* void, but will be held so, if, as is usually the case, it is of a nature to draw into discussion the character or feelings of third persons, or if the subject matter is of injurious tendency. In England, a wager upon a battle between two dogs was recently held void. So a wager upon the *sex* of a particular person.

6. A contract may be void, *for want of some formality* which the law requires. Thus there are certain agreements, which must be put *in writing*, and, if merely verbal, are held invalid. This is by virtue of a statute called the *Statute of Frauds*, which, originally enacted in England, has been substantially copied in nearly every State of the Union. It provides, in general, that no action shall be brought against *an executor or administrator*, to charge him personally upon his promise; upon a promise to answer *for the debt or default of another;* upon an agreement made *in consideration of marriage*, or *not to be performed within one year;* for *the sale of goods* of the value of *ten pounds*, or of *any interest in lands;* — unless such agreements be written and signed, or, in the sale of goods, some positive act be done to bind the bargain. Upon the construction of this statute, many questions have been raised, and various points decided. Its general provisions, however, are sufficiently intelligible without further explanation. In Chancery, after part-performance of a parol agreement, the whole will be enforced.

In general, the law requires no technical forms for the validity of a contract.[1]

III. *Performance and discharge of contracts.*

Contracts, valid at the time of making them, may become extinguished, invalid, or liable to be avoided, by some subsequent event.

1. If one contract to do an act, which was possible and legal at that time, but which, before breach, becomes *impossible by the act of God, or inevitable accident*, or *illegal* by an ordinance of the State; the obligation is discharged. But the promisor, in such case, must restore whatever consideration he has received, or render an equivalent in money. The *impossibility*, which discharges a contract, must be *absolute and unqualified;* as, for instance, the death of a person whose agency is necessary to its fulfilment. Any merely *temporary disability* does not have this effect. Thus, one who has contracted to sell teas of the first quality, is not excused from his bargain, by showing that there are none such in the market.

2. Where there are *mutual promises*, a neglect or refusal of one party to perform his part of the agreement, may operate to discharge the liability of the other. Whether mutual promises are *dependent or independent*, — that is, whether one is to be regarded as a *condition of the other*, or not; is to be determined, not by technical rules, but by the true intent of the parties, as apparent in the instrument. Where, however, the act in question is to be done, or may be done, *before the act of the other party;* or where the latter is only *part of the consideration* for the for-

---

[1] See *Forms of Deeds.*

mer, some benefit having been already received by the promisor; — he is independently liable, whether the other side of the bargain be fulfilled or not; and must resort to his action, to enforce performance by the other party. If, on the other hand, the acts are to be done *at the same time*; or *money is to be paid* as a consideration; or *lands are to be exchanged,* — the promises are *dependent and conditional.* If performance of any act or acts by one party is the condition of the other's liability, there must be an *entire performance,* before the latter can be called upon for any thing. Thus, if one engage as a servant for a year, and leave after six months, he shall recover nothing. But where the work agreed for has been done, though not *in the precise manner* stipulated, and is of some value to the other party; — a reasonable compensation may be recovered.

3. If a person contract to do a thing *at a certain time and place,* and if he be ready then and there to do it, and the other party fail to be present; the contract is terminated.[1]

4. A contract may be *extinguished,* by *payment.* If a person owes two debts to the same creditor, and pays a sum insufficient to satisfy both; the debtor may apply it to whichever of them he shall choose. If he makes no application, the creditor may do it. And if neither of them expresses an election, the law will appropriate the payment in such way as will best effect the ends of justice, and the implied intention of the parties. Thus the agreement of the sum paid with one of the debts, and not with the other; the circumstance that one is due

---

[1] See *Tender.*

from the debtor personally, and the other as executor; the legality of one, and illegality of the other, will determine the appropriation. If two debts be joined in one suit, and the execution recovered in such suit be satisfied only in part; a surety for one of the debts may insist upon a proportional application of the money to the debt for which he is liable.

After a certain time, the law *presumes payment* of a debt. Twenty years is the period established by the common law, in regard to *sealed instruments*; and in New York, this rule has also been applied to *judgments*. But in most of the States, a shorter time has been fixed for specialty debts, more especially for *official liabilities*.

For contracts *not under seal*, the usual limitation is six years; with many abbreviations of this period, however, in the several States, particularly with regard to *book-accounts*, which, in some of them, cannot be offered in evidence after the expiration of six months from the making of the charge.

The *statute of limitations* does not render a contract *void*, but only *voidable*, at the party's election. If he does not choose to avail himself of this defence, judgment will be rendered against him as for a recent debt.

The statute does not apply, where there are *accounts on both sides*, and any item is within six years; nor to the mutual *accounts of merchants*, in any case. But a *settlement* or *striking of a balance* between them, will bring the account within the statute, from that time. In case of concealment and fraud, the statute runs from the discovery of the fraud. The six years are reckoned to the commencement of suit, and not to the time of trial.

The *acknowledgment* of a debt within six years prevents the operation of the statute of limitations. To have this effect, however, it must, in general, be an admission of *existing liability*, and not merely of an *original contract*. In Massachusetts, by a recent statute, the acknowledgment must be in writing. A common mode of *implied* acknowledgment is an indorsement of interest or partial payments of the principal, by the maker or in his presence, upon the instrument.

Certain disabilities to sue, such as coverture, infancy, imprisonment, insanity, or long absence abroad, prevent the application of the statute.

The statute does not, in general, apply to *attested* instruments.

A *parol contract* may be *paid*, by giving *an instrument under seal*, or *a negotiable security*, for the same debt, whether executed by all or one of the former parties.[1] A new simple contract, *not negotiable*, will not have this effect. And no extinguishment will take place, if the new obligation be void, as where it is *usurious*; or given, without authority, by one person in another's name; or merely as additional *collateral security*.

5. A contract may be expressly *discharged* or *released*. But after breach of a contract, that is, after it is overdue, a discharge, to be valid, must either be made by a sealed instrument, or for valuable consideration. An agreement *not to sue* has the effect of a discharge. But an agreement not to sue *for a limited time* is no defence against a suit brought within

---

[1] See *Mortgage*, 5.

that time. The injured party must resort to his action for damages.

6. A contract, even written and sealed, may be *waived* by a new verbal agreement. For instance, if one contract under seal to build a house, and after part fulfilment, being dissatisfied with the price, refuse to go on, and the other party as an inducement verbally agree to pay him for his work and materials, and that he shall not suffer; the latter bargain is valid, and puts an end to the former.

7. A contract may be put an end to by *accord and satisfaction*; that is, by the offer and acceptance of something *different* from the agreement. A smaller sum cannot be a satisfaction of a larger, unless delivered at an earlier day, or another place, than the contract specifies. A *specific article* may always be a legal satisfaction, if accepted, of a money debt, though of much inferior value; for instance, a horse worth fifty dollars, of an obligation for a hundred dollars. A debtor's assignment of all his effects to a trustee, to raise a fund for paying a dividend to his creditors, is a satisfaction. And where several creditors, by mutual understanding, agree to give time to, or accept a composition from, the debtor, the agreement is binding on each.

8. Any *material alteration* of a written contract, made either by the holder or a stranger, will render it void. But not where the promisor consents to the alteration either expressly or impliedly, — as where blanks are left to be filled up; nor where a word is added which the law would supply, — as, for instance, the word "year" in the date of a note. The addition of *a seal* avoids the contract. *An erasure* is presumed to have been made after the signing. If there are several signers, and a part only

consent to an alteration; as to them it will not avoid the instrument.

IV. *Construction of contracts.* In the construction of all contracts, the situation of the parties, the subject matter of their transactions, and the whole language of their instruments, are to be taken into consideration, to determine the meaning of any particular sentence or provision. And when different instruments are executed at the same time, but are all parts of one transaction, the law will suppose such a priority in the execution of them, as shall best effect the intention of the parties.

Where a contract is made, and to be performed, *in some foreign place*, it shall be construed by the law of that place, — *lex loci contractûs*; and, if valid there, shall be enforced here, though contrary to our laws, and "vice versâ." Thus, a contract to pay a greater rate of interest than is legal with us. The rule does not apply however to contracts, the fulfilment of which would exhibit to our citizens an example pernicious and detestable, and which involve moral turpitude; as, for instance, an incestuous marriage, or a contract for the wages of prostitution. And as foreign laws are admitted, not "ex proprio vigore," from their intrinsic force, but only "ex comitate," out of courtesy; our courts will not sanction them if manifestly *unjust*. Thus a law, that the citizens of the foreign state shall be discharged from all debts due to persons out of the state, or authorizing such proceedings, under pretence of a bankrupt act, as would deprive foreign creditors of any share in the debtor's effects, — will be rejected by our courts.

The "lex loci contractûs" decides only the nature, validity, and construction of the contract. The form of action, the course of judicial proceedings, and the time when the action shall be commenced, must be directed exclusively by our laws. And, it seems, the "lex loci" does not govern, where one of our own citizens is a party to the contract.

In all transactions pertaining to *real estate*, the *law of the place where it lies*, — "lex loci rei sitæ," — shall be the governing rule. For instance, a deed of land must be executed with all the forms required by the laws of the country where the land is situated, or it will be everywhere held void. So the Supreme Court of the United States, in questions of real estate, always adopts the local law of a State.

Local or *commercial usage* may sometimes control the terms, or decide the effect, of a contract. For instance, the usage of *a bank*, as to notifying indorsers; of *a factory*, to require of its operatives a certain notice before leaving work; or of *a merchant*, to give a certain credit to his customers. But a usage, to be valid, must be either *actually known* by the party contracting, or else *so general*, as to furnish a presumption of knowledge. And the testimony to prove it must be *uncontradicted*.

CHAPTER VIII.

SALE.

A SALE is a transfer of chattels, for valuable consideration, from one person to another. In this country, no man can legally sell that which does not belong to him. By the common law, the sale of a chattel in open market or *market overt*, though made by a wrongful possessor, would in general pass the title as against the true owner. But with us *markets overt* are unknown; and a purchaser can only succeed to the rights of the seller, or, in common phrase, place himself *in his shoes*. This principle applies even to sales *on civil process*. Thus, if upon an execution against one man, the goods of another be taken and sold, the purchaser gains no title to them. But where property is sold after *capture* or *shipwreck*, under regular judicial proceedings, and according to the law of the place, the title is good against all the world.

To render a sale valid, the thing sold must have *an actual* or *potential existence*. If A sells his horse to B, and it turns out that the horse was dead at the time, though the fact was unknown to the parties, the contract is necessarily void.[1] Whether a sale of that, which does not exist at the time, but is afterwards created, will pass a property in the thing sold as soon as it comes into existence, is an unsettled point.

The validity and effect of a sale may be considered in several points of view.

I. Effect of a sale *between the parties*. — If one man agrees with another for goods at a certain price, he may not carry them away before he hath paid for them; for it is no sale without payment, unless the contrary be expressly agreed. If the seller says that the price is ten dollars, and the buyer says he will give ten dollars, *the bargain is struck*, and nei-

---

[1] That the same principle does not apply to *insurance*, see B. 4, ch. 12, 3, (1.)

ther of them is at liberty to be off, provided immediate possession be tendered by the other side. But if neither any part of the money be paid, nor any part of the goods delivered, nor an offer made, nor the agreement put in writing, it is no sale, and the owner may dispose of the goods as he pleases. When, by any one of these acts, the sale has been completed, the property of the goods is transferred to the buyer, and that of the price to the seller; who may maintain their respective actions therefor, subject to the seller's right of *lien*, or retaining possession, till the money is paid. If the sale is *on credit*, he has no such right; but in that case, though he have despatched the goods to the buyer, *the insolvency* of the latter will authorize him to stop them before they come into his hands. This is called *stoppage in transitu*. It does not avoid, but merely suspends, the contract; and either party may afterwards enforce it, upon offering to fulfil his part of the bargain, — the seller by tendering the goods, or the buyer by an offer of the money.

After sale, if the property perish in the seller's hands, the loss falls upon the buyer, and he must still pay the price.

Where property is of such a nature, and so situated, that personal possession of it is impracticable or inconvenient, — as logs lying in a boom, — it will be sufficient to show it to the purchaser. So, where a third person has a *lien* upon the property, it may be sold subject to the lien, and no delivery is necessary. So a regular bill of sale of a ship at sea, or an indorsement and delivery of a bill of lading of goods, will transfer the property. And, in general, where there can be no manual delivery, there should be a delivery of something as an *indicium* or token. If the goods are already in the buyer's possession, no delivery is necessary. If any thing remains to be done by the seller before delivery, — as if the goods be sold by *number, weight, or measure,* and have not been separated from the mass and identified, — the property has not vested. Delivery of the key of a warehouse in which the goods are kept; payment of warehouse rent by the purchaser; delivery of a sample, if part of the bulk of the property, or of an order upon the warehouseman; and marking the purchaser's name upon the article, have all been held sufficient to pass a property. But where certain *pew-panels* were to be paid for on delivery, merely leaving them at the meeting-house, the contractor not being present, was held not to change the title.

The nature and effect of *delivery* are usually brought in question, in controversies between the purchaser and *some creditor of the seller*, a point hereafter to be considered.

Where goods are sold *on a condition*, to be fulfilled before or at the time of delivery, — as for instance payment of, or security for, the price, — and are actually delivered; — unless the condition be waived, they may be reclaimed for non-performance of it, even from attaching creditors of the purchaser; though not, it seems, from subsequent *bonâ fide* purchasers. The same rule applies, where goods are obtained by *false representations* as to the circumstances of the purchaser. But only a reasonable time will be allowed for reclaiming them.

II. Effect of a sale *as to creditors of the vendor.* — A sale may be good between the parties, and yet *void as to the creditors of the vendor* or seller, as depriving them of the means of satisfying their just demands. A sale, thus void, is usually termed a *fraudulent conveyance.* The fraud may be *actual,* or only *constructive,* and, whether one or the other, will have the same effect upon the contract. The following circumstances constitute, or are evidence of, fraud against creditors.

1. If the seller and purchaser *combine in the purpose to secrete the property* from creditors; that is, if there is *a mutual fraudulent intent*; the sale is void, even though a valuable consideration be paid. And a knowledge, on the part of the purchaser, of the seller's fraudulent intent, may sometimes be *inferred* from the circumstances.

2. If the transfer is made *without consideration,* whether with a fraudulent intent or not, it is void as to creditors.

3. The seller's *retaining possession* of the property, after sale, is *evidence of fraud.* In most of the States, it is *conclusive* evidence; but in a few, merely "primâ facie" evidence, liable to be controlled by other proof that the transaction was an honest one. It is usual and advisable, where possession is to be retained after delivery, for the seller to take back *a lease* from the purchaser. Upon a sale *by civil process* or *execution,* transfer of possession is not so strictly required as in other cases; partly upon the ground of *humanity* to poor debtors, and partly because such a sale is in its nature *public.*

4. Any *secret trust* or reservation for the benefit of the seller, is strong, though not always conclusive,

evidence of fraud, more especially if the written instrument of conveyance is in its terms absolute.[1]

A *subsequent purchaser* from one who has conveyed property fraudulently, stands substantially on the same footing with a creditor, and shall hold it against the first purchaser. Whether the first purchaser himself can pass a good title to another person, not privy to the fraud, seems to be an unsettled point.

A conveyance will not be held fraudulent, if the debtor has other property sufficient to pay his debts.

III. Effect of a sale *as to creditors of the buyer.* — A contract may amount to a sale *as to creditors of the purchaser*, although between the parties it is a mere agreement for a future conveyance. Thus if A, with a fraudulent design to give a false credit to B, execute to him a bond for the conveyance of personal property, upon condition that he shall pay the price at a certain time, and the property be delivered to B, who keeps and uses it as his own; B's creditors may treat the transaction as a sale, and attach the property as his. But without such fraudulent intent, the property will not pass, although the proposed purchaser give his negotiable note for the price, and actually pay a part of such note.

IV. *Assignment for benefit of creditors.* — A common form of sale is, where a debtor, in failing circumstances, assigns his property to his creditors, or to a trustee for their benefit, in consideration of being discharged from their demands against him. This is usually done by *an indenture of three parts;* in which the debtor conveys the property to the trustees, the

---

1 See B. 5, ch. 18, VI.

creditors release their debts, and the trustees covenant to apply the proceeds, for the benefit of the signing creditors in the first place, and then of those who do not sign. A debtor may legally *prefer* one or more creditors, by conveying the whole property to them, and entirely excluding the rest. The *assent* of the creditors is essential to the validity of the assignment; so that a creditor, who attaches the property by a trustee process, will hold it in preference to one who subsequently executes the instrument.[1] *The legal estate* vests in the trustees; and a court of equity will compel an execution of the trust.

An assignment will be rendered *void* by any stipulation, condition, or reservation in favor of the debtor, which is fraudulent or oppressive. Thus if a debtor convey the whole of his property in trust for *a part of his creditors*, with a reservation that he shall receive back a portion of the proceeds to his own use, the assignment is void. So also a condition, that whatever share would belong to a signing creditor, shall on his refusal be paid to the debtor himself, has been held to avoid the assignment. Otherwise in Massachusetts.

Delivery of the instrument of assignment is, it seems, sufficient to pass the property; and, if it be found in the hands of the trustee, who takes possession of the effects, and enters upon the execution of his trust, this will be sufficient evidence of the delivery and acceptance.

V. *Warranty*. In every sale of chattels, if the possession be at the time in another person, and there be no covenant or *warranty of title*, the rule of

---

[1] Held otherwise in the United States Court.

law is, "*Caveat emptor*," — let the buyer take care; and he buys at his peril. But if the seller has possession, he is understood to *warrant* the title, in consideration of *a fair price*. If there be a failure of title to only *a part* of the property, the sale may be *rescinded*, provided that part appears to be so essential to the residue, that it cannot reasonably be supposed the purchase would have been made without it. Thus, in case of the sale of a pair of carriage-horses, and a good title to only one of them, the buyer may rescind as to both.

With regard to *the quality* of the goods, unless there be an *express warranty*, or *fraud* on the part of the seller, the buyer shall suffer from any deficiency. This rule does not apply, however, where goods *of a certain character* have been either ordered or offered for sale, and those actually delivered do not answer the description. A sale *by sample* is a warranty, that the goods sold are the same *generically* and *specifically* as the sample, and equally sound throughout; but not that there is *no latent infirmity* alike in the sample and the goods themselves. But it has been held, that where one sells articles *of his own manufacture*, he impliedly warrants that they are fit for the use for which he knows they are intended. A mere *indefinite description* is no warranty, — as for instance "*good fine wine*."

Direct misrepresentation by the seller avoids the sale. *Mere concealment* does not, unless the defect were *a latent one*, known to the seller, but not known, nor liable to be discovered with reasonable care, by the purchaser. Even a warranty will not cover defects, that are *plainly the objects of the senses*; as, if a horse be warranted perfect, and wants a tail or an ear. Fraud may be *inferred*, not only from false representations, but from trivial facts and circumstances, as where a seller, *by his acts*, produced an impression in the mind of the buyer, that he was purchasing a picture which belonged to a person of great skill in painting. A mere false assertion of value, when no warranty is intended, is no ground of relief; nor even a false affirmation that a particular sum had been bid for the property. But a sale of land has been held void, where *the amount of rent* previously paid for it was misrepresented; upon the ground that this was a private matter, which the seller had peculiar means of knowing.

Where a buyer would *rescind* a sale on the ground of fraud, he should do it in reasonable time after discovery of the defect, by restoring whatever he has received on his part, and claiming restitution of the price. He may, however, treat the contract *as subsisting*, and sue for the damages sustained by him; and if there were an express warranty, this is the only proper remedy.

CHAPTER IX.

BAILMENT.

Bailment is *a delivery of goods in trust*, upon a contract, express or implied, that the trust shall be duly executed, and the goods then restored by the bailee. Bailment is of five kinds.

I. *Deposit*. This is a bailment of goods *to be*

kept gratuitously. A depositary, without any special undertaking, and without reward, will not be answerable for the loss of the goods, unless there be *gross negligence*, which is considered equivalent to *a breach of faith*; and the degree of care necessary to avoid this imputation, will be measured by, though it need not equal, the carefulness which the bailee uses towards the like goods of his own. If, however, he specially undertakes to keep the goods safely, he will be liable for any loss which may happen from the want of *common prudence.* So, if he himself proposes to keep them, or if the deposit is made for his special accommodation, he will be held to the exercise of *ordinary care.*

II. *Mandatum*, or *mandate.* This is when a man undertakes, without reward, to do some act for another in respect to the thing bailed. In connexion with this species of bailment, there is the following important distinction. If one make a gratuitous engagement to perform a certain act for another, unless it be a part of his professed employment, the contract is not binding; but if he actually enter upon the execution of the business, and through negligence do it amiss, he is responsible for damages. In other words, he is liable for *misfeasance*, but not for *non-feasance.* A mandatary, however, cannot be held to any more than ordinary reasonable care, — such as a prudent man would take of his own property; unless he voluntarily offer, or specially undertake, to perform the work.

III. *Commodatum.* — This is *a loan* of property, to be used by the borrower without paying for it. Being made for the sole benefit of the bailee, he is bound to exercise, in preserving the property, not merely *ordinary*, but *the greatest care*, and is responsible for the slightest neglect. He cannot apply the thing borrowed to any other purpose than that for which it was lent, nor keep it beyond the time agreed. If he does, he becomes responsible, though the loss happen without any fault on his part. Ordinarily a borrower is not liable for a loss by external and irresistible violence, or *vis major*, unless the accident be owing to his own imprudence; as if he borrow a horse, and, riding at a late hour of the night, or over an untravelled road, is attacked by robbers; — or unless he practises some deceit to procure the loan.

IV. "*Pignori acceptum*," *pawn*, or *pledge*. — This is a bailment of goods *by a debtor to his creditor*, to be kept till the debt is discharged. It being alike beneficial to both parties, the pawnee is responsible only for the want of *ordinary care*. If the property be such as is injured by use, he cannot use it, and if otherwise, is liable at all events for any loss happening while it is in use. Where, however, it is of such a kind as to be a charge in keeping, he may take its products, as for instance the milk of a cow; but must apply the net profits to reduce the debt.[1] On tender of the debt, the bailee's property ceases. If he refuses to give up the pledge, he becomes *a wrongdoer*, liable absolutely for a loss. If a pawn be stolen, the bailee is "primâ facie" answerable; but not if he can prove due care for its preservation.

Delivery is essential to a pledge. In this it differs from *a mortgage*, which may be good without de-

---

[1] Same law in regard to real estate. — See *Mortgage*, 4.

livery.[1] A mortgage is *an absolute pledge*, to become *an absolute interest*, if not redeemed at a fixed time. The legal property passes, with *a condition of defeasance.* A pledge of goods is *a deposit of them as security.* The general property does not pass, but remains in the bailor; and if the debt be not paid at the time appointed, the pledge does not become the bailee's absolutely, but he shall have recourse to legal process, or give reasonable notice to the owner, in order to sell it. A pawn may by agreement be made to cover *future advances*; but will not receive this construction, unless there be an express contract to that effect. If goods be deposited by a debtor in the hands of his creditor, for a particular purpose, or on a particular trust, but without reference to the debt; the creditor cannot treat them as pledged, and retain them till the debt is paid.

In the nature of a pledge, though arising from a different source, is the right of what the law calls *lien. A lien* is *a right to detain property* until some charge or claim is satisfied, in general relating to the identical property which is detained. Thus a tailor has a lien upon a garment made by him for the price of making it; a carrier upon goods for the price of transporting them; and, in general, any one, who performs a service with respect to any article of personal property, has a lien upon it, till he is paid for such service. The property, however, must belong to the person, for whom the service was rendered; — otherwise, it cannot be retained against the true owner, except in the two cases of *inn-*

[1] In Massachusetts, a mortgage of chattels is invalid, unless it be publicly recorded, or the mortgagee take and retain possession of the property.

keepers and *common carriers*, who, upon peculiar principles of public policy, can assert the lien for their dues against all the world. The vendor of goods, as has been shown in a previous chapter,[1] has a lien upon them, before delivery, for the price. In chancery, the seller of real estate has a similar lien.

The law, in some instances, allows *a general lien*,— that is, *for a general balance of accounts*. The distinction, in this respect, in favor of some employments over others, seems to be founded on the consideration of the usage of trade, to *give a continuing credit*, instead of receiving immediate payment in each case. The right of lien, either general or special, may arise from the particular mode of dealing between the parties in previous instances.

The law implies *waiver* of a lien, where there is *an express credit, a distinct security taken*, or the possession acquired *for another specific purpose*, and that only. Thus the owner of a ship, hired by charter-party, has no lien upon the cargo for the hire, though he come into possession of it. So there is no lien, where a party never had possession, or voluntarily parts with it;— though that of a servant is sufficient. So when the party fails to enforce his lien in reasonable time, and the property passes to a *bonâ fide* purchaser without notice, the lien is held to be waived.[2]

In Massachusetts, Maine, Pennsylvania, and probably some other States, a special statute gives to *mechanics* and "*material-men*," or furnishers of materials, a lien upon the buildings which they erect or provide for, together with the land; depending, how-

---

[1] See p 88.

[2] See B. 4, ch. 12, (4.), for an exception in the case of *vessels*.

ever, upon their observance of certain prescribed and public formalities. In some of the States, also, a lien of the same nature is given upon *ships* under similar circumstances.

V. *Locatum*, or *hiring for a reward.* — This is where one gains, for a pecuniary compensation, the temporary use of a thing; or receives it, for the purpose of performing some labor, or bestowing some care and attention, upon it; or where goods are delivered to a public carrier or private person, to carry them, for reward, from one place to another.

1. In case of a *letting to hire*, the hirer is bound only to *ordinary care* and diligence; proportioned, however, to the value of the article and the means of security which he possesses. Substantially the same principles apply to the hiring of real estate by *lease*, which will be hereafter mentioned.[1]

By any *misuse* of the thing hired, or deviation from the contract, the hirer loses the privileges of a bailee, and becomes responsible at all events. For instance, one who hires a horse to go to one place, and drives him to another, must pay the value of the horse, if killed, though by inevitable accident.

Under this title may be considered the subject of *interest*. Interest is a compensation paid *for the use of money*. The letting of money is not strictly a *bailment*, because the particular money hired is not to be restored, but only an equivalent sum, in amount and value.

The *rate* of interest in most of the States is six per cent. per annum. In New York it is seven per cent.

---

[1] See *Lease*.

The rate of interest will always be governed by the "lex loci contractûs," — the law of the place where the contract was made and to be performed.

Interest is recoverable, *after a demand*,[1] upon all debts *payable on demand;* in all cases, on judgments, or after the day of payment, if one is appointed; and for *money paid*, from *the time of payment.* Interest may be sued for without the principal, where the latter is not due.

The reservation of a higher rate of interest than that prescribed by law, is termed *usury.* This, in some States, is an indictable offence; besides rendering the contract void, or subjecting the lender to a restitution of the interest, together with an additional and often severe penalty.

A bill or note, usurious in the making, is in general void, even in the hands of an innocent indorsee, as against the maker.[2] But it is valid against the indorser.

Where a transaction is substantially a loan of money, the law will disregard the particular form which it is made to assume for purposes of evasion, and pronounce it usurious, if such is the fact.

If money be lent *on risk* at more than legal interest, and the risk affect *the interest only*, it is usury.

But sometimes the hazard may affect *the principal sum*, as well as the interest, and may be greater than the legal rate will compensate. This gives rise to certain lawful contracts of a peculiar nature, which will be noticed hereafter.[3]

2. Where *labor* or *care* is to be bestowed on the

---

1 *The commencement of suit* is equivalent to a demand.

2 Otherwise in New York.

3 See B. 4, ch. 13.

thing delivered, for a pecuniary compensation, the bailee must exercise *ordinary care*, and *a degree of skill* equal to his undertaking. The work must be done in *a workmanlike manner*. This rule applies particularly to the undertakings of all *mechanics* and *artificers*.

Under this head, may be stated the principles applicable to *inn-keepers*, whose liability is strict and peculiar. An inn-keeper is responsible for the *acts of his domestics*, and for *thefts*, and is bound to take *all possible care* of the goods deposited in his house or entrusted to his family or servants. And he is chargeable, although not informed that the goods are in his house, nor guilty of any negligence. He is regarded as *an insurer*, responsible for any injury or loss, not caused by *the act of God* or *the common enemy*,[1] or *the neglect or fault of the owner of the property*. *An inn* is a house kept open publicly, for the lodging and entertainment of travellers in general, for a reasonable compensation. The person losing his goods, however, need not, in order to charge the inn-keeper, be either a traveller, or himself a guest, provided the property be entrusted to the inn-keeper; as where one leaves his horse at an inn to be fed, without having his own lodging or refreshment there. When a guest has the exclusive keeping and occupancy of a room, the inn-keeper is not liable. Nor where the former takes upon himself the care of the goods, or, under circumstances of suspicion, neglects to use ordinary caution.

3. "Locatio operis mercium vehendarum." This

---

1 See *Common Carrier*.

is a contract relating to *the carriage of goods* for hire. A carrier, who acts as such in a particular case only, is answerable for the want of *ordinary care.* A *common carrier* is one who undertakes, for hire, to transport the goods of such as choose to employ him. By the English law, it matters not whether the transportation be by land or by water; but, in some of the States, a distinction has been made in favor of the latter.

A person of this description is answerable for all losses, which arise from any other cause than *the act of God* or of *the public enemy* — even from inevitable misfortune or irresistible violence. *The act of God* is such an event as could not happen by the intervention of man; as lightning, tempest, or the sudden failure of the wind. But if goods be destroyed *by necessity,* as by throwing them overboard from a vessel for the sake of preservation in a storm, the carrier is not liable.

A carrier need not be informed of the peculiar value of an article delivered him; but any fraudulent concealment, for the sake of paying a less price, will discharge his responsibility. If a carrier receives goods directed to be carried in a certain position, — as, for instance, a box marked "glass, — with care, — this side up," and violates this direction, he will be liable for any loss or damage, unless he can clearly show, that it was in no degree attributable to his breach of contract, but caused solely by *the act of God,* or *a public enemy,* or the act or fault of the owner himself.

The liability of a carrier does not commence till actual delivery to him, unless by usage it be sufficient to leave the goods at a particular place; and then he must have notice. His liability does not end, it seems, till delivery at the consignee's residence or place of deposit. It is the modern practice, for common carriers to limit their responsibility, by public, special notice of the extent to which they will be answerable. The goods, in such case, are understood to be delivered on the footing of a special contract; but the notice, to have effect, must be brought home to the knowledge of the owner, and be clear, explicit, and consistent; and the bailee, though discharged from his obligation as insurer, is still held liable for gross negligence or misfeasance in him or his servants. It has been held, that the strict responsibility of a carrier does not apply to the carriage of *negroes*; they being regarded rather as passengers than as goods.

The contract of *bailment* transfers a special qualified property from the bailor to the bailee, together with the possession; and the latter, as well as the former, may maintain an action against such as injure or take away the goods. But a judgment in favor of one, is, it seems, a bar to any suit by the other.

A bailor cannot, in general, sue the bailee to recover his goods, till after a demand for them.

CHAPTER X.

BILLS AND NOTES.

THE most common and important kind of *simple contract* is that sometimes called "paper credit," including *bills of exchange* and *promissory notes.*

A *bill of exchange* is a written order or request, by one person to another, for the payment of money to a third person. If A, living in New York, wishes to receive one thousand dollars due him from B in London, he obtains this sum from C who is going to London, and gives him therefor *a bill of exchange* upon B for the money. A is called the *drawer*, B the *drawee*, or, after acceptance of the bill, the *acceptor*; and C the *payee.* Where the drawer and drawee reside in one State, the bill is an *inland bill*; if in different States, it seems to be a point somewhat unsettled, whether it shall be held an *inland* or a *foreign one.* The payee may, by *indorsement*, or writing his name on the back of the bill, assign over his whole property in it to another person; the former is then called *indorser*, the latter *indorsee*; and it may be again so assigned, "ad infinitum." The payee or indorsee is to go to the drawee in reasonable time, and offer the bill for acceptance. If he accept it verbally, or in writing, he becomes liable to pay it.[1] The usual mode is merely to write his name on the bill, or the word "accepted."

---

[1] In New York, only a written acceptance, or a destruction of the bill, or refusal to return it for twenty-four hours, will bind the drawee.

A previous authority to draw bills; a promise to the holder, or to the drawer by him communicated to the holder, to accept; or even *the acts* of the drawee, as keeping the bill long in his hands, may amount to an acceptance. It may be *conditional*; and a *verbal* condition may be proved to limit a written acceptance, as against a holder who had notice of the limitation. An offer to pay the bill at a future day, which the holder rejects, will not make an acceptance.

The acceptor is bound, though he accepted *without consideration.* In such case, he is called *an accommodation acceptor.* A third person, after protest for non-acceptance by the drawer, may accept and pay the bill *for the honor of the drawer* or an indorser, and will have a claim against that party as well as all prior parties on the bill. This is termed *an acceptance supra protest.*

If the drawee refuses to accept the bill, the holder may *protest* it for non-acceptance,—a formal proceeding before a *notary public,* for the purpose of notifying and charging the drawer. And he may immediately sue the drawer, though the bill is not due. The same course is pursued, if, after accepting, the drawee neglects or refuses to pay the bill. In both cases, the bill must be demanded of the drawer as soon as conveniently may be,—he being liable to pay it only on this condition. If duly notified, the drawer is answerable not only for the amount of the bill, but for additional damages and costs. The drawer is not discharged by want of notice, if he had no funds in the hands of the drawee; the object of notice being to give him an opportunity of seasonably withdrawing his funds, for his own security. Notice from the drawee himself of non-acceptance is not sufficient; it must come from a party to the bill. If the bill be an indorsed bill, the indorsee may call upon the drawer or any of the indorsers, on failure of the drawee to meet it; every indorsement being considered as *a new bill,* drawn by the indorser or the acceptor, in favor of the indorsee, who therefore need not call upon the drawer, to charge the indorsers.

The English law, requiring *a protest* of foreign bills, has been adopted in many of the States, but the Supreme Court of the United States have held it unnecessary.

The above principles are exclusively applicable to bills of exchange. There are others, more numerous, which pertain alike to bills and to promissory notes. These will be stated as concisely as possible.

A promissory note, or *note of hand,* is a promise in writing to pay a certain sum, at a certain time or on demand, to a person therein named, or his order, or to the bearer. An English statute, adopted wholly or partially throughout the Union, makes promissory notes, payable to order or bearer, *negotiable* like bills of exchange. This is said to be according to *the custom of merchants,* or *the law merchant,* which however is nothing but a branch of the general law of the land.

1. *Form* of bills and notes.—A bill or note is not confined to any set form of words; but, in order to be negotiable, must be exclusively and absolutely for *the payment of money.* Thus a note payable in bank-bills, or in goods and to bearer, has been held not negotiable. Bills and notes must also be payable *absolutely,* and not *upon a contingency*; though if the

event be certain, the time may be *uncertain;* as, for instance, the death of the maker's father. The above-named exceptions can never be taken against the original payee or promisee; but affect merely *the negotiability* of the instrument.

It is usual to insert the words *value received.* These words are not absolutely necessary, but only impose upon the maker, in order to avoid payment, the burden of proving a want of consideration; although, even if they are wanting, it is not clear that a consideration must be proved by the payee. The want of consideration is no defence against an indorsee.

2. *Negotiation* of bills and notes.—A writing in this form, "Good for one hundred dollars on demand," is not *negotiable*; and no one can maintain an action upon it, except the person to whom it was given.

The only way of *assigning* a note payable to order, so that the assignee may sue upon it in his own name, is by *indorsement.* If indorsed *in blank,* that is, merely by writing the payee's name upon it, or to the indorsee by name, without adding the words "or order"; the note is still further negotiable in his hands,—it being a settled principle, that a security negotiable in its creation must ever afterwards remain so, unless there be a special indorsement *by the payee* to the contrary.

Each indorser becomes liable to all subsequent holders. If the note be paid and taken up by *the last indorser,* he may again transfer it to a new indorsee, who may maintain an action upon it in his own name against any prior party. But if paid by any other indorser than the last, the note is no longer negotiable ; because, if it were, the new holder might hold liable parties whom such indorser could not, and who were discharged by the payment. Hence if transferred by such indorser, a suit will lie only in his name. A subsequent indorser who takes up the note, may recover from a prior one, without proving that he, the plaintiff, was duly notified and therefore legally liable.

A note payable to *a fictitious person*, may be sued by an ignorant or *innocent* indorsee, as *payable to bearer*.

When a negotiable security is indorsed, "Pay the contents to my use"; this is not *an assignment*, but only *an authority* to receive the money.

A note jointly held by two persons, not partners, cannot be transferred by one alone. An *infant promisee* may pass a note, even to one who knows of his infancy, by his indorsement. So one of two *partners*, or *an agent* of the owner.

A bill or note cannot be indorsed *for a part only of what is due upon it;* otherwise the promisor might be subjected to two actions instead of one. A blank indorsement may be filled up by the holder with his own name, even at the moment of trial; and if he put his own name immediately under the first indorser's, this will not discharge the others. After a blank indorsement, the note is like one payable to bearer, and passes by delivery. The holder may constitute himself or any other person assignee; and the court will not inquire, whether he sues for himself, or as trustee for another. An action upon a note will lie, in the name of one who has no interest in it, for the promisee's benefit. The holder may strike out the indorsement to him, though full, and all prior indorsements except the first, and upon that charge the maker or indorser. The first indorser is liable to every subsequent *bonâ fide* holder, though the note were forged or fraudulently circulated.

In case of blank indorsement, possession is evidence of title; but if the indorsements be all filled up, a prior indorser, coming into possession of the instrument, has sometimes been required to prove that he had paid and taken it up. The Supreme Court of the United States have held such proof unnecessary.

Upon the principle of *protection to mercantile paper*, an indorsee may recover upon the note, though it have been paid, provided he took it fairly *before it became due*; and *the burden of proof* is on the maker, to show a payment before the transfer; and not on the holder, to prove the reverse. The indorser himself is a competent witness to prove the time of transfer. In a suit by the indorsee against the maker, no claims of the maker against the indorser can be inquired into; nor the consideration of the note. To the latter principle there is one exception; where a note, given for a particular consideration, is declared by statute *absolutely void*; in which case it will be void in the hands of any one. Gaming and usurious notes are examples, under both the English and American statutes. Nor does the principle apply, where the indorsee is in fact the original holder, the indorser merely putting his name upon the note for the accommodation of the maker.

If the indorsee take the note *after it is due*, the maker may defend as he might against the indorser. It has been an unsettled point, when a note, payable *on demand,* shall be held *overdue.* It is a question of law, depending upon the particular facts of each case. From eighteen to two months have, in various instances, been held an unreasonable delay.

A note may be indorsed so as to exempt the indorser from liability, by adding, "at his own risk," or "without recourse."

3. *Demand and notice.* — The indorser of a note is holden to pay it on the implied condition, that the indorsee shall present it to the promisor when it is due, and demand payment, if it can be done by using due diligence, and give seasonable notice to the indorser of the promisor's failure; and if the indorsee do not comply with this condition, the indorser is discharged, unless he have waived it.

A demand upon the maker, in order to charge the indorser, must not be made until the day the note is payable, and must in general be made on that day. But if the maker live at a great distance from the holder, a reasonable time will be allowed after the note becomes due, to transmit it for payment. If a note be made payable on a day and at a place certain, a demand need not, and cannot legally, be made at any other time or place; but a readiness then and there to receive the money will be sufficient to charge the indorser. Whether *the maker* will be liable, without a demand at the place, seems somewhat unsettled.

Any person having possession of the note, with a letter or verbal request from the indorsee, may legally demand payment, without a special power of attorney. A demand upon one of several promisors is sufficient. If a person go with the note to the maker's place of business, in business hours, for the purpose of demanding payment, and find it shut, and no one there to answer inquiries; this will be equivalent to an actual demand.

Notice to the indorser, of non-payment by the maker, may be given either on the same day with the demand upon him, or the day after. And if the indorser live in another town, it will be sufficient to put a letter in the post-office on the next day. If he be absent, and have no domicil or place of business, it will be sufficient if the notice be given him as soon as he returns.

In some of the States, the rules of demand and notice have not always been strictly enforced, partly upon the ground of usage, and partly from the imperfect facilities of communication in a new country.

The usual condition of an indorser's liability may be *modified* or *waived* with his consent, either express, or implied from his knowledge of the usage or rules of those to whom the note is indorsed or negotiated for collection. Thus if a note be made payable at a bank, it must be considered as having reference to the rules and practices there prevailing, and a notice conformable thereto will be sufficient. So if the regular time of notice occur during certain *holidays*, when no business is transacted, — as, for instance, the Christmas holidays in Havana, — a delay will be excused.

If the indorser, knowing that he is discharged from his liability, promise to pay the note; it is a waiver of the usual condition, and the promise will be binding. So if he receive security of the maker to meet the indorsement. But he will not be bound because, under an erroneous impression that he is liable, he takes measures for his own indemnity.

4. *Discharge* of bills and notes. — *A release* or *credit*, given by the holder of a note to any of the parties, even after legal demand and notice, will discharge all those subsequently liable; that is, all subsequent indorsers, if given to a prior one, and all the indorsers, if given to the maker, — because the subsequent parties thereby lose either their claim or chance of security against the prior ones. A mere *gratuitous indulgence*, which does not interfere with an immediate right of action, will not have this effect. Even an express discharge of the maker will not release an indorser, if the latter expressly or impliedly assent to it; as, for instance, by becoming party to an instrument of assignment, in which such discharge is contained.

5. *Time of payment* of bills and notes. — A note payable *on demand* is due and may be sued immediately, without a previous demand. If payable in a certain number of days *from the date or day of the date*, this day shall not be counted one. By the English law, now generally or universally adopted in this country, *three days of grace* are allowed, that is, the note does not become due, till three days after the time stipulated for payment. If the last day be Sunday, it is due on Saturday. When a note is payable *by instalments*, they may be sued for as fast as they fall due. So *annual interest* may be recovered, before the principal is due.

6. *Remedies* upon bills and notes. — The indorsee may have a several action on the note, at the same time, against the maker and each indorser. He can however recover but one satisfaction of his debt. If the note were *void in its creation*, the indorsee may in general recover from the indorser, though not from

the maker. If the indorser and indorsee live in different towns, an action may be commenced against the indorser, immediately after notice has been put into the post-office, and before he can have received it by due course of mail.

7. *Collateral liabilities.* — In connexion with the subject of bills and notes, may properly be considered the different forms, in which one man may incur liability for another, and the peculiar legal effect of each.

A surety is one who signs an instrument *with the maker*, but *as surety*. A surety is originally liable to the holder, precisely like the maker; and his suretyship will avail him, only as furnishing a claim against the maker, for any damage or loss sustained by him in consequence of his liability. Subsequent events, however, may discharge the surety, which will not affect the principal. *Mere delay* in calling upon the latter for payment, will not discharge the former; nor *a renewal*, without consideration, and according to usage, which leaves *a present right of action*; — as by a bank: but an express *extension of credit* will. So, any *variance of the contract, which increases his risk*; or the assumption of *new and material obligations* by the principal, without the surety's consent; will discharge him, however general may be the terms in which the contract is expressed. Thus, if a bond is given by the cashier of a bank, with sureties, for the faithful performance of his duties *so long as he shall continue in that office*, and the office is *an annual one*;—the sureties will not be bound after his *re-election* at the commencement of a new year. So if a surety be erroneously informed by the creditor, though without intentional deception, that the debt has been paid, and in consequence loses his chance of securing himself; he is discharged.

Another form of liability, is where a person puts his name *on the back of the note* at the time of making it, or afterwards, according to previous agreement, without any words written over it. In such case, he may be charged like a surety or original promisor; the holder filling up the blank at pleasure with suitable words. Such an indorser is usually termed *an accommodation indorser.* Like any other indorser, he is liable to all subsequent parties.

But if such a signer expressly *guaranty* payment of the note, his liability is of a different nature. A guarantor *warrants the solvency of the promisor*; and is discharged only by the joint effect of negligence on the part of the holder, and an actual loss or prejudice to himself in consequence. If previous parties are solvent when the note becomes due, and become insolvent subsequently, the guarantor will be discharged, unless there were a seasonable demand and notice; but these are not necessary, when the maker and indorsers were insolvent at the maturity of the note. If a note be signed by one person, as surety, and *guaranteed* by another, and the former take it up; he cannot call upon the latter to reimburse a share of the money paid.

The most common form of *guaranty* is that given by one man for *the general solvency* of another in trade, or for his *paying debts to a certain amount.* In the latter case, if the party in trade has once taken up goods to the amount stipulated, and paid for them wholly or in part; it seems to be somewhat unsettled, whether the guaranty is discharged to the amount of such payment, or whether it may still subsist as before. This contract however will, in general, be strictly construed. When advances are made, *notice* should be given in reasonable time to the guarantor.

CHAPTER XI.

PARTNERSHIP.

I. *Nature and requisites* of partnership.

PARTNERSHIP is a contract of two or more persons, to place their money, effects, labor, and skill, or some or all of them, in lawful commerce and business, and to divide the profit and bear the loss in certain proportions. One party may advance funds, and another his personal services or skill; and their connexion will make a partnership. There can be no partnership without *a community of profit.* The parties must be jointly concerned, not only in the purchase, but in *the future sale.* A joint purchase, with a view to separate and distinct sales by each person on his own account, is not sufficient. But though the purchase be on separate account, yet if the interests of the purchasers are afterwards mingled, with a view to a joint sale; a partnership commences from the time of such union. The members of any large *unincorporated association* are partners. They may limit their responsibility, upon contracts of the association, by an explicit stipulation with the other party; but such limitations are looked upon unfavorably, as contrary to the policy of the law, and must be strictly proved. *Incorporated companies* are not partnerships, and the stockholders are not liable as partners, unless the act of incorporation or a general law expressly so provide. It seems that, apart from any agreement to the contrary, each partner shall share in the profit or loss of the concern, in proportion to the value of what he brings into it.

There may be *a general partnership at large*, or it may be limited to *a particular branch of business*, or to *one particular subject*. The usual form of partnership is where two or more persons are both *nominally and really* connected in business, and interested in the profits. A *dormant partner* is one who is thus interested, but who *conceals his name*. A dormant partner is equally liable, when discovered, as if his name had appeared in the firm; and although he was not known to be a partner at the time of contracting the debt. The reason is, that, by partaking of the profits, he diminishes the fund which ought to be applied to payment of the company debts. And however small the share which he receives, he is still liable *in solido*, — for the whole. A distinction has been made, however, between one who receives, as a compensation for services, *a share of the profits*, as such; and one who merely receives *a sum in proportion to them*. The latter will not be held as partner. A contract of this kind will not, in any case, constitute a partnership as *between the parties*; but only create a liability *to third persons*. In New York, the rules of dormant partnership have been modified by a late statute.

A *nominal partner* is one, who has no interest in the trade, but *suffers his name to appear* to the world as a partner. Such an one, also, is liable for all the debts of the firm, upon the ground that his name gives them credit, and is relied upon by creditors for payment.

A very recent act, in Massachusetts, provides for the formation of *limited partnerships*; by virtue of which, persons may become interested in a business, by furnishing funds to carry it on, without subjecting themselves to liability beyond the amount contributed. To secure this privilege, the contract of partnership must be recorded in *the registry of deeds*, and published in a newspaper.

One who joins a partnership, does not, without a special promise, become bound by its *previous debts*.

II. *Rights and duties* of partners.

1. *Their interest in the stock in trade.*

Partners are *joint tenants* of their stock, without the right of *survivorship*. On the death of one, his representatives become *tenants in common* with the others.

No partner has an exclusive right to any part of the joint stock, until a balance of accounts be struck between him and his copartners, and the amount of his interest ascertained. Each has *a lien* upon the stock, for any balance due him from the others on account of partnership transactions, as against creditors of the latter; so that the joint property cannot be validly *attached* for a separate debt of one.

The doctrine of joint ownership is not applicable to *real estate* purchased by partners in business. They hold it, as any other persons would, without reference to the partnership. And no one can claim, as *dormant partner*, any interest in lands expressly conveyed to another, though purchased with partnership funds.

2. *Rights and duties of partners as to each other.*

One partner cannot sue another, for any thing concerning the partnership, before dissolution and settlement of the joint concerns, except to call him *to render an account.* And if the same individual belong to two firms, neither can sue the other *at law,* though it may be done *in Chancery.* But, after dissolution, one partner may maintain a suit for any balance due from the others. And if there is a written contract, each may at any time sue another upon his *express covenants.* So where the debts due the firm are *desperate,* one partner may sue another before final settlement; especially if he has offered to relinquish all his interest in them.

3. *Rights and duties of partners as to third persons.*

The act of each partner, in transactions relating to the partnership, is considered *the act of all,* and binds all. He can buy and sell goods, make contracts, pay and receive, draw, indorse, or accept bills and notes, for the company. In all negotiable paper, the signature of one binds the whole, even though he sign in his individual name, provided it appears on the face of the paper to be on partnership account: if it does not thus appear, there is some doubt whether the firm can ever be bound. If partnership security be taken from one partner, *for a private debt* of his own, the creditor knowing that the subject matter of it was out of the scope of the partnership dealing; it is *a fraud,* and the firm shall not be bound:—without such knowledge, they will be bound. It will depend, however, upon various minute circumstances, whether the creditor shall be bound to show that it was, or the firm, that it was not, a partnership transaction. If goods sold *come to the use of the firm,* they are liable at all events. When the security is *a negotiable note,* it will be good in the hands of *an indorsee,* unless fraud be clearly proved against him. If a partner borrow money, representing that it is to go to the use of the firm, and give their note for it, they will be bound, whether it is thus applied or not.

A partner may contract on his own account, and make himself alone liable, for goods bought for the firm, if the seller choose to accept him. But a credit, given to one partner on his own separate account, is not a discharge of a demand against the firm, unless it were intended or accepted as such.

The right of one partner to bind the firm may in some instances be controlled by the express dissent of the latter; as where, contrary to the partnership agreement, one buys goods, and the rest have given previous notice to the seller of the agreement. Whether, if there are more than two, the dissent of one can avail against the will of the majority, seems somewhat questionable.

One partner may in general *pledge* as well as *sell* the common property. But he cannot bind the firm by *a guaranty* or *suretyship* for a third person, without express or implied authority; nor by *an instrument under seal,* unless it be a release of debts, or some paper connected with proceedings of bankruptcy, or unless the others are present or expressly assent.

III. *Dissolution* of partnership.

If a partnership be formed *for a single purpose or transaction,* it ceases as soon as this is completed; if *for a definite period,* at the end of that time. If no period be fixed, any partner may withdraw when he pleases; though for all antecedent debts, the firm still remains liable. And it seems to be the prevailing opinion, that the same right of withdrawing exists, though the connexion were formed by a written instrument, for a fixed time. The withdrawing partner will subject himself to damages for breach of the agreement; but, as to the rest of the world, the partnership ceases.

A partnership will be dissolved, by *the death, insanity*, or *physical inability* of any member; by *the marriage* of *a feme sole* member; by *bankruptcy* or *insolvency*; in some instances, by *judicial decree* of a Court of Equity, — though only a strong case of injury, danger, or fraud will justify such interference; — or by *a war* between the two governments, of which the partners are respectively members.

When a partnership is ended, no individual can make use of the joint property, but for the purpose of settling the partnership affairs, and winding up the concern. The power of one to bind the rest ceases; he cannot even indorse notes previously made, nor circulate them, though previously indorsed. On a dissolution *by death, the survivor* settles the affairs; — all suits for or against the firm must be brought in his name; and he is held to account with the representatives of the deceased for his share of the effects and profits.

In payment of debts, *the joint creditors* have a primary claim *upon the joint fund*, and their debts are to be settled, before any division of the funds.

Public notice must be given of the dissolution. Otherwise, the firm may be bound by a contract of one member, with persons not apprized of the event. As to all who have previously dealt with the partnership, in order to avoid such liability, *actual, personal notice* must be shown.

CHAPTER XII.

MARITIME CONTRACTS. SHIPPING.

THERE is a peculiar class of contracts, of the most frequent occurrence and the highest importance in a commercial community, called *maritime contracts*. These, however, cannot be intelligibly and satisfactorily treated, without a previous explanation of the law of *shipping*; which will accordingly make the subject of the present chapter.

1. *Title to vessels.* — This is usually acquired by *a bill of sale*, although a verbal contract and delivery of possession are all that is absolutely necessary to pass the property.

A sale under *the decree of a Foreign Court* having admiralty jurisdiction, will also pass the title. So *a capture and condemnation.*

When a ship is *at sea*, delivery of *the grand bill of sale*, — that is, the original conveyance from the builder, — or of other title documents, passes the property; subject, however, to any transfer lawfully made by the master, before notice of the former conveyance, and upon condition of the buyer's taking possession in reasonable time after her return.

For the encouragement of domestic trade and navigation, the laws of the United States confer peculiar privileges upon *American ships*, on condition that they are *registered* with the collector of a port in the mode thereby provided. No foreigner can be entitled to these privileges. Every transfer of title, unless by act of law, as, for instance, by sale on execution, requires some alteration in the registry; and a secret conveyance to a foreigner forfeits the vessel. Certain oaths are required before registry. Coasters are *enrolled* and *licensed*, instead of being *registered*. The certificate of registry must be set forth in a conveyance of the ship, in order to entitle her to a new registration. The want of a register is no ground of forfeiture, but merely excludes American privileges.

Registry is not a voucher required by *the law of nations*, as evidence of a ship's national character, but only by our own statutes. Nor is it of itself any evidence of ownership.

The State legislatures have, on some points, regulated the subject of vessels.

2. *Ship-owners.* — *The owner* of a ship is answerable for all necessaries supplied and repairs made to her, by order of the master, unless there be a special contract with the latter by the creditor. He is also liable, for expenses incurred by *a consignee*, if conformable to the usage of the place to which the ship is sent, — as for instance, those of the master's last sickness and funeral, and for all contracts made by the master *according to custom*, though not strictly necessary, — as, for instance, the contract termed *mateship*, by which one whaling-ship meeting another forms a partnership in the proceeds of the expedition.

The *mortgagor* of a ship is ordinarily regarded as the owner. So also is one, who *charters* her for a particular voyage, appoints the master, and exercises general ownership, "pro hac vice," — for that purpose. Sometimes a vessel is let, with an agreement, that the owner shall in some way be compensated by *the profits*. Whether this will make him liable or not *as partner*, will depend on the particular terms of the contract.

Part-owners of a ship are *tenants in common*; and when one of them is appointed to manage her concerns for the common benefit, he is called *the ship's husband*, who may, however, be some third person. A maritime court has the power of authorizing a majority of ship-owners to employ the vessel, against the will of the rest, giving them proper security for her safe return, or an equivalent compensation.

A part-owner cannot, like a partner, dispose of any more than his own share of the property; but may bind the rest for whatever is necessary to the preservation or proper employment of the ship. Ships may, however, be owned, like other chattels, in partnership, and the law of partnership will then apply to them. *Part-ownership* is the title, generally, to cargo as well as ship.

A part-owner cannot bind his fellow by a contract of *insurance*.

3. *Master of a ship.* — The *master* of a ship has an implied authority to bind the owner, by contracts relative to the usual employment of the vessel. He will also be bound himself, unless the credit be given to the owner alone. The power does not exist, where it is not absolutely necessary, to procure supplies or repairs. It includes authority to bind the ship and freight by *a charter-party*, that is, a contract of letting and hiring; to *hypothecate* or pledge the ship, freight, and cargo, for raising money to complete the voyage; and also to sell a part of the cargo, if absolutely necessary for carrying on the residue. But, without such necessity, no local usage will justify the sale. If several *liens* or incumbrances be created at different periods of the voyage, and the value of the ship is insufficient to satisfy them all; the

last will have priority, as being the means of saving the ship.

A master cannot bind the owner by a contract of *insurance*.

A master is discharged from liability, after taking *a pilot* on board, within the usual limits of his employment. And the owner becomes responsible for the pilot's conduct.

4. *Seamen.* — For the protection and benefit of *seamen*, the laws of the United States require the master to enter into a written contract with them by *shipping articles*, so called; and provide a summary remedy, for recovery of their wages, and for quitting an unseaworthy ship. Suitable penalties are also imposed upon them for desertion and other misconduct.

A master has over his seamen a very strict authority. If necessary, he may *chastise* or *imprison* them, or authorize an inferior officer to do it; but will be held to severe damages, if he go beyond the limits of reason and moderation. The master may also for just cause *discharge* a seaman, whether a common sailor or some subordinate officer; but will be bound to receive him again on his making due satisfaction. A seaman who becomes *sick* during the voyage, is entitled to medical aid at the owner's expense, in addition to his wages.

As to *the wages* of seamen, the general principle is, that *freight is the mother of wages*; and consequently, if no freight be earned, no wages are due. This rule applies, only when the voyage is defeated by some *natural peril or unavoidable accident*, as for instance, fire, tempest, or capture; and not by the *fraud or misconduct of the master*. In the latter case, wages are recoverable for the time of actual service, with some additional allowance. Wages are due, at every *delivering port,* as well as every *port of destination,* in the course of the voyage; even though, by a contract between the master and owner, the whole voyage is treated as one, and the freight made payable accordingly; and even notwithstanding an express agreement of the seaman to the contrary. If the ship be *captured,* a *recapture* and completion of the voyage will restore the right to wages (deducting salvage[1]) for the entire voyage, although a seaman be himself detained by the captor. If freight be earned in part, wages are recovered in proportion. By act of Congress, *one third of the wages* is due at every port of delivery.

Seamen have a claim for wages against the owner of the ship. The wages of *a master* are not subject to the same restrictions and limitations with those of seamen.

Seamen have *a lien* upon the ship, to be enforced in *the admiralty court,* for their wages. This takes precedence of all other claims whatsoever, and does not depend, like other liens, upon possession.

If a vessel be *chartered,* and for non-payment of their wages by *the charterer,* the seamen enforce their lien upon her against the general owner; he shall recover all money paid them from the charterer.

5. *Affreightment.* — This is a contract, between the owner of a vessel and other persons, to convey their goods in his ship, for a compensation which is called *freight.* It may be made either by *charter-party* or in some other mode.

---

1 See *Salvage.*

A charter-party, is a written and sealed agreement for the exclusive *hiring* of a ship; and contains mutual stipulations between the owner and hirer. The latter may *underlet*, like the lessee of a house. A vessel so hired is said to be *chartered*.

If a vessel be hired at so much a month, the hirer shall pay for the whole time during which he retains her, though, in consequence of an embargo, or capture, she is during a part of the time wholly useless to him.

The owner is bound to have the vessel *seaworthy*[1] through the voyage, unless she be damaged by perils of the sea; also to have her in readiness at the appointed time for loading. The freighter also is bound to *load* in a certain time. Any delay in this respect is termed *demurrage*, and justifies a rescinding of the bargain. The owner must furnish all requisite papers for the advantage and security of the ship. After the cargo is embarked, he becomes *a common carrier*, with all the liabilities incident to that employment,[2] unless the goods are clandestinely received by the master, and the owner of them is himself on board. He is bound to sail, as soon as wind and tide will permit, if the weather be not very tempestuous; and to proceed by the direct course to the destined port, unless some strong necessity prevent. If the ship becomes disabled, the master is bound, if possible, to complete the transportation in another vessel, and may charge for any increased freight. If the owner of the cargo dissents from this course, the whole freight may be recovered; and if he accepts the cargo

---

1 See *Seaworthiness*. 2 See *Common Carrier*.

at any intermediate port, a proportional amount of freight shall be paid.

A bill of lading is a contract for conveyance of the cargo, and, though signed by the master, binds the ship-owner. There are usually three copies of it; one for the freighter, a second for the master, and a third for the consignee or agent abroad. The bill of lading is made payable *to order* or *assigns*; and a transfer of it passes the property of the goods.

Where there is no charter-party, but the vessel is open to all merchants who choose to employ her; she is called *a general ship*. Substantially the same principles apply to both descriptions of vessels.

In order to claim *freight*, the goods must be delivered at the port of destination named in the charter-party; and, unless by express stipulation, nothing shall be recovered, till the entire contract has been fulfilled.

In some instances, however, delivery of a part of the cargo will give title to a proportional freight. This is where the ship is chartered generally, to be paid according to the quantity of goods. It is otherwise, where she is chartered for a certain sum. If the outward and homeward voyages are spoken of as parts of one voyage, this will be the construction in regard to the claim of freight. And *vice versâ*, where they are mentioned as distinct voyages. The same circumstances, which prevent a recovery of freight, will justify an action to regain it, if paid in advance.

Dead freight is the freight paid, where a return cargo was agreed for, and is not carried; in which case, the same compensation shall be recovered, as if it were actually carried.

The master has a lien upon the cargo for freight; which he may preserve, by entering the goods at the public depository in his own name. By the usual terms of the bill of lading, the *consignee*, who receives a cargo, becomes responsible for the freight; but not a person who purchases from him. A delivery to the consignee does not discharge the consignor. Freight commences when the ship *breaks ground.* Any temporary obstacle to the voyage, — as, for instance, *an embargo,* — does not break up the contract; but the voyage may be performed whenever the obstacle is removed, unless the goods are *perishable.* In general, there is no deduction from freight on account of a deterioration in the goods, unless occasioned by some fault of the master.

6. *General average* is *a contribution,* made by all parties concerned in a voyage, towards a loss sustained by a part for the benefit of all. As where goods are thrown overboard to lighten the ship, which is called *jettison.* The case, however, must be one of extreme necessity; and the least precious articles must be first sacrificed. So, if a ship be injured by a peril of the sea, and go into port to repair, the wages and provisions of the crew are a subject for general average. In what cases this right exists, has been a matter of much conflicting opinion. It does not exist, unless the preservation of a part of the property is effected by a sacrifice of the rest. For instance, if the crew, the ship being in imminent danger, take to the boat, carrying with them some articles of the cargo, and afterwards to save the boat throw them overboard, and the ship with the rest of the cargo is saved; there shall be no contribution for the goods thus lost.

7. *Salvage* is a compensation for preserving a ship or cargo. *The rate* varies with circumstances, but never exceeds *one half* the value of the property. It may be allowed to strangers, or, in case of extraordinary danger and effort, to the seamen of the preserved ship.

8. *Maritime remedies.*—The rights, arising out of marine contracts or services, are in general a subject of *Admiralty jurisdiction*, and enforced by the Circuit and District Courts of the United States. The mode of proceeding in these courts is materially different from that in the courts of common law. The process is *in rem*,—that is, *acts upon the thing itself* in connexion with which the claim arose, and enforces the claim by *a sale or forfeiture* of the property. This remedy, however, does not in most cases supersede an action at common law. Thus a seaman has a claim for wages, either against the master, the owner, or the ship, at his election.

CHAPTER XIII.

BOTTOMRY, RESPONDENTIA, AND INSURANCE.

I. Bottomry is in the nature of *a mortgage of a ship*: when the owner hires money, to enable him to carry on his voyage, and pledges the keel or *bottom* of the ship as security; with an agreement, that, if the ship be lost, the lender shall receive nothing, but if she return in safety, that he shall receive the stipulated premium, which always exceeds the legal rate of interest. This is everywhere a valid contract; and binds the ship and tackle, if she return, as well as the person of the borrower. A contract of bottomry is valid, though the lender is to be repaid from the earnings, before the expiration of the contract, and what is thus paid to be kept at all events; and though a mortgage of land be given as additional security.

II. *Respondentia* is where one borrows money for the prosecution of a voyage, to be repaid with a high rate of interest, if it terminate safely, and, if otherwise, to be wholly lost to the lender.

III. The abovementioned contracts are comparatively of rare occurrence, and therefore of minor importance. Belonging to the same general class, though not precisely analogous, is the contract of *insurance*, than which, in a mercantile community, there is none more frequent or of greater consequence.

1. *Nature and effect of insurance, and parties to the contract.*

Insurance is a contract, whereby one party, for a stipulated premium, agrees to indemnify the other against certain perils of his property. *Marine* insurance is an insurance *against the perils of the sea*; and is that branch of the subject, in relation to which the principles of law have been chiefly discussed and settled. Insurance *against fire*, and insurance *upon lives*, though usual and important contracts, do not demand a distinct notice.

The written instrument, in which a contract of insurance is contained, is called *a policy*; and the insurer, *an underwriter*.

All persons may be *insured*, except *alien enemies*,

or citizens of a hostile country. Different persons, having distinct interests in the same property, may be insured, each for his share,—as for instance a mortgagor and a mortgagee.

Either corporations or individuals may be *insurers.*

The description of the property need not, though it should be, very nice and accurate. An insurance may be valid, though neither the ship, master, port, nor consignee be specified. If upon goods, they may be transferred from one ship to another. If upon the body of the ship, all its appurtenances are covered. The insurance may be "for all whom it may concern." So it may be and usually is, "lost or not lost," and will cover a prior loss. *Freight* cannot be insured under the name of *property*; nor *live animals*, as *goods or cargo*; nor *provisions* for their support, *as cargo*.

A policy, like other contracts, may be *assigned*;[1] but a suit must, in general, be brought in the assignor's name.

Policies are either *open* or *valued.* An *open policy*, is one in which the value of the property insured is not fixed. A *valued policy* is one in which the value is fixed, and will be the measure of indemnity to be recovered in case of *total loss.* The valuation is held conclusive, unless there be some fraud. But it will be the measure of damages, only so far as *a risk has been incurred.* Therefore, if a part of the goods were never put on board, or landed before the loss, a proportional deduction shall be made from the policy. And in case of partial loss, adjusted by *average and contribution*, neither party is concluded by the valuation.

A *double insurance*, is where one obtains two

---

[1] See p. 44.

insurances on the same property or interest, either by the same or separate policies. In such case, he may sue both underwriters, though he can recover but one satisfaction. The insurers are bound to contribute equally, unless some special clause provides otherwise; and if one pay the whole, he shall recover a share from the other. Provision is usually made, however, that the insurances shall take effect in the order of their dates. In New York, it is understood that *mercantile usage* somewhat controls the effect of such a stipulation.

There may be separate policies against different risks. Thus there may be one against *capture*, and another against *perils of the sea.*

2. *What may be insured.*

A trade *illicit* or prohibited in the State where a policy is made, or sought to be enforced, cannot be validly insured; but its illegality in the foreign country to which or from which it is carried on, — as in cases of smuggling, — will not avoid the policy, provided the insurer was apprized that such trade was to be undertaken. So an insurance in a neutral country of goods *contraband of war*, — that is, goods which furnish aid to one belligerent, and may therefore be seized and confiscated by the other, — is a valid contract. So also an insurance against loss arising from acts of government, — as, for instance, an embargo. Clearing out for a foreign port is no evidence of an intention to engage in an illicit trade at such port.

Seamen's wages may be insured after they are due, — not before.

Freight, or the compensation to be paid for the use of a ship in carrying goods, may be insured, after it has commenced, — which will be, after the goods have been put on board.

Profits may be insured; that is, all beneficial interests, by way of commissions or otherwise, in a cargo. The interest must in general be such, that a loss of the property would involve some loss, or the interception of some profit, to the party insured. For instance, an insurer may himself procure insurance of his own liability. A mere *wager policy*, or *a bet* upon the return of the ship, without any interest, is in Massachusetts and Pennsylvania void; though in New York it has been held valid.[1]

Policies usually contain *a memorandum*, providing that, for certain articles, nothing shall be recovered, in case of a *partial loss*. These are commonly *perishable goods*, liable to loss from their own nature as well as other causes. If only a part of them are lost, though totally, the preservation of the rest will prevent any claim upon the insurer. In case of *a total loss* of the voyage, by shipwreck or otherwise, *memorandum articles* stand on the same footing with others.

3. *What will avoid an insurance.*

(1.) A policy is *avoided* by any *misrepresentation* or *concealment* in regard to a fact which is material to the risk. In this respect, insurance stands upon a more purely equitable footing than any other contract known to our law.[2]

These causes will avoid the contract, although the loss occur from a source entirely unconnected with the matter misrepresented or concealed, and though the misrepresentation or concealment happen through neglect or mistake. If there be *fraud*, the *materiality*

---

1 Otherwise, it seems, by the Revised Statutes.
2 See p. 74.

of the fact does not come in question; otherwise it does. In some cases, misrepresentation even upon a material point, — as, for instance, the time of sailing, — will not avoid the policy, if innocently occasioned by false information from others.

There are some material facts, which the insured is not bound to communicate. Such are all topics of general speculation and intelligence; matters of opinion; loose reports; and the general course of trade and of the proposed voyage. Such also are all matters covered by a *warranty*, either express or implied.

A false representation, made to the first underwriter, will avoid subsequent insurances upon the same policy; but not those by other policies, though upon the same property. The rule does not extend to representations made to any intermediate underwriter.

(2.) *Breach of warranty. Warranty* is either implied or express.

There is an *implied warranty*, on the part of the insured, that the ship is *seaworthy*, that is, soundly and substantially built; properly equipped, manned, and stocked with provisions; and provided with a trust-worthy commander; and that the cargo is carefully and properly stowed. This warranty applies only to the *commencement* of the risk. But if the vessel become unseaworthy during the voyage, any unreasonable neglect to repair her will avoid the policy, if the loss happen through such neglect. If a vessel spring a leak and founder, in moderate weather, the loss will be presumed to arise from unseaworthiness; but if she is apparently seaworthy at the time of sailing, and never afterwards heard of, the insurers are liable. Unseaworthiness at the commencement of the voyage will have no effect, if remedied before the loss. If a ship be *surveyed* (according to the common usage), and condemned as unseaworthy, this is strong evidence, though not conclusive, for the insurer, in a suit against him. Seaworthiness is not warranted while the ship remains in port.

The usual *express warranties* are; that the ship *was safe at such a time*, would sail *with convoy*, or *by such a day*, that the *property is neutral*, or *the trade lawful*. The warranty of neutrality requires the insured to pursue the conduct, and, when necessary, to exhibit the documents and vouchers, of a neutral.

In general, a policy of insurance, like other written contracts, cannot be varied or controlled by verbal or *parol* evidence.[1] Upon this principle, a *warranty* must be in the policy itself. But *misrepresentations* may be proved by any kind of competent evidence, whether written or unwritten.

(3.) *Deviation* avoids an insurance.

Every departure from *the usual track* of the voyage, specified in the policy, is a deviation, however short the time or distance. Necessity alone justifies such departure; and nice questions constantly arise as to the limits of this exception. Obtaining new seamen, the crew being sick; avoiding capture, if there be a reasonable fear of it, or an obstruction by ice; compulsion by the crew; the procuring of information which is important to the voyage; and some other similar circumstances, will justify a departure as *necessary*.

Where the policy reserves liberty to touch at intermediate ports, they must be visited in the order named, or else in geographical order.

---

[1] See *Parol Evidence*.

If the insurance is from one port to another, *and a market*, in a particular country, the ship may go to any port in the country which furnishes a market, without first going to the one named; but, after visiting others, she cannot go to the port named. Liberty to *touch* at a port does not in general authorize *trading* there; but the mere selling of a part of the cargo will not avoid the policy, unless it cause delay or increase the risk, or be foreign from the purpose for which the leave was granted.

Deviation may consist in *unnecessary delay in port*, or in any other act which, without just cause, increases or changes the risks insured against.

4. *Risks covered by an insurance.*

The phrase "perils of the sea" applies to accidents, which are neither caused, nor can be foreseen or prevented, by man; and to such only as are in their nature *extraordinary*. The misconduct of mariners, the loss of an anchor, or the spontaneous combustion of some substance on board, for instance, are not dangers covered by the policy; because they result from the ordinary use of the ship. Nor does the insurance apply, unless the peril insured against is *the immediate cause* of the loss. For instance, if a ship be stranded and afterwards captured, the loss is not held to be by stranding.

"*Bilging*," when named in a policy, must consist in *a breach of the vessel*, and not in a mere straining and opening of her seams.

Besides the general clause, "perils of the sea," policies of insurance usually contain more special enumerations of probable marine risks; such as piracy, theft, acts of government, fire, capture, and barratry. *Barratry* is the wilful misconduct of the master or mariners; as, for instance, entering a foreign port without instructions, and selling the ship and cargo; incurring extreme danger of capture; or engaging in an illicit trade.

5. *Commencement and termination of the risk.*

The time when a policy commences, depends upon *the subject matter* insured, and *the phraseology* made use of.

If *upon a vessel, from a certain place,* the risk begins when she *breaks ground.* If *at and from,* it includes all the time that she is in port, if at home; and also, according to the weight of authority, when in a foreign port. The risk usually continues *twenty-four hours* after arrival at the port of destination. Insurance upon a vessel *while at sea,* will cover her in a foreign port, if she is there in prosecution of the voyage proposed.

The risk upon *a cargo* usually commences, when the goods are put aboard the ship; and continues, till they are removed. A temporary landing from necessity, will not affect the insurance; and usage may extend its operation to the transportation from the ship to the shore in another vessel. If the policy be upon the voyage *out and home,* on cargo to a certain value, it will cover to that extent every cargo put aboard during the voyage. If goods are insured *to a port of discharge,* the policy will continue in force, though the discharge be not made at the first port of arrival; but not if the vessel has begun to unload, or *broken bulk,* at such port. A delivery of goods to the consignee terminates the voyage, though made at another port than the one specified.

6. *Total loss and abandonment.*

A *total loss* consists, either in *the destruction* of the

thing insured, or in such a damage *as renders it of little or no value.* In other words, a loss is *total,* when the voyage is wholly lost or defeated, or not worth pursuing, and the projected adventure fustrated; or when circumstances render such an issue highly probable.

In such case, the insured may *abandon* all his interest in the property to the insurer, and require payment as for *a total loss in fact.* If the loss is actually total, of course no abandonment is required. The insured may elect to *repair* at the insurer's expense; but the latter has no such right against the will of the other party. A loss cannot be constructively total, unless the insured has power to abandon. Thus where he has mortgaged the ship since the insurance, and thereby lost the control of it. *Submersion* is not conclusive evidence of a total loss.

No particular form is required for an abandonment; nor need it be in writing. But it must be *explicit and absolute,* and must set forth the reasons upon which it is founded. It must also be made in *reasonable time* after the loss. The sale of a ship by the master, from necessity, may make a total loss, without abandonment. And the judgment of disinterested and competent *surveyors* will be strong proof of such necessity. The master, in case of sale, should retain the money for the insurers.

Abandonment vests the property in the insurer. When once rightfully made, it is binding and conclusive, and no subsequent event will change the effect of it; that is, it will remain valid, although the loss prove to have been less than was fairly and reasonably supposed at the time. But if the insurer elects to repair the vessel, and does it for *less than one half* the value, he may in reasonable time avoid a total loss by restoring the ship.

Substantially the same rules apply to both ship and cargo. Perhaps the loss of the latter must be more nearly total, to justify an abandonment, than that of the former. Mere *delay of the voyage* is not sufficient, unless the goods are *perishable.* In all cases, a diminution in value to the amount of more than one half will justify an abandonment, whether the interest be ship, cargo, or freight. The value is *the general market value.* And the amount of injury is determined by the cost of repairs at the port where they become necessary.

Capture is a ground for abandonment, before *condemnation* of the vessel. But the insured may safely wait for a condemnation. Subsequent restoration, or reversal of the decree of condemnation, will not avoid the abandonment.

The usual evidence of loss is *the protest of the master*; or, if this cannot be had, the *affidavit or statement of the pilot.*

After abandonment, the master of the vessel becomes *agent for the insurer,* and the insured is no longer bound by his acts. If the loss, however, prove not to be total, the property remains that of the insured. And any unqualified act of ownership by him will be a waiver of the abandonment.

7. *Partial loss and average.*

A partial loss, or *particular average,* consists in *some injury* to the thing insured, short of a total loss, which the insurer is bound to make good, provided it exceeds a certain amount,— usually *five per cent.*

General average results from the expense, sacrifice, or damage, incurred by the owner of ship, freight, or cargo, for the owners of the others, in saving their property; and furnishes a claim against the insurers of the latter for their proportion of indemnity. *An adjustment* of general average, at a foreign port, is conclusive upon the insurer, as well as the parties. The basis of it is the value of the property at such port. *Repairs* to the ship, in their nature permanent, are not a subject of general average; it is otherwise with those which are necessary for the ship's return, and of temporary use.

In case of partial loss, the practice is to pay *the cost of the goods and the expenses incurred*, so as to place the insured *in his original position.* If goods arrive damaged at the destined port, the standard is the difference, in the market price there, between sound and damaged articles.

Where a vessel is damaged, and, before any repairs have been made, is totally lost; the whole damage will be ascribed to the latter peril, and no deduction allowed from the policy for the diminished value of the vessel.

An adjustment of a loss cannot be set aside or opened, except for fraud or mistake, or an imperfect disclosure of the facts. In a partial loss, the rule is, to apply the old materials towards payment of the new, deducting *one third new for old* upon the balance.

For all necessary repairs made by the master, the insurers are liable.

8. *Return of premium.*

Where an insurance is *void* "ab initio," from the beginning, or where the risk has never commenced; *the premium shall be returned to the insured.* As, for instance, where the insured had in fact no interest in the property, although he supposed himself to have an interest, or where from any cause the voyage is never commenced ; or there is a breach of warranty, without fraud, which avoids the policy. In such cases, the insurer retains *one half per cent.* for his trouble. If the voyage is divisible, and only a part of it performed; a proportional share of premium only shall be retained. *Fraud and illegality* preclude any claim for a return of premium, notwithstanding they avoid the policy.

BOOK V.

RIGHTS OF THINGS REAL.

CHAPTER I.

INCORPOREAL HEREDITAMENTS.

Real property, in the technical phraseology of the law, consists of *lands, tenements, and hereditaments.* The precise legal meaning of these terms need not be explained, being of little practical consequence. The first is the least comprehensive, including only *corporeal* property; while the two last embrace also *incorporeal.*

Tenements and hereditaments are either *corporeal* or *incorporeal.*

Corporeal hereditaments are confined to *land*, which includes not only the ground or soil, but every thing attached to it; whether by the course of nature, as trees, herbage, and water, or by the hand of man, as houses; and which has an indefinite extent, upwards as well as downwards, so as to embrace every thing terrestrial under or over it; as for instance, woods or mines. Standing ripe corn, however, or any other *annual product*, is *personal estate*; passing to the executor instead of the heir, and liable to be taken on execution like other chattels.

An *incorporeal hereditament* is *a right issuing out of a thing corporate*, or concerning, or annexed to, or exercisable within, the same. Thus, for example, *a rent*, issuing out of a house,—the house being the substance or thing corporeal, and the rent the invisible right which adheres to it. Most rights of this description are also termed in law "easements." Incorporeal hereditaments may be classed as follows.

I. *Commons. The right of common* is a right which one man has *to use lands of another*, in pasturing his cattle, catching fish, providing necessary fuel, or repairing his implements of husbandry. This right, though an important one in the early ages of English law, is little known or used in the United States, and therefore may be passed over, with only a brief notice of a single branch of the subject, viz. *common of fishery.*

Common of fishery, or *piscary*, is a right of fishing in the water covering or running through the soil of another person; and may be divided into a right *common to all*, and a right *exclusively in one or a few individuals.*

The owners of land on the banks of *fresh water rivers*, above the ebbing and flowing of the tide, have the exclusive right of fishing opposite their respective lands, "ad filum medium aquæ,"—to the thread of the river. But if *navigable*, this right is subject to that of the public to use the river as *a common highway*; and any obstruction is *a nuisance.* And the owner of the land has not a right wholly to obstruct the fish, whereby owners above on the river may be prevented from enjoying a similar privilege.

The right of fishing *in the sea, in the bays and arms of the sea, and in all tide-waters*, is in general common and public; but in some instances may belong by prescription or usage to particular individuals.

Both the above rights may be, and in many of the States have been, modified and restrained by the statute law. Thus, in Massachusetts, the regulation of the subject has been given *to the several towns*, within their own limits. And in Pennsylvania and South Carolina, the public right of fishery is held to apply to *large fresh-water rivers*, as well as those in which the tide ebbs and flows. Proprietors of land, adjoining a navigable river, have the exclusive right to draw the seine and take fish on their own land; but though the seashore, between high and low water mark, be held by grant as private property, the common right still exists to go there and fish, unless there be an individual claim *by prescription*. The conveyance of *land covered by a pond* passes the fishery.

II. *Aquatic rights.* Proprietors of land bounded on the salt water, own to *high-water mark*; and, in Massachusetts, by an old statute, to *low-water mark*,[1] provided it is not more than one hundred rods below high-water mark, and subject to the public right of a convenient passage along the shore. *The shore* is the space between high and low water mark; hence if in a deed this be named as the boundary, the conveyance reaches only to high-water mark.

Navigable rivers which flow through a territory, and the navigable waters included in bays and between headlands and arms of the sea, belong to the sovereign of the adjoining territory.

The open sea is public property, except that part within *a cannon-shot*, or *one marine league*, from shore;

---

1 It has sometimes been held, that the title to the land between these two *points is a movable freehold*, — changing in the tide.

but, in some instances, the United States have asserted their right much beyond this limit.

Grants of land, bounded on rivers above tide-water, carry the exclusive right of the grantee to the centre of the stream, subject to the public right of passage.

Every proprietor of land on the bank of a river, has a right to the use of the water, *as it was wont to run,* without diminution or alteration; and no owner has in general a right to use it, to the prejudice of other owners above or below him.

Ownership of the bank gives no title to the water itself, but a simple *usufruct* or enjoyment while it passes along; unless by virtue of a grant, or an uninterrupted enjoyment for twenty years,[1] which is evidence of one. These principles do not, however, debar a proprietor from using the water in a reasonable manner, for domestic, agricultural, or manufacturing purposes, though he may cause some slight diminution; but only from shutting the gates of his dams and detaining the water unreasonably, and from letting it off in unusual quantities, to the annoyance of his neighbour. An exclusive enjoyment for twenty years, without interruption, raises a presumption against a right in any other person, which might have been, but was not asserted. But *the mode of using the water* cannot, under such a title, be *materially varied,* to the prejudice of other owners; though the mill need not be *of the same description* as that originally established.

The owner of a mill-site, who first occupies it by erecting a dam and mill, will have a right to the

---

1 In a few of the States, less time is required.

use of water sufficient to work his mill, notwithstanding he may render useless the privilege of an owner above or below him. So, if a former mill have been abandoned, another owner may improve his privilege, as if the first had never been built. A mere suspension of occupancy, however, without the intention to abandon, will not give this right. The owner of an ancient mill may lawfully enter upon the land of another, and remove an obstruction, by which the water is interrupted, or diverted from flowing to the mill by its ancient course.

To sustain an action, a mill-owner must prove *an actual damage* to his privilege. Mere theoretical or constructive injury is not sufficient.

At common law, the owner of *land overflowed* by means of the erection of a dam, may recover damages for the injury. In Massachusetts and several other States, a special remedy has been provided for this wrong by statute, which supersedes the common law action.[1] But if the legislature authorize the erection of a mill-dam of certain height across a navigable river, without providing any remedy for *flowage*; the only remedy is an action at common law.

Every owner of a mill or dam holds it on the condition, that a sufficient and reasonable *passage-way* shall be allowed *for the fish*; and this limitation, being for the benefit of the public, is not extinguished by any neglect in compelling the owner to comply with it. In Massachusetts, the Legislature have

---

[1] In Delaware, one mill-owner, injured by the act of another, may have a special jury to view the premises, who, if necessary, shall *abate* or remove the wrongful erection. In Illinois, an owner on one side may, by the same means, run a dam across the stream.

from time immemorial taken measures to regulate the site and dimensions of these passage-ways.

The owner of a mill may erect a dam above and remote from it, to create a reservoir of water for the use of his mill. A mill-owner, who has a right to the surplus water only which may remain after another mill is supplied, is bound to shut his gate when there is not water enough for both; and the owner of the latter must remove any obstruction, erected during a deficiency, whenever there shall be enough for both.

Uninterrupted enjoyment for twenty years, will give the same right to *a spring of water*, which issues above ground in a man's land, as it would to a stream or river; so that an adjoining owner cannot cut a drain to divert the water.

III. *Ways. A right of way* is the right of going over another man's ground; and is either *private* or *public*.

1. *A private way* may be grounded *on a special permission*; as when the owner of land grants to another a liberty of passing over it, to go to church, to market, or the like; in which case, the grant is particular and confined to the grantee alone, dies with him, and is not assignable. Or it may be granted or reserved to *one and his heirs*, and will then descend to heirs, like any other inheritance.

A way may be also *by prescription*:[1] as if all the inhabitants of a village have immemorially used to cross such a ground for such a purpose; for this usage supposes an original grant.

A right of way may also arise *by operation of law*.

---

[1] See B. 5, ch. 17, (4.)

If one man grants another a piece of ground in the middle of his field, he impliedly gives *a way* to come at it over his land. So if a man have several distinct parcels of enclosed land, and sell all but one, which is surrounded by the others; it seems that a right of way *from necessity* impliedly remains to the grantor. But if one take a conveyance of land, which is surrounded on all sides by land of his grantor *and others*; he can enforce his right of way against no one but the grantor. A sheriff has, by implication, the power to annex a convenient right of way to land which he sets off on execution.

A right of way may also be *annexed to an estate*, and will then pass by assignment, when the land is sold to which it is annexed.

If a right of way be from one close to another, and both become united in the same person, the way is *extinguished by unity of possession.* It seems however, that this principle does not apply to *ways of necessity.* And a way, thus extinguished, may be afterwards revived by a severance of the two estates; as where, on the owner's death, one is assigned to one child and the other to a second. Nor will a way be extinguished by an occupancy of the land *under a defective title.* If the owner of two adjoining closes, over which ways have been used by him, convey one of them; the ways will not pass under the general clause relating to *privileges and appurtenances.*

The duty of *repairing* a private way, falls, in general, upon the proprietor of the easement, and not the owner of the land. Hence the former has no right to go upon the adjoining land, even though the way be impassable, unless it was rendered so by the owner of the land. It is otherwise where a *highway* is impassable; so, it seems, in case of a *way of necessity*.

A person cannot claim a way over another's ground, *from one part thereof to another*, but only *from one part of his own to another*, or *to the highway*. And the claim of a right of way by one man over another's land, "in any direction most convenient to the former, and least prejudicial to the latter," is void, for unreasonableness and uncertainty. But one may claim a right of way over another's close "in all directions," as appurtenant to his own adjoining land. If one has a right of way over another's close *to a particular place*, he cannot use the way to go beyond it.

2. *Public ways* consist of *town ways and highways*.

Town ways are those laid out by a town, nominally for the use of its inhabitants. But they need not be confined to this object; since the real utility of a road to a town may consist less in its being used by the citizens, than in facilitating the intercourse of strangers with them. Town ways seem to hold an intermediate place between private and public ways; having some of the characteristics of both.

Highways are those, in which the citizens generally have a right to pass; and are laid out and supported, for the benefit of the community, by public authority. The care and control of highways is a subject for the most part regulated by special statutes. The laws of the different States in relation to it, with a general similarity, are yet so various in their details, as not to admit of particular notice in this work.

By the location of a highway over the land of any person, the public acquire *an easement*; but *the soil and freehold* remain to the owner, and he may put the land to any use, and derive from it any profits, consistent with the easement. Thus he may sink a drain below the surface, taking care to cover it securely; and has a right to the herbage growing by the side. And if the way is at any time *discontinued*, he will hold the land free from incumbrance.

No man can be deprived of his lands for public uses, without being paid for them a reasonable compensation. And where *the common convenience and necessity* are not sufficient, to warrant the laying out of a new highway wholly at the public expense, the law does not authorize it, in consideration that individuals have agreed to contribute. But such agreement will not invalidate the proceeding, unless it was founded on this basis, and the public use was only a colorable object.

The law of the road, as it is called, prescribes the relative duties of travellers, passing each other in vehicles on the highway. In Massachusetts, they are required by statute to take *the right hand side*; and a penalty is provided for breach of the law.

In many States, the law requires the erection of *guide-posts* upon highways.

The repair of highways is imposed upon *towns*. Towns are subject to *indictment* for not repairing highways; and also, in general, made liable to *damages*, for any injuries happening in consequence of defects or obstructions, which arise from a neglect of this duty, — provided they have had reasonable notice thereof. In Massachusetts, *double damages* are recovered. They are not answerable, however, where the injury might have been avoided by ordinary care. But travellers are not required to look far before them, for obstructions which ought not to exist.

When a highway is unlawfully *obstructed*, any passenger has a right even to enter upon private lands, for the purpose of removing the obstruction. A *navigable river* is in this respect like a highway, and cannot be obstructed by a bridge or otherwise, without authority from the legislature.

Non-user or disuse of a highway, for a long time, has been held to *forfeit* it, and to bar an indictment for not repairing or for obstructing it. So permitting the public to use a way for a long time, may give a right against the owner of the soil.

A highway may be *discontinued* by public authority.

Under the head of highways, may be mentioned *turnpikes* and *railroads*; which are laid out for public use, but owned usually by corporations, expressly instituted for that purpose, and authorized to exact *toll* from travellers.

IV. *Rents.* *Rent* is a certain profit, in money, provisions, chattels, or labor, issuing out of lands and tenements in retribution for the use.

Rents, though classed with incorporeal hereditaments, may be more intelligibly considered hereafter, in connexion with the subject of *leases*;[1] which constitute a part of the extensive system of *real estate corporeal*, to be treated of in the next chapter.

---

[1] See *Lease*.

CHAPTER II.

REAL ESTATE CORPOREAL.—FREEHOLD ESTATES.

Real property is divided, with respect to the nature and quantity of interest in it, into *estates of freehold*, and *estates less than freehold*. The former are again divided into *estates of inheritance*, and *estates not of inheritance*. *Freehold estates* will be treated of in this chapter.

I. *Estates in fee*. *A fee* is *an estate of inheritance*, belonging to the owner and transmissible to his heirs, and which may continue for ever; and is either *a fee simple*, or *a qualified fee*.

1. *A fee simple* is *a pure inheritance*, or *absolute ownership*, clear of any qualification or condition; and, upon the death of the proprietor, gives *a right of succession* to all his heirs. Whenever a person grants an estate in fee simple, he can make no further disposition of the land, because he has already granted the whole. In *devises*,[1] however, and deeds deriving their effect from *the statute of uses*,[2] an estate in fee may be made defeasible, on the happening of some future event.

Unlimited power of alienation is an inseparable incident to this estate. Hence all conditions or local customs restrictive of this power are void. But a condition against alienation *to a particular person* has been held valid; and an estate in fee may, by devise, be made inalienable, for lives in being and twenty-one years and nine months afterwards.[3] *Per-*

---

1 See *Devise*. 2 See *Use*.

3 In New York, this rule has been modified by statute.

petuities, by which lands are locked up from all transfer, are regarded as against the policy of the law, and therefore allowed only to the extent above mentioned.

In general, to create an estate in fee, the word "heirs" must be used; and no other expression, though indicating ever so clear an intent, will be in law sufficient. Thus a conveyance to one "and his generation, to endure so long as the waters of the Delaware shall run,"—was held to give only *a life estate.* To this rule however there are some exceptions; as in certain kinds of *release*, in *partition, devise*, and *grants to a corporation.*[1] And, in many of the United States, this strict rule has been dispensed with by positive statutes; which provide that *the whole* of a grantor's estate shall pass by the deed, unless it express an intention to the contrary.

A grant to one and his heirs, of all *the trees and timber* on certain land for ever, with liberty to cut and carry them away, gives the grantee *a fee* in their present and future growths, and an exclusive right to the soil, so far as necessary for the support of the trees. Standing trees may be validly *reserved* by a grantor from the conveyance.

2. *Qualified, determinable*, and *conditional fees*, are estates which *may last for ever*, but *are liable to be determined* by some act or event. Thus a limitation to one and his heirs, *tenants of a certain estate*; or *so long as a certain church shall stand,*—passes *a qualified fee.*

If the event marked as the boundary becomes *impossible*, as, for instance, if a third person who is to

---

[1] See *Release, Partition, Devise, Corporation.*

do a certain act has died without doing it,—the estate ceases to be determinable, and changes to *a fee simple*; but till then, it is in the grantee, subject to a possibility of *reverting* to the grantor.

To this class belong *estates tail*; limited to *the heirs of the body*, instead of the heirs generally, and not subject to be disposed of by the holder beyond his own life. These occupy a prominent place in the law of England; but, being less consonant with our institutions, have been abolished or modified in nearly every State of the Union, so as to become a comparatively unimportant subject of attention.

In New Jersey and Connecticut, estates tail become estates *in fee simple* in the heirs of the original owner. In Massachusetts and Maryland, they may be conveyed, and in Rhode Island conveyed or devised, so as to pass *a fee simple*. In Massachusetts and Virginia, they are also made liable for the tenant's debts. In New York, estates tail are converted into estates in fee. But when lands are given to one *and the heirs of his body, remainder to another and his heirs*, for the sake of giving effect to the remainder, the former does not take the absolute title. In Pennsylvania and Delaware, an entailment may be destroyed by the old fictitious process, now generally obsolete, of *common recovery*.

Estates tail are either *general* or *special*; the former, where lands are given to one *and the heirs of his body*; the latter, where the gift is to *particular heirs of the body*, as, for instance, *by a certain wife*. They are also either *male* or *female*;—and, in each case, none of the other sex can ever inherit, nor any one derived from them. Thus, an estate *in tail male* can never go either to a daughter or the son of a daughter.

II. The other kind of *freeholds*, are *estates for life.* These may arise, either from *the act of parties,* or *operation of law.*

1. *A life estate* may be created, *by act of parties,* either by *an express grant* for the life of the grantee, or of a third person, or both; or by *a general grant,* no limit being specified, which cannot pass an inheritance for want of the word "heirs."[1] So an estate limited *upon a contingency,* — as to a woman during her widowhood, — is *a life estate,* though it may terminate sooner than the grantee's life.

If one holds an estate *for the life of another,* — termed an estate *pour autre vie,* — and dies before the latter; the interest *survives* to the representatives of the former, and is variously disposed of by the statutes of the different States. In New York, it is held *a chattel real,* and, in Massachusetts, goes to *the heirs,* like real estate.

2. Estates for life created by *the act of law,* are two, — *curtesy* and *dower.*

Tenant by the curtesy, is where a man marries a woman *seised* or possessed of an inheritance, and has by her issue born alive, which is capable of inheriting the estate. In this case, *on the wife's death,* he holds the lands for life, as *tenant by the curtesy.* The common law on this subject remains in force in nearly all the States. In general, the wife must have been *actually,* and not merely *in law, seised of the land;* that is, she must have had *actual possession.* The rule, however, does not apply to *waste lands;*

---

1 For exceptions to this rule, see *Remainder, Devise.*

nor where there is an outstanding *lease for years,* (the possession of the tenant being equivalent to that of the owner herself); and, in Connecticut, is wholly exploded. In some cases, a husband may have curtesy, even out of an estate which comes to an end by the wife's death, as in case of *an estate tail,* which has failed by the death of issue and her subsequent decease, — because, *during the marriage,* all the circumstances existed requisite to this claim. A husband is not debarred from curtesy, by living in *adultery* with another woman. It is otherwise with the wife's right of *dower.* If the marriage were *void,* there can be no curtesy; otherwise, if only *voidable,* and not annulled during the life of the wife.[1] The husband, by the birth of a child, becomes tenant by the curtesy *initiate,* and may do many acts to charge the lands; — but his estate is not *consummate* till the death of the wife.

Courts of equity allow curtesy of *trusts,*[2] and other interests, which, though *mere rights* in law, are deemed *estates* in equity.

Dower. (1.) *Nature and requisites of dower.*

Tenant in dower, is where a husband is seised of an estate of inheritance, and dies. In this case, the wife shall have *a third part* of all the *lands and tenements,* or *real estate,* whereof he was seised at any time during the coverture, *for her life.* This right is paramount to debts and all other claims, — according to the old legal maxim, "There be three things favored in law; *life, liberty, and dower.*" The common

---

[1] See p. 17. [2] See *Trust.*

law rule has been somewhat modified in this country. In Georgia and Vermont, if there are no children, the widow may elect to take one half the real and personal estate after payment of debts, in lieu of dower. In the States of Ohio, Tennessee, North Carolina, Vermont, and Connecticut, the right is limited to lands of which the husband *dies seised.* In some other States, it may be barred by sale of the property *on mortgage* or *judicial process*; is subject to the husband's *debts*; and does not apply to *wild lands,* the clearing of which by a tenant for life would be a wrong to the owner of the inheritance. Upon a similar principle, there shall be dower in *a mine* or *quarry,* if it has been *opened* either wholly or in part; but not otherwise. In Massachusetts, there shall be dower of wild land, which was used by the husband, as an appendage to a dwelling-house and cultivated lands, for fuel and repairs. In Virginia and New York, the widow may have dower in *the proceeds of a contract,* by the husband, for *purchase of lands.*

Seisin in law, on the part of the husband, is sufficient to give dower; that is, a *right* to lands without *actual possession,* as, for example, that of *an heir,* before he has entered upon the estate which descends to him. But there is no dower in *a reversion or remainder,*[1] *after a freehold estate.* Thus, if a third person has a life-estate in the land, and the husband has the inheritance expectant upon it, the widow will not have dower. Nor shall there be dower, where he has only *an instantaneous seisin*; as if he takes a deed of land, and immediately mortgages it back. *An equity of redemption,* or right to redeem lands mortgaged, is

---

1 See *Reversion, Remainder.*

subject to dower, whether it existed before marriage, or arose after, from a mortgage signed by the wife. But the widow of *a mortgagee* has no dower, unless the mortgage have become absolute during his life. The widow of *a mortgagor* cannot redeem, without paying the whole debt; in which case, she shall hold the estate till reimbursed a fair proportion. But she may redeem before any *assignment of dower*; and if the administrator, or a purchaser of the equity of redemption, redeem, she may claim dower on paying her proportion of the debt, estimating it upon the principle of *life annuities*.[1]

(2.) *Extinguishment of dower.*

Dower *may be defeated* by every subsisting claim or incumbrance, existing before marriage, which would have defeated the husband's estate; as, for instance, by *an entry* of his grantor for *breach of condition*,[2] or *the happening of a contingency* to which his right is subject; though not by *a determination* of the estate *according to its own limitation.* Thus, though an estate tail ceases by the tenant's death without children, the widow may still have dower. There can be no dower in land, of which the husband was seised *wrongfully*, or of which he was the *actual* but not the *legal* owner.

No act of the husband alone, after marriage, can deprive the widow of her dower. She may *release* it, by joining him in conveyances of the estate, with an express relinquishment at the close; which is the usual form in this country.

Dower may be barred by *a jointure*; which is the settlement upon the wife of a freehold estate for life,

---

[1] See *Equity of Redemption.* [2] See *Entry for Breach of Condition.*

to take effect upon the husband's death. If made *before marriage*, it is an absolute bar; if *after*, she has her election between them.[1] And if the title to lands, given as a jointure, prove at any time defective, the widow may claim her dower. In some of the States, jointures may consist of *personal estate*. A jointure *during widowhood* is good; because, if it end before the wife's death, it will be by her own act. In regard to *the value* of a jointure; it is expressed, as "a competent livelihood," and must bear a reasonable proportion to that for which it is a substitute. If the husband merely *covenants* for a jointure, instead of making an actual conveyance, chancery will carry the agreement into effect after his death. It will also remedy any deficiencies in the instrument by which a jointure is created.

A woman is in general barred of dower by *adultery*, unless there has been a subsequent voluntary reconciliation with the husband; but not of her jointure. *Divorce "a vinculo"* also bars dower; but not *a separation "a mensâ et thoro."*[2] In New York, a divorce for adultery is a bar to a jointure as well as dower.

Any provision made by will expressly *in lieu of dower*, if accepted by the wife, will be a bar of her dower: she may make her election, but cannot take both. The same will be the case, if there is a manifest intention to that effect, arising from an inconsistency between the provisions of the will and the claim of dower. The courts, however, uniformly lean against giving this effect to a devise, except under very strong circumstances. In Equity, a legacy given to the

---

1 In New York for one year. 2 See p. 17.

widow, as the price of her release of dower, must be paid in preference to other legacies. She is regarded in the light of *a purchaser*. If the provision in a will is more beneficial than dower, it will be presumed that the widow elects it, although she dies before any positive expression of her intent. If an assignment of dower be made *against common right*, or differently from the legal mode, as, for instance, by conveying a part of the lands to the widow *in fee*, and she voluntarily release her right of dower in the rest; she will be bound by the release, although the lands assigned to her are under incumbrance, and she be *evicted* or expelled therefrom. But, in general, an eviction from the lands assigned will entitle her to be endowed anew in other lands.

(3.) *Assignment and recovery of dower.*

A widow, having the right of dower, cannot lawfully enter upon any lands of the husband, until her dower has been *assigned* according to law.[1] This is done at common law *by the heir*; but in this country, almost universally, by *commissioners* appointed by the Probate courts, on petition of the widow and notice to the parties interested. The latter proceeding, however, does not supersede the right of bringing a suit for dower at common law, after demand, or in equity, where courts of chancery exist; and such suit is the only remedy, where dower is claimed in lands of which the husband *was not seised* at his death; as, for instance, those which he conveyed to a third person without the wife's joining in the deed. In the assignment of dower, the widow is not entitled to one

---

[1] In many of the States, provision is made for her support, for a certain period after the husband's death; particularly for the privilege of occupying his mansion-house.

third of the land *in quantity*, but to so much as will yield *one third of the income*. If *improvements* have been made *by the heir*, she shall have the benefit of them; but not if made *by a purchaser* from the husband. Whether any increase of value from external circumstances shall be allowed her, seems doubtful. If the dower arises from *an incorporeal hereditament*, one third of the profits is assigned; and if the property is indivisible, — as, for instance, a mill, — either one third of the profits, or the use of it for one third of the time. When the husband was a *tenant in common* with others, the widow has one third of his share still in common; but if *partition* were made after the marriage, only a third of the portion which was assigned to him. *An infant heir* may assign dower by his guardian, and without any instrument in writing; the widow being understood to hold *by law, and not by contract*. After assignment, she is considered as being in possession from the husband's death. In a suit for dower, *damages* are recovered for detention, as well as the land itself.

To all estates for life, there are certain *incidents*, either *permissive* or *prohibitory*, which will be briefly enumerated.

1. Tenant for life may take reasonable *estovers*, or wood, from off the land, for fuel, fences, and other agricultural erections or improvements. But he cannot, under this pretence, destroy the timber, nor permanently injure the inheritance.

2. *The representatives* of tenant for life may take the *profits of growing crops*, in case the estate terminates by his death before they can be gathered.

These are called *emblements*; and consist only of annual products, and such as are raised by yearly expense and labor, as grain; but not of fruits, grass, &c., though annual, because they are spontaneous. The same right exists, when the tenancy terminates *by act of law*, as when the grant was to husband and wife *during coverture*, and they are divorced; but not if it ends *by the act of the tenant*, causing a forfeiture of the estate.

3. Tenants for life can make *under-leases*, and the under-tenants have the same right with themselves. They are also entitled to *emblements*, though the estate be ended by the act of the tenant for life himself; because for such an act they are not accountable.

4. If an estate for life be *charged with an incumbrance*, as for instance a mortgage, the tenant is bound to *keep down the interest* from the rents and profits, but has nothing to do with the principal sum. Hence, when he pays the latter, he stands creditor to the estate in fee to that amount, unless he manifest a different intention.

5. Tenant for life cannot lawfully commit *waste* upon the estate, either *voluntary* or *permissive*; as by cutting down timber, suffering buildings to decay, or doing or suffering any other permanent *strip* or injury. If *the timber* is expressly included in *the lease* or conveyance to the tenant for life, neither the lessor nor lessee can cut it down; the act would be *a trespass* in the former, and *waste* in the latter. *Timber trees* are those *used for building*; and the question, in each particular case, is determined by local usage. But it is also waste to cut down trees standing *in defence of a house*; or to cut down trees *for fuel*, when

there is sufficient dead wood on the estate. Working old mines is not waste; opening new ones is. The American doctrine on this subject is somewhat varied in several States from the English law; having been gradually accommodated (chiefly with respect to the right of *clearing woodland*) to the circumstances of a new and growing country.

In general, a tenant is responsible for waste by whomsoever committed; with the exception, as in the case of *common carriers*,[1] of the acts of God or the public enemies, or of the owner or *reversioner* himself.

If a lease be made "without impeachment of waste," as is often done, the tenant has the same power to cut timber, &c. as an owner in fee; excepting that a court of chancery will restrain him from malicious and fraudulent destruction of trees unfit to be cut down. Such a tenant has no interest in the timber while it is standing; nor can he convey any interest in it to another person.

The law of waste applies to *tenant for years*,[2] as well as for life; but not to tenant at will,[3] in whom such an injury is *a trespass*, and terminates his estate.

The law against waste is both *preventive* and *remedial*; providing *an injunction* from a court of Equity, to prohibit and stop the commission of it, and also an action for damages, which is the remedy usually adopted. By the ancient law, still in force in many of the States, the reversioner might bring *an action of waste*, in which he recovers *the place wasted, with treble damages*; but, in Massachusetts, if the waste were committed by *tenant in dower*, with only *single*

---

1 p. 102. 2 ch. 3, (1.) 3 ch. 3, (2.)

damages. In case of forfeiture, if waste be done "sparsim," or here and there, all over a wood, the whole wood shall be recovered; or if in several rooms of a house, the whole house; but if upon an end of the wood, or a single separate room in a house, — only these parts are forfeited.

By an old English statute, the destruction of a house *by accidental fire* was *permissive waste*; but this has been altered by a later one, which is probably adopted or copied in most of the States; though a general *covenant to repair* still obliges the tenant to rebuild after a loss by fire.[1] In New York, it seems, the tenant is still liable for this kind of loss. Any insurance upon the property would undoubtedly inure to his benefit.

Particular statute provision has been made, in Massachusetts, New York, and other States, to prevent waste upon land, for the recovery of which from the occupant, a suit has been commenced by an adverse claimant.

CHAPTER III.

ESTATES LESS THAN FREEHOLD.

1. *Estates for years.* *An estate for years* is a right to the possession of land *for a certain time*, and is usually created by *lease*,[2] with the recompense of *rent.* This title applies, though the time be less than a year. And, upon the maxim, "That is certain which can be rendered certain," a lease for so many years

---

[1] See *Covenant in Lease.*

[2] See *Lease.*

as A shall name, is good; but a lease for so many years *as A shall live*, is void, as an estate for years, though with us it might be a good life-estate. Tenancy for years is an inferior title to a life-estate, however long it may last; being in its nature *a chattel interest*, and not *real property*.[1] Upon this principle, — unlike *freehold* estates, which could formerly be created only by manual delivery or *livery of seisin*,[2] and cannot now be made to commence "in futuro"; an estate for years may begin at any future time. If no day of commencement be named in the lease, it begins from *the making* or *delivery*. So if the date be impossible, as the 30th of February; but if uncertain, as where the year is omitted, the lease will be void.

Tenant for years is not, in general, like tenant for life, entitled to *emblements*, because he may know when his estate will terminate.

2. *Estates at will.* — *An estate at will* is where lands and tenements are let by one man to another, to have and to hold *at the will of the lessor*. Such tenant hath *no certain, indefeasible estate*, — nothing that can be assigned by him to any other; because the lessor may put him out whenever he pleases. But every estate at will is at the will *of both parties*. The tenant is always entitled to *emblements*, unless he quit of his own accord; and to *reasonable notice* for the purposes of removal. The estate may be terminated by *implication*, as well as express notice; thus, by the death of either party; any act of immediate ownership on the part of the lessor; a partition of land

---

[1] By a late statute, in Massachusetts, long leases are invested with the incidents of real estate.

[2] See *Livery of Seisin*.

held in common; or desertion, assignment, or waste, on the part of the lessee. If rent be payable at certain intervals, and the lessee terminate the estate, he is required to pay to the end of the current term.

In England, where there is a *demise* or letting for no certain period, the courts have, in modern times, construed it as a tenancy *from year to year*, requiring *six months' notice*; especially if an annual rent be reserved. But perhaps there is no fixed rule on the subject, in this country. In some of the States, an express statute makes all *unwritten leases* tenancies at will;[1] and there, the tenant is entitled only to reasonable notice; and in New York, Pennsylvania, Massachusetts, and Maryland, *a summary process* is provided, for regaining possession, after giving a short warning to quit. In Massachusetts, the same remedy has been very recently extended to other cases of unlawful occupancy.

3. *Estates at sufferance.* — *An estate at sufferance*, is when a person comes into possession of land by lawful title, but keeps it after the termination of his estate; as if one, having a lease for a year, continues to hold when the year has expired. But the holding over of an estate acquired *by act of law*, — as, for instance, by a guardian, — does not make an estate at sufferance. This estate is a *mere naked possession*, arising from the *laches* or neglect of the landlord, who may enter at any time, using such gentle force as may be requisite, and put an end to it; but, before entry, cannot sue the tenant as *a trespasser*. If a lessee hold over, after the expiration of his term, the law implies a new contract, similar in its terms and

---

1 In New York, an unwritten lease for one year, or less, is valid.

conditions to the original one; but not such a renewal of the original one, as will charge *a surety* in the lease. In New York, a tenant at sufferance is made liable to pay *double the rent reserved.* The same summary process, provided for the termination of estates at will, applies also to a tenancy at sufferance.

CHAPTER IV.

ESTATES UPON CONDITION.

An estate upon condition is one, whose existence depends upon the happening or not happening of some uncertain event, whereby the estate may be either originally created, enlarged, or finally defeated. The conditions pertaining to estates may be either *implied* or *express*.

Implied conditions are those *annexed inseparably* to an estate, from its very essence and constitution, though not expressed in words. Thus, the condition annexed to the grant of a public office, or *a franchise*, that the grantee shall *duly execute it*, and *forfeit* it if he does not. So the condition, that the owner of *a life-estate* shall forfeit it, by attempting to convey an inheritance; which, however, has been much qualified in this country.[1]

Express Conditions are either *precedent* or *subsequent*; the former operating *to vest*, the latter *to de-*

---

[1] See *Forfeiture*.

feat an estate. Thus, if a life-estate be granted to A, upon his marriage with B, the marriage is a condition *precedent*; but if an estate be granted, reserving rent, and in case of non-payment, that the owner may *re-enter*, this is a condition *subsequent*.

A condition differs from *a limitation*. The latter expressly confines the duration of the estate to the happening of the event referred to; as when land is granted to one, "*while* he is unmarried," or "*until* he receives a certain sum." In such case, the estate ends, as soon as the contingency happens. But where the estate is strictly *upon condition*, — as, for instance, *upon condition* to be void on payment," &c., or "*so that* A remain unmarried," — there must be *an entry* or *claim* by the grantor, to revest the title. If, however, upon breach of condition, the estate be limited over to a third person, — as where a man devises land to his heir, on condition that he pay a sum of money, *otherwise to A;* the gift is held *a limitation*, and the property vests in A upon non-fulfilment of the condition. So when the estate granted is an estate *for years*, the same consequence follows a breach, without an entry by the reversioner.

One who enters for condition broken, becomes *seised* or *possessed of his first estate*, and avoids, of course, all intermediate charges and incumbrances, — as, for instance, that of *dower*.

So long as a condition subsequent remains unbroken, the grantee has an estate of the same nature as if there were no condition, and it may pass by conveyance, devise, or descent.

Conditions, impossible at the time, or which afterwards become so, contrary to law, or repugnant to the nature of the estate,[1] are void ; and, if precedent, no estate passes, — if subsequent, the estate is absolute. In the latter case, where literal performance has become impossible, the condition should be performed as near the intent as practicable.

There are no technical words, which distinguish a condition precedent from a condition subsequent. It is matter of construction, depending upon *the intention.* Precedent conditions must be literally performed, before the estate will vest. On the other hand, a condition subsequent must happen strictly according to the terms of the grant, before it shall defeat the estate; and, in some instances, where *a pecuniary satisfaction* can be made, a Court of Chancery will relieve against a breach of the condition, which happened without the party's fault. On the same principle, that which is in form *a condition*, so that a breach would forfeit the whole estate, is sometimes construed as *a covenant,* on which the only remedy is an action for the actual damages sustained. But where one conveyed a house, "*on condition,* that no windows should be placed in the north wall within thirty years," and windows were made within that time ; it was held, that this could not be construed as a covenant, and the estate was wholly forfeited.

A party can never avail himself of the same clause, as making both a condition of forfeiture, and a covenant for damages. Thus, if one covenant *not to sue* his debtor, and then sue him, and the debtor set up this covenant as *a release* ; he cannot afterwards treat it as *a promise,* and claim damages upon it.

---

[1] For instance, a lease for two years, *provided the lessee occupy but one ;* or a grant in fee-simple, on condition the grantee's widow shall not have *dower.*

For the purpose of *avoiding maintenance*,[1] and the purchase of *pretended titles*, the benefit of a condition cannot be reserved *to any third person*, but only to the grantor and his heirs; that is, there cannot be a condition, that, on a certain contingency, a third person shall have the right to enter upon the land. If, however, the grantor afterwards *convey* the whole of his *reversionary right*,[2] the condition passes with it; but if only a part, the condition is destroyed. A condition must determine *the whole estate*. Thus, in a lease for ten years, a condition, embracing only five, is void; but if it is merely confined to *a portion of the land*, as, to five acres out of ten, the condition is good.

All persons are bound by conditions annexed to estates; even those in general disabled to bind themselves, — as, for instance, *femes-covert* and infants. And any one, interested in the estate, may perform them. Thus, for example, a purchaser from one, who himself purchased on condition subsequent. An heir may perform a condition, though not named, if a time is limited for performance; otherwise, though named, he cannot.

Where no time is specified for performing a condition, *a reasonable time* will be allowed.

A condition annexed to *a bequest or devise*, whereby it is to be defeated by *the marriage* of the legatee or devisee, is void, being *in restraint of marriage*, and against the policy of the law; unless, upon such termination, the estate is immediately given over to another person, in which case it may be valid.

In general, *a devisee* is bound to take notice of

---

1 See *Maintenance*.

2 See *Reversion*.

any condition annexed to his devise; but if a devisee is also *heir at law*, he shall not lose the estate by non-performance of the condition, until after he has been notified of it.

CHAPTER V.

MORTGAGE.

THE most usual form of *estates on condition*, is where one man conveys land to another, *by way of security* for a debt, or other promise, and to become void, or be reconveyed, on payment or fulfilment of it. This is called *a mortgage*. There is no branch of the law of real property, which embraces more important interests, or which is of more practical application. Of a title so extensive, only a very general and comprehensive view can here be taken.

1. *What constitutes a mortgage*. To constitute a mortgage, *a particular form* is not absolutely necessary, though usual and proper. The common form is *a warranty deed*,[1] containing, and subject to, the proposed condition. But the latter may be valid, if written on the back of the deed, though without signature or seal, or in a separate instrument called *a defeasance*, which is part of the same transaction with the deed. In a Court of Chancery, whenever it appears from written, or perhaps even *parol* or verbal evidence, that land is conveyed to secure the payment of money; the conveyance will be treated as a

---

1 See *Warranty Deed*.

mortgage, whatever may be its form, and *the right of redemption* considered as an inseparable incident, even though it is expressly waived or surrendered.

2. *Effect of a mortgage.* — Although a mortgage purports to convey *a present estate in fee*, defeasible on the performance of a certain condition by the *mortgagor*, or party who makes the mortgage; yet it is settled, that the *mortgagee*, or person to whom it is given, instead of having an estate defeasible on performance of a condition *subsequent*, has *the right of acquiring an estate* on a certain contingency, and that the condition is a *precedent* one. As *between the parties* and their representatives, the legal freehold passes, the mortgagor being as a tenant *at sufferance*, or *at will*, to the mortgagee; who may enter and take possession at his pleasure, without giving notice to quit, unless there be an agreement to the contrary; or claim the rents of a lessee. But, as *between the mortgagor and all other persons*, the mortgage is considered only as a pledge, and the mortgagor the owner of the estate. Thus he is a *freeholder*, with all the rights pertaining to that character. He may sell in fee, subject to the condition, or make a second mortgage; and the purchaser or second mortgagee may redeem. The estate descends to his heirs, who may also redeem, or call upon the administrator to do it.[1] For a dispossession of the land, the mortgagor may bring his action against the wrong-doer, who cannot set up the mortgage against him to disprove his title. The interest of the mortgagor may be, while that of the mortgagee cannot be, taken *on execution*.

---

[1] Upon the ground, that *the personal estate* was augmented by the mortgage, and should therefore go to discharge it.

A mortgagor, however, though regarded as the *legal owner*, cannot do any thing to *impair the security*. A Court of Chancery will issue an injunction against him to stop the commission of *waste*; and, in some instances, the mortgagee may maintain an action against a third person for any injury to the estate. But the mortgagor cannot be compelled to make repairs.

3. *Rights and duties of a mortgagee.*

A mortgagee, though the mortgagor be in possession, may convey the lands, subject to the condition, to a third person; and it will be regarded as the *conveyance of an estate*, and not the mere *assignment of a security*, so that the grantee must bring an action, if at all, in his own name.[1] But if the mortgagor is *disseised*,[2] the mortgagee is also, and cannot convey his interest.

A mortgage, being usually an accompaniment to a note or other personal security, is treated, like that, as *personal estate*; and, on the mortgagee's death, passes to his executor or administrator, or else to *the heir* in trust for him. If there be no personal security, and no covenant in the mortgage itself, the mortgagee has no personal claim for the debt, but his only remedy is on the land. In some of the States, it is usual to add to the mortgage *a power of sales* in case of default; or a process in equity is provided for the same purpose. If this take place, the mortgagee becomes *trustee* for what remains after paying the debt. He also becomes a trustee, after receiving payment from the mortgagor.

A mortgagee has a right to take down and carry

---

1 See p. 44. 2 See *Maintenance.*

away any buildings erected by him, which can be removed without injury to the soil.[1] But he will not be allowed, on settlement, for any *new erections*, unless absolutely necessary, or permanently beneficial, — as, for instance, an aqueduct required to furnish water; nor for *insurance*. He will be held to *account for the rents and profits* received by him with interest, and for all that by reasonable care and diligence he might have obtained. In Massachusetts, a commission of five *per cent.* is allowed; but this is not the usual practice.

A mortgagee, before entry, cannot claim from the mortgagor any part of the rents and profits.

The mortgagee may pursue his legal remedies upon the mortgage and the personal security at the same time. But he cannot, in general, cause *the equity of redemption* to be sold, to satisfy a judgment upon the personal security; because he might thus abridge the right of redemption at his pleasure, — a less *time* being allowed by law to redeem a right in equity sold, than to redeem a mortgage.

Where *negotiable notes* are secured by mortgage, and *assigned* without the latter, the mortgagee becomes a trustee for the assignees, and holds the mortgage for their benefit.

If the mortgagee resort to an action, *before condition broken*, to obtain possession of the estate; he recovers it *generally*, as in any other case of a title to real property; but if *after condition broken*, in Massachusetts and other States, the judgment is *a conditional one*, that he shall have possession, unless the mortgagor pay the debt, interest, and costs within a certain time.

---

[1] See pp. 42, 48.

Though a mortgagee has an undoubted legal right, unless restrained by statute, or agreement, to enter before condition broken; yet in ordinary cases it is not an advisable proceeding, because he will be held to account very strictly for all that might have been made from the estate.

4. *Rights and duties of the mortgagor.* — Until the condition of the mortgage is *broken,* — as, for instance, (if the debt is a *note*) until the day of payment has passed; the rights and remedies of the mortgagor are *legal, not equitable*; so that, by performing the condition, he may revest the estate in himself, and regain possession of the land either by entry or by legal process.

But when *the condition is broken,* the estate, *at law,* becomes absolute in the mortgagee; even though the mortgagor still retain possession; he being understood to occupy, under these circumstances, merely by indulgence of the mortgagee. But *in equity,* in all the States, whether they have distinct *Courts of Chancery* or not, the mortgagor is allowed a certain time after breach of condition to regain or *redeem* his estate. This right is called *an equity of redemption.* No words in the deed, however explicit, are allowed to impair or abridge it. The maxim of law is, — "Once a mortgage always a mortgage." The time limited, varies in the different States, from one year in New Hampshire, to twenty years in New Jersey, — after entry by the mortgagee for breach of condition. Entry may be made, either by the mere act of the mortgagee, sometimes termed *in pais* or in *the country*; or by virtue of *a judgment* recovered against the mortgagor. If the mortgagee enter before, and continue to occupy after, condition broken, the time of redemption does not begin to run, till he has notified the mortgagor that he shall thenceforth hold for the purpose of *foreclosing* or gaining an absolute title. But if he first enter *after breach*, the time runs from his entry, although no notice be given. After the requisite time has elapsed, the mortgage is said to be *foreclosed*, and the mortgagee becomes absolute owner.

Redemption is effected by *a bill in equity*. In this process, the mutual accounts of the parties are adjusted; payment of debt and interest being required on the one side, and an account of rents and profits on the other. If the mortgagor have conveyed the estate to several persons, either may redeem, — but only by paying *the whole debt*, looking to the rest for contribution of their share. So a widow entitled to dower;[1] a purchaser of the equity at an execution sale; or a second mortgagee, that is, a mortgagee of the first equity of redemption, — may redeem the mortgage. If one person, jointly interested with others, redeem the whole, he becomes, in relation to them, *an assignee* of the mortgage, and may hold the estate till their share is paid.

If a mortgage is given to secure payment of a note payable *by instalments*, the non-payment of any instalment as it becomes due is a breach of the condition. And if an action be brought for such breach, and judgment recovered, conditioned to pay the amount due, the mortgage will still remain as security for future instalments. If a mortgage be given *to indemnify a surety* from his liability, and the mortgagor do not pay the money at the time stipulated, so that the mortgagee is exposed to suit; it is a breach of

---

[1] See Dower.

the condition. If the indemnity is against *actual loss or damage*, mere exposure to suit is no breach.

5. *Discharge of mortgages, and extinguishment of equities of redemption.*

A mortgage will not be held *discharged*, where such was not the intention of the parties, by the giving of *a new security* for the debt, even though it be *of a higher nature* than the former one, — as, for instance, *a bond* instead of *a note.*[1]

If a mortgagor, before condition broken, *tender payment*, and the mortgagee refuse to accept it, *the land is discharged*, though the debt remain. If the mortgagor release by deed to the mortgagee all right and title to redeem, such release will make the latter absolute owner. And *the surrender* or giving up of *a bond of defeasance* will have the same effect. But not *an assignment* of such bond to an assignee of the mortgage; for the bond is *a chose in action*, not assignable in law,[2] and cannot be converted into a conveyance or release of the equity. An equity of redemption cannot be extinguished by *parol agreement*; because it is such an *interest in land* as is within the statute of frauds.

In several of the States, a mortgage may be discharged by a short memorandum upon the margin of the public record of deeds.

---

1 See *Discharge of Contract.*

2 See p. 44.

CHAPTER VI.

REMAINDER AND REVERSION.

After considering estates with reference to *the quantity of interest* which the owners have therein, we are now to speak of them in another point of view, viz. with regard to *the time of enjoyment*, when *the actual occupancy or receipt of the profits* takes place.

Estates are either *in possession*, or *in expectancy.* Of the former there is nothing peculiar to be observed, since all the estates hitherto spoken of are of this description. There are two kinds of *expectancies*; one *created by act of parties*, called *a remainder*; the other *by act of law*, called *a reversion.*

I. An estate *in remainder* is one limited to take effect and be enjoyed *after another is determined.* As if a man, seised in fee-simple, grant land to A for twenty years, and *after the end of said term* to B and his heirs for ever. Here A is tenant for years, *remainder to B in fee.* But both these interests are in fact *a single estate*; the term and the remainder, when added together, being equal only to one estate in fee. Hence no remainder can be limited after the grant of an estate in fee-simple; because tenant in fee has the whole. Hence also there must necessarily be some *particular estate precedent to the remainder*; otherwise, the latter would be an estate in possession.

An estate created *to commence at a future time*, can only be made of *chattel interests*, unless there be a prior particular estate; since every *freehold* estate takes effect immediately or not at all.[1] Therefore, though *a lease for seven years, to commence after a year*, is good; *a conveyance to one and his heirs for ever*, thus to commence, is void. But if a prior estate for years be created at the same time, the possession of the tenant will be considered as that of the remainder-man, and the whole will be valid. The particular estate is said to *support* the remainder. *A lease at will*, being so slight and uncertain an interest, is not sufficient to constitute such support. If the particular estate is *void in its creation*, or by any means *defeated afterwards*, the remainder is defeated also. Thus, where the former is for the life of a person not in being, it is void, and the remainder with it. So, where the particular estate is an estate for life *on condition*, upon breach of which the grantor enters and avoids it, he thereby destroys the remainder likewise.

The remainder must commence, or pass out of the grantor, at the same time with the particular estate; and it must vest in the grantee, either during the continuance of the particular estate, or the instant it terminates. Thus, if A be tenant for life, remainder to B in fee; B's remainder is vested in him at the creation of the particular estate to A: or if A and B be tenants for their joint lives, remainder to the survivor in fee; here, though during their joint lives the remainder is vested in neither, yet, on the death of either, it vests instantly

---

[1] For the reason, that at common law freeholds were conveyed only by actual delivery or *livery of seisin*. (See *Livery of Seisin. — In Futuro.*) In New York, the rule in the text has been changed.

in the survivor; therefore both these are good remainders. But if an estate be limited to A for life, remainder to the eldest son of B in fee, and A die before B has any son; here the remainder will be void, —for it did not vest in any one during the continuance, nor at the termination, of the particular estate; and though B should afterwards have a son, he will take nothing. This leads us to speak of what are called *contingent remainders.*

Contingent remainders are those limited to take effect, either to *an uncertain person,* or upon *an uncertain event.*

If A be tenant for life, remainder to B's eldest son, *then unborn,* in fee; this is *a contingent remainder,* for it is uncertain whether B will ever have a son. This species of remainder must be limited to some one, that may by *common possibility* be in *esse* or existence, when or before the particular estate terminates. Thus, in the case above stated, if there is such a person as B at the time of the conveyance, the remainder is good; but if not, it is void, because *two contingencies* must happen before it can take effect, which is too remote a possibility. Upon the same principle, a remainder limited to an unborn son *of a particular name,* is void; because it is contingent whether the son will be born, and also whether he will bear that name.

In this connexion, it is proper to remark upon what is usually termed "the rule in Shelly's case." By this ancient decision, the principle was first settled, that when one takes an estate of freehold, and in the same instrument there is a limitation by way of remainder to *his heirs* or *the heirs of his body,* as a class of persons to take in succession; instead of making *a contingent remainder* to the heirs, it gives him the whole *as an inheritance*, in *fee-simple* or *fee-tail*. The rule is subject to some exceptions, and in New York has been abolished, and in Massachusetts altered in relation to *devises*, by statute. In Kentucky, a posthumous child may take by way of remainder, precisely as if born before the parent's death.

A remainder may also be *contingent*, where the person is certain, but the *event upon which it is to take effect* uncertain. As where land is given to A for life, and, in case B survives him, then with remainder to B in fee. This remainder, during the joint lives of A and B, is *contingent*; and if B dies first, it never can vest in his heirs, but is for ever gone; but if A dies first, the remainder becomes vested.

The true criterion of a *contingent remainder* is, that it could not take effect, if the particular estate should come to an end *immediately after creating it*; — as, for instance, a remainder *to the heirs of A*, A being then alive, and of course having no heirs; so that, if the prior estate should then cease, the remainder would be void. A remainder is not *contingent*, because it may possibly never take effect; for this may be said of any remainder. For instance, if it be to A for life; A may die, before the particular estate terminates, and yet this is a *vested remainder*.

The law favors *vested estates*; and words are frequently used in conveyances, which, instead of creating contingencies on which *remainders are to become vested*, only indicate the time when *vested remainders shall become estates in possession*. Thus, a devise to executors *till A is twenty-one, then to him and his heirs*, gives A a *vested remainder* during minority, and a *vested estate* afterwards.

Contingent remainders of *freehold* cannot be limited on any particular estate *less than freehold.*— Thus if land be granted to A *for ten years*, with remainder in fee to *the right heirs of B*, this remainder is void,—but if granted to A *for life*, with a like remainder, it is good. The reason is, that a freehold estate must always take effect *at the time of conveyance*,—it cannot commence "*in futuro.*"[1]

Contingent remainders may be *defeated*, by destroying or determining the particular estate upon which they depend, before the contingency happens. For instance, if there be tenant for life, with remainder to his oldest son unborn in *tail*, and the tenant for life, before any son is born, *surrender*[2] *his estate*; he thereby defeats the remainder. In such case, therefore, it is necessary to have *trustees to preserve the contingent remainders*; in whom there is vested an estate in remainder, for the life of the tenant for life, to commence when his estate terminates. Upon its terminating *otherwise than by death*, the estate of the trustees, for the residue of his natural life, will then take effect, and become a particular estate in possession, sufficient to support the contingent remainders.

The doctrine of contingent remainders has been in Virginia modified, and in New York almost entirely abrogated, by statute.

By *devise*,[3] remainders may be created in some

---

1 See *In Futuro*. 2 See *Surrender of Estate*.

3 See *Devise*.

measure contrary to the rules above laid down. Such remainders are termed *executory devises.*

An *executory devise* is such a disposition of lands by will, that thereby no estate vests at the devisor's death, but only on some future contingency. It differs from a remainder in two points.

1. It needs no *particular estate* to support it. Thus, if one devise land to a *feme-sole* and her heirs *upon her day of marriage*; it is a good freehold to commence "in futuro," and, till the marriage takes place, the estate descends to the devisor's heirs.

2. A fee, or other estate, may be limited *after a fee.*[1] Thus, if one devises land to A and his heirs, but, if he die before twenty-one, then to B and his heirs; this remainder, though it would be void in a deed, is good as *an executory devise.* Within what limits, however, such a devise must be made, so as to avoid *a perpetuity*, has been already stated.[2]

II. The other species of *expectancy* is *a reversion.*

A *reversion* is either *the residue of an estate left in a grantor,* to commence in possession, after the termination of some particular estate which he has conveyed, or *the residue of an estate which descends to heirs,* subject to some particular devise, or some temporary interest created by act of law. Thus, if the owner in fee grant an estate for life, *the reversion* of the fee is, without any special reservation, vested in him by act of law. So, if an owner in fee devise an estate to one for life, or if the owner's widow is *endowed* out of his land, his heirs are owners of *the reversion.*

A usual incident to reversions is *rent*: that is, the

---

[1] See p. 152. [2] See p. 153.

particular tenant holds, under a condition and promise of *paying rent* to the reversioner. The reversion and rent, however, may be separated; — either may be granted away without the other, by special words. By a general grant of the reversion, the rent will pass as incident; but not the converse. And if a part of the reversion be conveyed, or taken on execution, a part of the rent will accompany it. The tenant may safely pay rent to the former owner, till he is notified of the transfer.

Although there is a substantial distinction between remainders and reversions, which the law, in general, is careful to uphold; yet, when a *devisor*, after several intermediate estates, limits the ultimate remainder to *his own right heirs*, the remainder is void, and the reversion *descends* as it would have done without such limitation. Thus, if one devise land to A for life, remainder to B for life, remainder to *his own heirs at law*; the latter are *reversioners by descent*, and not *remainder-men by devise.*

In connexion with remainders and reversions, it may be remarked, that whenever a greater estate and a less coincide and meet in one and the same person, without any intermediate estate, the less is immediately annihilated, or, in legal phrase, *merged*, that is, sunk or drowned, in the greater. Thus, if there be tenant for years, or for life, and the reversion in fee-simple descends to or is purchased by him; the term for years or life-estate is *merged in the inheritance*, and shall never exist any more. But to have this effect, the two estates must come *to one and the same person, in one and the same right.* Therefore if tenant for years dies, and makes the reversioner *his executor*, whereby the term vests in the latter; the term shall not merge, for he hath the fee in his own right, and the term in right of the testator, subject to his debts and legacies. *A trust* or *equitable estate* will *merge* in the legal estate, if they become united in the same individual. Thus where a mortgagee, having the legal estate, takes a release from the mortgagor, who has only an equitable one, the latter merges in the former, and the ownership becomes absolute in one person.

Reversioners and *remainder-men* may maintain an action for any wrongful act which does permanent injury to their property, — as, for instance, the cutting down of trees. And the tenant in possession may at the same time have another action for *the immediate injury.*

In New York a process is provided, by which reversioners and remainder-men may call annually for the production of the tenants for life, upon whose estates their expectancies depend, and whose residence is unknown or concealed. In Rhode Island, a tenant for life is presumed to be dead after an absence of seven years.

CHAPTER VII.

USES AND TRUSTS.

A USE is where the *legal estate* in lands is *nominally in one person,* but another is *beneficially interested* and to receive the profits. At common law, the latter, in such case, had no estate of any kind which the law would recognise; but the whole was in the former, who might fulfill the trust or not at pleasure. Afterwards Chancery assumed jurisdiction of the subject, and compelled an execution of the trust. And, by a statute of Henry VIII., called *the Statute of Uses*, and adopted through the United States, the party beneficially interested, or *cestuy que use*, is constituted *the legal owner*; so that the trustee cannot in any way control his rights, nor is the estate subject to any claims against the trustee,—as, for instance, dower or forfeiture,—but is subject to all claims against the *cestuy*, as if he were the sole owner.

Although the statute thus *executes* the estate in the *cestuy*, so that he has the same interest as if there were no trustee; yet the original and peculiar qualities of uses, which distinguish them from legal estates, still remain. They cannot indeed be created or conveyed without *formal words of limitation*, — as, for instance, the word "heirs" in granting *a fee*: but they may be conveyed, *after a limitation in fee*;[1] or *in futuro*, without any prior estate; or with *a power of revocation*, reserved to the grantor or a stranger, to recall and change the uses. Thus a conveyance to A, *for the use* of B and C after they are married; or *to the use* of B and his heirs till C shall pay a sum of money, and then *to the use* of C and his heirs, — is good. So if a man make a conveyance, *to the use* of his intended wife and her eldest son for their lives; upon the marriage, the wife takes the whole use, and, upon the birth of a son, it is executed jointly in them both. This is called *a shifting use*. And whenever the use limited by the deed

---

[1] See p. 152.

expires, or cannot vest, it returns back to the grantor after such expiration or during such impossibility, and is called *a resulting use.* Thus if a man conveys to the use of his intended wife for life, with remainder to the use of her first-born son in tail; — here, till he marries, the use *results back* to himself; after marriage, it is executed in the wife for life; and, if she dies without issue, the whole *results back* to him in fee.

Under certain circumstances, the *Statute of Uses* does not apply, and a use is as at common law. This is usually called *a trust. A trust-estate,* is *a right in Equity* to take the rents and profits of lands, of which *the legal estate* is vested in some other person. This happens, — 1. When a use is *limited on a use,* the technical words of the statute being held in such case inapplicable. Thus, a conveyance to A for the use of B *for the use of C* gives C only *a trust.* 2. Where the trustee is required to do what he cannot do, without a legal ownership and possession, — as, for instance, to *pay over the profits.* 3. Where the trustee's estate is *less than freehold*; because he cannot then be considered as *seised,* in the words of the statute, — as, for instance, where an estate is conveyed to A *for fifty years* for the use of B *for life.*

Courts of Equity consider a trust-estate as equivalent to the legal ownership, governed by the same rules of property, and liable to every charge *in Equity,* which the other is subject to *in law.* The trustee is regarded as merely *the instrument of conveyance,* and can in no shape affect the estate, unless by alienation for valuable consideration to a purchaser without notice of the trust; which, as the *cestuy* is generally in possession of the land, is a thing that can rarely happen. The trust will *descend*, may be *conveyed*, or *incumbered*, is liable to *curtesy*, though not to *dower*,[1] and chargeable upon *the heir* of the trustee. In Massachusetts, a trust cannot be taken on execution against the *cestuy*. It is otherwise in New York, and probably most of the other States.

No particular form of words is requisite to create a trust, if the intention be clear. But the declaration or creation of the trust must be proved by *some writing*, signed by the disposing party; or, if it be lost, by evidence of its contents. This rule does not in general apply to *resulting trusts*. In Equity, where an estate is purchased in the name of A, and the consideration[2] actually paid at the time by B, there is a *resulting* trust in favor of B. The mere *want of consideration* will not make the grantee a trustee for the grantor. If a trustee purchase *with trust-money*, a trust *results* to the owner of the money. It is to be observed, however, that trusts are almost exclusively a subject of *Chancery jurisdiction*,[3] and cannot be enforced, to any considerable extent, in those States which have no court with full Chancery powers. It has been held, in Massachusetts, that even *resulting trusts* must be evidenced by writing. If an agent take a security to himself for a debt due his principal, sue it in his own name, and cause the execution to be levied on the debtor's lands, the principal acquires no trust interest in them, unless the agent declare in writing that the judgment is his property. So, if a grantee of land give to another person, who furnished the money, a bond, to convey the land to any one whom

1 In Virginia and Kentucky a trust is subject to dower.

2 See p. 75.

3 See *Chancery*.

he should appoint; this gives the latter no trust estate. But where the owner of land gave a bond to secure it to another, who entered accordingly and received the profits, it was held a good trust.

In case of an *executed use*, the estate of the *cestuy* cannot continue beyond that of the trustee. Thus if land is conveyed to one person *generally*, for the use of another *and his heirs*, the former takes only a life-estate, and the use also terminates with his death. But if the beneficial interest is a *trust*, the legal estate will be enlarged into a fee, to make it commensurate with the trust, and the trustee's heirs will succeed to his office.

An executor, purchasing an estate of the deceased person, which is sold by *order of court*, becomes *a trustee* for the heirs or devisees, who may compel him to convey to them, or account for the proceeds, if he have resold it. Such purchase is not *void*, but only *voidable* by the *cestuys*.[1]

Where the management of the estate is left to the trustee's discretion, gross negligence or fraud alone will make him liable for losses. In Massachusetts, five per cent. on the value of the property is allowed the trustee for his services.

In New York, uses and trusts have been to some extent abolished by statute. They are still retained, for the purpose of selling lands for the benefit of creditors or legatees. And, in such case, the trustee has the whole estate, subject to the right of enforcing the trust in Chancery. The estate of a trustee ceases with the purposes of the trust; and, on the death of a trustee, his heirs do not succeed to the office, but it vests in the Court of Chancery.

---

[1] See *Void and Voidable.*

CHAPTER VIII.

JOINT TENANCY AND TENANCY IN COMMON.

1. An estate *in joint tenancy* is where lands or tenements are granted to two or more persons, *to hold jointly.*

Joint tenants must have *the same interest*; thus one cannot be *tenant for life* and the other *for years.* But if land be granted to A and B *for their lives, and to the heirs of A*; A and B are joint tenants of the freehold during their respective lives, and A has *the remainder in fee.*

Joint tenants must also have *the same title,* — they must claim under one grant or one *disseisin*;[1] and their estates must be vested *at the same time.*

Joint tenants are said to be seised "per my et per tout," by the half and by all; that is, each of them has *the entire possession,* as well of every parcel as of the whole. Hence, if an estate be given to *a man and his wife,* they are not properly joint tenants; for husband and wife, being considered *one person* in law, cannot take the estate *by moieties,* but both are seised of *the entirety,* and neither can dispose of any part without the other's assent. So, if an estate is conveyed to a man and wife, and another person, they take together one moiety, and he the other. But a marriage between two persons, after the conveyance, will not create this peculiar ownership.

---

[1] See *Disseisin.*

From these principles of a thorough and intimate union of interest and possession, it results, that the rights, liabilities, and acts of one joint tenant are construed in law as those of all. But one cannot do any act which may tend to defeat or injure the other's estate. Thus an action lies *for waste* by one against another; also, an action to recover any excess of profits received by one over his share.

The distinguishing characteristic of this estate is, that, when one tenant dies, the other takes his share *by survivorship* (unless it has been previously disposed of), free of all charges and incumbrances, even that of *dower*. But one may *convey* his share, and the grantee becomes *a tenant in common* with the other. So one may make *a lease*, even to commence after his death. And, in chancery, *a mere covenant to convey* may be sometimes held a *severance* of the joint tenancy.

In the United States, the title by joint tenancy is very much reduced in extent, and the incident of *survivorship* still more extensively destroyed. In many of the States, a joint tenancy cannot be created but by express words, which are very rarely used; and, in many others, survivorship is abolished, except in the case of *joint trustees and executors*. This alteration, however, does not affect conveyances to *husband and wife*. And *joint mortgagees* hold as joint tenants; because the surviving one could alone sue for the debt, and the collateral security should accompany the principal demand. But, *after foreclosure*, they become *tenants in common*.

2. *Tenants in common* are those who hold together by *unity of possession*, whether by the same

title or not. This estate may be created by *descent*,[1] *deed*, or *will*. Tenants in common have *several and distinct freeholds*. Each one is considered to be *solely seised of his share*; and there is no *survivorship* among them. All joint estates are, in most of the States, construed to be tenancies in common, unless special words require otherwise. A conveyance of "a moiety of a piece of land in quantity and quality," creates a tenancy in common between the grantor and grantee.

There are some principles alike applicable to both the kinds of estate above treated of.

One joint tenant or tenant in common cannot convey a distinct portion of the estate, by *metes and bounds*, so as to prejudice the others, but only so as to preclude or *estop* his own title. And the levy of an execution would have the same effect, in this respect, as a conveyance. In either case, the other tenant may claim the same undivided interest *in the whole*, which he had before the transfer. But if a division is afterwards made, and the portion transferred is allotted to the one whose interest was disposed of, his grantee or creditor may claim it in his right or stead.

Such tenants may compel each other by legal process to *make partition* of the estate, or may do it voluntarily; but a *parol* or verbal partition is void, notwithstanding a subsequent several occupancy. Lands lying in common are subject to partition, notwithstanding the proprietors are *a body politic*, and have from time immemorial managed and divided the

---

1 The technical name for *heirs* holding together, is "parceners," or "coparceners."

lands at public meetings. But this process lies, only where the applicants have merely *a share of the lands*; not where they *claim the whole* in common, because then they may divide amicably.

The possession of one joint tenant or tenant in common is *that of all*; and the taking of the whole profits by one does not amount to an *ouster*[1] or dispossession of the rest; — though any acts, indicating an intention to claim the whole estate, will have that effect, and drive the others to their action at law. If one occupies a particular part of the premises by agreement, it is a trespass for the others to disturb him. One may, in general, compel the others to pay their share of the expense of *repairs* upon the property.

When *an action is brought* by *joint tenants* against a third person, they must all be parties to it. If by *tenants in common*, — for any injury to, or claim arising from, the estate, as for instance *trespass* or *rent*, they must sue together; but in *real actions*, to recover the estate itself, the actions are separate. In some of the States, special statutes have changed this rule.

CHAPTER IX.

TITLE TO REAL PROPERTY.

A TITLE is the means, whereby the owner of lands has the just possession of them.

The lowest and most imperfect degree of title,

---

[1] See *Ouster*.

consists in *mere naked possession*, without any shadow or pretence of *right* to hold the land; as where one man by force or surprise turns another out; or where, after an owner's death and before entry of the heir, a person gets possession of the land. Such an act of dispossession is called in general *a disseisin.* The rightful owner may regain his estate by entry or action; but, till he does, actual possession is *primâ facie* evidence of legal title in the occupant.

The next step to a good and perfect title is *the right of possession.* Thus, in case of an unlawful entry as above stated, the legal owner, though the *actual possession* be lost, has still left in him *the right of possession.* This right may be either *apparent* or *actual.* Thus if *a disseisor*, or wrongful possessor, die, the land descends to his heir, and he has *an apparent right*; while *the disseisee*, or rightful owner, has *the actual right*, which however he cannot, in general, assert *by entry*, after a certain time, but only *by an action at law.*

If the owner neglect to assert his title for a certain time, the occupant gains *the right of possession* in addition to *the possession itself*; but what is called *the right of property* still remains to the former, and he may regain his estate by another form of action. The several periods of *limitation* will be more particularly considered hereafter. [1]

One in possession of land, claiming to hold it in fee, is *seised* of the land, either *by right* or *by wrong. Entry* is in some cases necessary to a legal seisin; in others not. Thus, an heir is not seised, after his ancestor's death, nor a judgment creditor, of

---

[1] See *Real Action.*

lands levied on,[1] till after entry or some equivalent act; but a purchaser, from one who is seised, by a deed duly executed, acknowledged, and recorded, becomes seised without entry. When one enters on land, *claiming no title*, he gains no seisin but by *ousting* the occupant, and not beyond his actual possession. But if there is *a claim of title*, entry on *a part* will give seisin of all to which the title extends. In case of *concurrent actual possession*, the *legal* possession is in the party rightfully seised. A disseisin cannot be effected, but by acts either *public* in their nature, or of which the owner has *notice*.

CHAPTER X.

TITLE BY ACT OF LAW.

1. *Descent*. This is the title, whereby a person, on the death of his ancestor, acquires the estate of the latter by *right of representation*, as *heir*. In the United States, the English law of descents, in its most essential features, has been almost universally rejected, and each State has established a law for itself, substantially conformable to that which regulates the *distribution of personal estate*. For a general view of the rules on this subject, reference is made to page 66. *The executor or administrator* has no control of lands, unless they are required for payment of debts.

By the English law, real estate descends only to the heir of the person *last seised*; so that, if a father

---

1 See *Execution*.

dies, having *a right* to an estate, but never having had *actual or constructive possession*, his son does not take it, — but the heir of the person who last had possession. But this rule does not prevail in the United States. Every thing descends to the heir, to which the ancestor had *a title of inheritance*, without regard to occupancy.

Descended lands are in general liable *for the ancestor's debts*; but not till the personal estate is exhausted.[1] In Virginia, it seems, lands are liable for no debts but those *by specialty*,[2] in which the heirs are expressly bound. In North Carolina, the proceeding against them is in *Chancery*.

Posthumous children, or those born after the father's death, are, in general, entitled to an equal share with others.

2. *Escheat*. When the owner of land dies, leaving no heirs, it reverts or *escheats* to the people, as forming part of the common stock to which the whole community is entitled. The same thing happens, when the relations are *aliens*, and therefore incapable of holding real estate. In such cases, the lands vest immediately in the State, and the attorney-general may sue for them. In some States, lands escheat to *the town*, instead of *the Commonwealth*.

3. *Forfeiture*. For the law relating to *forfeiture for crimes*, reference is made to page 51.

In England, if a tenant for life or years undertake to *convey a greater estate than he has, he forfeits his estate* to the remainder-man or reversioner. The rule has not been generally adopted in this country, but still prevails in Massachusetts. It does not apply

---

[1] See p. 62. [2] p. 71.

to conveyances of *incorporeal estates*, nor *by way of use*; nor where the tenant conveys *all his interest*, though he *covenant that he has a fee*,—for by these a man can pass only *his actual interest*; whereas, in the former case, his absolute conveyance operates *a disseisin* of the reversioner or remainder-man. When a tenant for life forfeits his estate, the remainder-man *may enter immediately*; but *need not*, till the death of the former: that is, *the statute of limitation* will not run against him till that event takes place.

4. *Prescription* and *Custom*. Title by *prescription*, is where one claims real estate, upon the ground that he, and those under whom he holds, have *immemorially used to enjoy it*. All prescription must be either *in a man and his ancestors*, or in a man *and those whose estate he hath*; and if it be the former, the ancestor's possession must have been *within sixty years*.

A prescription must always be laid in him that is *tenant of the fee*. The holder of any less estate cannot, of course, claim by *immemorial occupancy*, except as holding under the owner in fee.

Only *incorporeal hereditaments* can be claimed by this title,—as a right of way or common; but not lands and other *corporeal substances*, of which more certain evidence may be had.

Nothing, which could not be the subject of *a valid grant*, can be prescribed for,—prescription being founded on the supposition of *a lost grant*. So nothing can be prescribed for, which must arise *by matter of record* or judgment of court.

Under prescription in a "que estate," or as belonging to a particular estate, such things only can be claimed, as are incident, or *appurtenant, to lands*; but if one prescribe in himself *and his ancestors,* he may claim any thing of an incorporeal nature.

In general, *an adverse enjoyment for forty years* will give a prescriptive right. But such right cannot grow either out of an *unknown* or a *permissive* enjoyment for any length of time; because it is founded upon *an implied admission* of title by any opposing claimant, which cannot exist, where he is *ignorant* of the occupancy, or *suffers it under himself.*

Immemorial usage being the foundation of prescriptive right, the common law is not of course strictly adopted in this country. The length of time here held equivalent to it, is somewhat indeterminate; but this is not practically of great consequence, because an adverse title may be gained, *upon the presumption of a grant, in twenty years.*

A prescription must have *a continued and peaceable usage and enjoyment.* But where a title has been once thus gained, it will not be lost by any *temporary interruption.* A prescription must be *certain*; *not unreasonable,* though it may be *unusual or inconvenient,* as, for instance, for a way through a church; *not for a wrong or nuisance,* as to lay logs in the highway; nor *against an act of the legislature,* unless merely declaratory of the common law. The *antiquity* of a usage is regarded as strong evidence of its *reasonableness.*

There may be prescriptive *obligation* as well as right. Thus where lands are divided by *a fence,* the owner on one side may be prescriptively bound to repair it.

The above remarks apply, in general, to *customs* as well as prescriptive rights. *Custom* is a *local,* prescription a *personal,* usage. A usage for the inhabitants of a certain parish to water their cattle at a certain pool, is *a custom*; a usage for the owners of a certain estate to have a right of way over another estate, is *a prescription.*

A custom to take any thing from another's land,— for instance, to take fish from his fishery,—is void. A prescription "que estate" might be good for the same privilege.

Different persons may have the same right by different titles; as, for instance, a right of way; one by grant, a second by prescription, and a third by custom. But one custom cannot be contradictory to another. Thus if there be a custom that one shall have windows looking upon another's ground, the latter cannot claim another custom to stop them, but should dispute the existence of the former.

CHAPTER XI.

TITLE BY DEED.

THE most usual title to real estate is by *alienation, conveyance,* or, as it is commonly termed, *purchase*; though the latter word technically includes all titles but that by *descent.*

A resolve of the Legislature, or *the vote of a town* or other civil corporation, though without any price or consideration, will be sufficient to transfer real estate. But the usual form of alienation is *by deed.* At common law, lands could not be conveyed without actual delivery, or *livery of seisin*; but, in this country, a deed regularly executed, acknowledged, and recorded, will, in general, pass a title, though the possession remain unchanged. In Virginia, it seems, *livery of seisin* is still sometimes required.

I. *Nature of Deeds.* — A *deed* is *a writing*[1] upon paper or parchment, *sealed and delivered* by the parties. If there are more parties than one to be bound, — that is, if there are *mutual* grants or obligations, — each party has a copy, and the deed is called *an indenture*; if only one party, it is a *deed-poll*, and is received only by the grantee or purchaser. The common law, by *a seal*, intended an impression upon wax or wafer, or some other tenacious substance. In the southern and western States, however, the courts allow a *flourish* at the end of the name, or a circle of ink, or *scroll*, as a substitute. A piece of paper annexed to an instrument by a wafer is a seal. In New York, a *private* seal must be upon wax or a wafer, but a *public* seal may be impressed directly upon the paper. If an instrument with but one seal be signed by several, it will be considered the seal of each; and if actually sealed, though it conclude "given under our hands," without adding "and seals," the omission will not be material.

II. *Delivery of Deeds.* — *Delivery* is essential to the validity of a deed. The deed may be delivered to the grantee himself, or to any other person authorized to receive it. It may be delivered to *a stranger*, as "an escrow," to be kept by him till certain conditions are performed, and then given up to the grantee, before which time, no estate passes.

---

[1] It has been held that *printing* is equivalent to writing.

But, in some instances, the instrument takes effect from the first and not the second delivery. Thus, where the grantor is at the former time a *feme-sole*, and marries before the latter: — because the conveyance would be otherwise wholly invalid. But, if the instrument be delivered *as a deed*, though *to a stranger and on condition*; it is not *an escrow*, but the third person holds it *in trust* for the grantee immediately. After delivery, the estate vests in the purchaser, though the grantor keep the deed, or fraudulently obtain and destroy it. The deed of a corporation is valid without delivery. No particular form is necessary for the delivery of a deed. Any act is sufficient, which indicates an intention to put it in possession of the grantee. And the delivery may sometimes be *inferred* from the signing.

III. *Acknowledgment and Registry of Deeds.*— A deed must be *recorded* in a public registry, after *acknowledgment* or *proof* before some court or magistrate. If not recorded, it is good only *against the grantor and his heirs*, and void against *subsequent attaching creditors of the grantor*, or *purchasers*, having no notice of the first conveyance. But such notice may be *constructive* as well as actual; — as if the first purchaser be in the open and exclusive possession of the land, so as clearly to negative all other ownership. A purchaser, without notice of the former title, may make a valid conveyance to one who has notice of it. In some of the States, a fixed time is allowed for the purchaser to record his deed; and, if done within that time, no other title can interfere with it. Where no time is fixed, if the first purchaser delay unreasonably to put his deed on record, a second purchaser may hold the land,

26

though he knew of the former conveyance; and an ignorant second purchaser, who first records his deed, or an attaching creditor, shall hold the land, though the first be guilty of no delay in recording. Nor will the mere knowledge, that the first deed was about to be made, make any difference. Where *a mortgage* is made by an absolute deed and a bond back,[1] the bond must be recorded; or else the grantee may convey to an ignorant purchaser an absolute title.

Neither acknowledgment nor registration so authenticates a deed, as to dispense with proof of *its execution*, when offered in evidence. But if *a copy* is admitted, the original being lost, the registration is proof enough of the execution.

IV. *Component Parts of deeds.*—The essential parts of a conveyance are very brief and simple,—consisting of *the names of the parties, the price* or *consideration, the description of the land,* and *the quantity of interest conveyed.* Usage, however, has established certain additional forms, which, though not necessary to *pass* a title, are somewhat important for its perfect *distinctness and security.*

1. *Parties.*—It is not necessary, though an invariable practice, to mention either the Christian name or surname of a party, provided he be sufficiently designated in some other way,—as, for instance, "the wife of A," or "eldest son of B." So a conveyance to "the heirs at law" of *a deceased person* is good, as the individuals who are to take may be ascertained by extrinsic evidence; but a convey-

---

[1] See p. 171.

ance to "the heirs" of a person who is living at the time, is void *for uncertainty*.

A deed cannot bind a party who seals it, unless it contain words expressive of *an intention to be bound*. Where the estate belongs to *a feme-covert*, and the husband makes a formal deed, and she merely at the close relinquishes all her right and signs it, her estate will not pass. But it is otherwise, when one of two *joint tenants*, or a *remainder-man*, joins thus in a deed.

If *an attorney* have authority to convey lands, he must do it, not in his own name, but in the name of his principal, — unless he act in behalf of the public, in which case he may sign as agent. *A power of attorney* to execute a deed must itself be under seal.

2. A *consideration*, though usual, and usually expressed, is not necessary,[1] except in conveyances *to use*,[2] or to give validity to the deed against the claims of *bonâ fide creditors* or *subsequent purchasers*. If paid to a third person by the consent of the grantor, the effect is the same as if paid to himself.

3. *The description* must be certain enough to designate the property intended to be conveyed. But, though the estate will not agree with some of the particulars, yet, if it conform to others, the conveyance is valid. For instance, if one convey "a farm called A, in the occupation of B," when in truth it is occupied by C, — this mistake will not avoid the deed. As to *boundaries*; — *general courses and distances*, and even *a designation of the property*, — as, for instance, "the mansion-house and land thereto belonging," — are controlled by *known and fixed monuments*, if such are referred to, and there is a

---

[1] See p. 77. [2] See *Use*.

variance between the two: unless the intention of the parties appear to be clearly otherwise. The least certain and material, must yield to the most certain and material, parts of the description; though the whole will be effectuated, if possible.

The mention of *a certain number of acres*, does not amount to a covenant or *warranty*, that there is that quantity; especially if "more or less" be added, or the deed contain specific boundaries. But if the land be described as *bounded on a way or street*, this will make an implied covenant, that there is such an one, and the grantor will have no right to obstruct it. And where the quantity of land unreasonably varies from the deed, Chancery will afford relief. The deed may refer, for a description of the land, either to a plan, or another deed, or to the actual condition of the property. If reference be made to a monument, not existing at the time, but afterwards erected for the purpose by the parties, it will control the description, though varying from the lines.

Privileges naturally or necessarily *appendant to lands*, — as a natural water-course, or a light in a house, when the windows open upon other land of the grantor, — will pass under the clause of "appurtenances." *A right of way*, acquired by express reservation, will pass without this clause. In general, *land* cannot pass, but only some *incorporeal right*, as *appurtenant to land*. Where *a wharf and dock*, however, are conveyed "with the appurtenances," *the flats in front of the wharf* will pass — from necessity. So *a fence* standing upon the land. And the conveyance of a house, "with the appurtenances," will pass the garden, *curtilage*, and close adjoining the house and on which it is built; but no other land, though usually occupied with the house. Under the term "messuage" these will pass, without the addition of "appurtenances." The grant of a *mill* has been held to include the head of water necessary and previously used for carrying it on. So the term *saw-mill* passes the *mill-chain, dogs, and bars* connected with it; and the grant of *a factory* gives a right to the *machinery*. *Manure* has been held to pass with the land on which it lies.[1]

If there be a clear and express grant of an estate, any subsequent exception or reservation from it, in the deed, is void. But if the grant is in general terms, or in any way ambiguous and open to explanation, the exception shall take effect.

4. A conveyance usually contains several *covenants*, — viz. that the grantor is *lawfully seised* and *has good right to convey*, that there are *no incumbrances*, that the purchaser shall *quietly enjoy*, and that the grantor will *warrant* against all lawful claims.[2] From the last of these, such a conveyance derives the name of *a warranty deed*. In a *quit-claim deed* they are not inserted, — the grantor covenanting only against those *who claim under himself*, and not against *adverse and paramount titles*. Of the latter class, are all deeds given by *public officers*, such as administrators, sheriffs, &c.; who covenant only for the regularity of their own proceedings.[3]

---

[1] In *a devise, land* may pass under the word *appurtenances*, if such appear to be the testator's intention, as gathered from his own practice of using the property.

[2] In Pennsylvania, the words "grant, bargain, and sell" make *an implied warranty*, which may be controlled however by express covenants.

[3] See page 64.

The effect of the covenants in a deed, is to give to the grantee *a claim for damages*, if at any time *disturbed by an adverse claimant*. The *amount to be recovered* depends upon the particular covenant which is broken. In case of *an incumbrance*, the damages will be the sum paid for removing it, and, if not removed, only *nominal damages*;—if *a warranty*, in several of the States (though this is not the general rule), *the value of the land at the time of eviction* or dispossession;—and, *on the other covenants* and usually on the warranty, *the consideration paid*, with interest. Any *expenses of defending a suit*, brought by the adverse claimant, may also be recovered as damages,—but not *fees of counsel*, where the land was given up without suit.

If the grantee have conveyed the land to another person, the latter may recover upon some of the covenants as fully as the former might have done; they being said to *run with the land*. But the covenants of *seisin*, and of *a right to convey*, are personal to the first grantee; because, if broken at all, it is *at the time of the conveyance*, and they have become *choses in action*, which cannot be assigned.[1] An assignee *in law* may sue upon a covenant, as well as one who claims *by conveyance* from the first purchaser; as, for instance, a widow holding dower in the land, or one who purchases it at a sale on execution.

The grantee may recover damages upon the covenants, though he voluntarily surrender the land to the adverse claimant, without a suit;—provided the adverse title is good,—not otherwise. And the burden of proof is on the grantee, to show that the adverse title is good; unless a judgment have been recovered

---

[1] See page 44.

against him, and he gave notice to the grantor of the suit, so that he might defend it.[1]

The grantee cannot, to increase the damages, give evidence that the grantor *knew of the defect* in his title;—because this is ground for a distinct action.

5. *The conclusion* of the deed consists of the *date* and *attestation.* If not dated, it takes effect from *the delivery.* In Massachusetts, *witnesses*, though usual, are not necessary; but, in many of the States, the statute law requires two witnesses. In New York, *one* is necessary to give validity to the deed *against a subsequent purchaser.* In some States, certain kinds of deeds are required to be attested, and others are not.

The foregoing enumeration of the component parts of a deed is for the most part particularly applicable to original conveyances of *the fee simple.* Besides these, however, there is a variety of other deeds, which are of frequent use in this country, and require a short notice.

V. *The several Kinds of Deeds.*—1. *Absolute conveyances,* either of *warranty* or *quit-claim,* have been already sufficiently described. "Give, grant, sell, and convey," are the usual words of the former,—"release, remise, and quit-claim," of the latter.

2. *Lease.*—*A lease* is a conveyance of lands or tenements, (usually in consideration of *a stated rent,*) for life, for years, or at will; but always for a less time than the owner has in the premises. Leases, as they contain mutual obligations, are in the form of *indentures,* and signed alike by both parties.

Rent must be *reserved* or made payable to the

---

[1] See *Judgment.*

reversioner or *lessor*, or his representatives; not to a third person.[1] Thus if A leases land to B, the rent cannot be reserved to C. But, if the lease be made by a tenant for life, the rent may be reserved to *the remainder-man*, he being *a privy in estate*, or having an identity of interest, with the former.

If the lessor, being the owner in fee, *die before the rent falls due*, it passes to *his heirs*, as *incident to the reversion*, and they alone can sue for it; but, if he die *after* it falls due, it is *personal estate*, and goes to *the executor or administrator*, to be collected and disposed of like other chattels.

If the tenant is *evicted* or turned out from the land by *a paramount title* or by *the lessor*, before the rent is due; he will be discharged from the whole of it. But any wrongful dispossession by *strangers* will not have this effect, if there is *an express covenant* to pay the rent. So if a house leased be *burned down*, and the lease contain an express covenant; the rent shall be paid during the whole term.[2] Where the tenant is evicted from *part of the land*, the rent will be proportionably reduced. So when he *purchases* a part of the land; — unless the rent is payable in some indivisible thing, instead of money, — as a horse or a hawk, — in which case the whole will be extinguished.

From the above principles it results, that where

---

[1] For the reason of this rule see p. 170.

[2] It is an important and comprehensive principle, that, when one makes *an express contract*, he shall be held to fulfil it, though by inevitable accident he has been deprived of the benefits for which it was incurred.[3] But a mere *legal liability* will be discharged by such an event. Thus a lessee, after his house has been burned, is liable for rent only *upon his covenant*. The *legal liability*, formerly existing, and upon which an action of *debt* might be brought, — is extinguished.

[3] p. 80.

rent is made payable at a certain time, *no part of it* becomes due till that time arrive. It is *an entire debt*, which cannot be apportioned. For the same reason, rent differs from a debt "debitum in præsenti, solvendum in futuro," — due now, payable hereafter; as, for instance, a note payable *on time*. The liability is *a contingent one*. Where no time is fixed, rent is due according to *the usage* of the country or place. If there is no usage, it is due at the end of *a year*. In the city of New York, rent is made payable, by statute, *quarterly*.

A lease usually contains *a condition*, that if the rent shall not be paid when it falls due, the lessor may *re-enter* upon the land, and "hold till he is paid," or "avoid the lease." If the former expression is used, the tenant may have his land again on payment of the rent; if the latter, the entry terminates his estate. Such entry cannot in general be made, till after *demand of payment*, on the land, and before sunset of the day when it falls due, that the money may be counted. The demand must be at the most public and notorious place, — thus, the front door of a house, or, if there is no house, at the gate of the land. In some of the States, it is expressly provided, that upon non-payment of rent, the landlord may recover the land in an action of ejectment, without either demand or entry. In Vermont, the tenant may stop the proceedings, by paying the rent into court at any time before judgment.

A lessee for years may either *assign* to another his whole interest, or *underlet* for a shorter term than his own. An assignee will be liable for the rent to the lessor; but an underlessee, only to the first tenant, of whom he hires. In case of assignment, without the lessor's consent, the original lessee still remains liable for the rent, upon his covenant. But an assignee, who again assigns, is no longer liable. The usual covenant in leases, against *assigning or underletting*, has merely the effect of subjecting the tenant to an action for damages, if he violate the covenant. But *a condition* against it, would enable the lessor to re-enter and avoid the lease.

An assignee is bound by some of *the covenants* in a lease, but not by others. He is bound by all covenants which *run with the land*,—as, for instance, to *pay rent*, *repair*, or *reside upon the premises*; but not by *collateral* or *incidental* stipulations pertaining to the estate, as *to build a wall*, unless *assigns* are named in the lease; nor, in any case, to do an act which does not *pertain to the estate*,—as, for instance, to build a wall *on other land*, though *assigns* are mentioned.

A lessee cannot defend against an action for rent *by denying the title* of the lessor. He is *estopped* by the act of hiring, and his occupation of the premises. He may, however, deny *the particular title* which is claimed; as, for instance, if the claimant sues *as heir* to the lessor, it may be shown, that, under the circumstances, *the executor* should have brought the action. If a tenant at will or sufferance expressly *renounce* the title of his landlord, the latter cannot recover rent for his subsequent occupancy.

Whether an agreement shall be construed as *a present lease*, or only *a provision for a future one*, depends rather on the apparent *intention* of the parties, than on the particular words used. Words of *present demise*, however, generally import an immediate lease.

Where a lease is made "for seven, fourteen, or

twenty-one years," it is not void for uncertainty; but, if continued by the lessee over one period, extends to the others. And, it seems, he alone has the liberty of determining its extent.

The words "grant and demise," or "hold and occupy during the term," make *an implied covenant of quiet enjoyment*, on the part of the lessor, for breach of which damages may be recovered. Otherwise, when there is an express covenant against *eviction* "by the lessor or any claiming under him," — this expression limiting and controlling the implied covenant.

A landlord is not bound, it seems, to make any *repairs*, unless expressly agreed for; and no evidence will be received of *a verbal contract* to make them.

The statute law, in some States, requires *registration* of long leases, to make them valid against subsequent purchasers or lessees, or against creditors.[1] In Massachusetts and Maryland, the term is seven years; in New York, three; in Connecticut, one; in Kentucky and Virginia, five.

3. *Confirmation.*

A confirmation is a conveyance, whereby *a voidable estate* is made *sure and unavoidable*, or *a particular estate increased.* The words used are "give, grant, ratify, approve, and confirm." If tenant for life lease for forty years, and die during the term, the reversioner has a right to avoid the lease; but, if he have *confirmed* the estate of the lessee for years, before the death of the tenant for life, the title for years is thereby made good. So, if there be tenant for life,

---

[1] See supra, III.

remainder in fee ; a deed of confirmation to the former, from the remainder-man, will give him the fee.

Where one has conveyed land to which he had no title, a subsequent deed of *release* to him from the true owner will operate as *a confirmation*, for the benefit of the former purchaser.

4. *Partition.* *Partition* is the mutual conveyance, which takes place between *joint tenants*, &c., for the division of their estate ; and has been already sufficiently noticed.[1]

5. *Surrender.*

A surrender is the yielding up of *a particular estate*, to the immediate reversioner or remainder-man ; whereby it becomes *merged* and extinguished in the larger estate.[2] The words used are "surrender, grant, and yield up." But a surrender may be *implied*, as well as express. Thus, *the taking of a new lease* is a surrender of an old one, though the first is for life, and the last for years, and conditional, or to commence "in futuro." But the mere cancelling of the old one, or a new one for any cause invalid, will not have this effect.

6. *Defeasance.*

A defeasance is *a collateral deed*, made at the same time with a conveyance, and containing certain conditions, upon the performance of which the estate then created may be defeated. This kind of deed has been sufficiently noticed under the head of *mortgage*.[3]

7. *Covenant to stand seised.*

A covenant to stand seised to uses, is where one, seised of lands, covenants, in *consideration of blood*

---

[1] p. 192. [2] p. 184. [3] p. 171.

or marriage, that he will *stand seised thereof* to the use of his wife,[1] child, or other relative. Such a transfer, as has been already seen,[2] will be immediately *executed by the Statute of Uses,* and have all the effect of a direct conveyance. And, if one convey to his son in fee, to hold *after the grantor's death,* covenanting that he shall then have the land; though this is void as a grant, being to commence *in futuro,* it will be good as *a covenant to stand seised* to his own use for life, and to that of the son after his death.

The abovementioned forms of conveyance are, in legal practice, strictly observed, and appropriated each to its own specific object. But still, when a deed is intended as one form of conveyance, and cannot so operate for want of the proper phraseology; — it will, if possible, be construed as another, rather than held wholly void.

VI. *Void and Voidable Deeds.* — 1. *From the nature of the thing conveyed. Reversions and vested remainders* may be granted; but *contingencies and mere possibilities,* though they may be *devised, inherited,* or *released to a party interested in the estate,* cannot be *conveyed,* unless coupled with some present interest.

By the English law, every grant of land is void, if, at the time, the land is in the actual possession of another person, claiming a title *adverse to the grantor,* or if *a suit is pending* in relation to it. Such a transaction is even a criminal offence; being regarded as *an encouragement of litigation,* and called, in the first case *maintenance,* and in the latter *champerty.* This

---

[1] In this mode a man may convey to his wife, contrary to the general rule. See p. 18.

[2] p. 186.

principle has been adopted in most of the States. As the conveyance, in such case, is *a mere nullity,* the title continues in the grantor, so that he may enforce it by suit; and the void deed cannot be set up by the adverse occupant as a defence. But, as between the parties to the deed, it operates as *an estoppel,* and bars the grantor, whenever he acquires a title. A grant of lands *by the Commonwealth* will pass its title, notwithstanding an adverse possession; because the Commonwealth cannot be *disseised.* In New York, one disseised may *mortgage* his estate.

2. *For fraud or illegality.* Deeds of land, like sales of chattels, if made *without consideration,* or with *a mutual fraudulent intent,* are void, *as to creditors or subsequent purchasers* of the grantor. The principles applicable to this subject have been already stated.[1] In conveyances of land, however, unlike those of chattels, any *secret trust* is conclusive, and not mere *primâ facie,* evidence of fraud; and, since deeds are required to be publicly recorded, the circumstance of the grantor's *continuing in possession* of the land does not affect the validity of the conveyance. A deed is not invalid as to creditors, merely because no consideration is *expressed.* It will be *presumed,* and the want of it must be proved.

In New York, when a first grantee is guilty of no fraud, but merely takes without consideration, his estate will not be defeated by a subsequent conveyance to one who knows of the former. A similar rule prevails in some other States.

The possession of the fraudulent purchaser is no *disseisin* of the grantor; but he holds *under the*

---

[1] See p. 90.

grantor, and a second conveyance is valid to defeat his estate. If the first purchaser were a disseisor, *holding adversely*, the second deed would of course be void.[1]

In some States, a very severe penalty is inflicted upon any party to a fraudulent conveyance.

In general, when *the consideration of an executory contract is illegal*, this is a good defence against an action brought upon it.[2] But, on the same principle — "Potior est conditio defendentis," — *a conveyance* of land, for such consideration, cannot be avoided by the grantor; because, in order to do it, he must be *plaintiff* instead of *defendant*.

3. *For incapacity or want of consent*. The same circumstances incapacitate a person for making a deed, as for entering into any other contract. For instance, *infancy*;[3] *imbecility, and undue influence*; and *duress*, or compulsion. But no one can avoid a deed for these causes, except the grantor himself, by a *re-entry* upon the land within a certain time. And, before such re-entry, he cannot make another valid conveyance, — being *disseised*;[4] nor, in case of *imposition*, can the grantor reclaim the estate from a third person, who has purchased it from the first grantee, ignorant of the unlawful transaction.

The deed of *a non compos person* is *voidable*, or, if *under guardianship, absolutely void*.[5]

---

[1] Supra, (1.) [2] See p. 78.

[3] In Vermont, *a feme-sole* may convey lands, at the age of *eighteen*.

[4] See supra, (1.)

[5] The distinction between *void* and *voidable* consists in several particulars. A *void* deed is *a nullity from the beginning*, — but a *voidable* one is good, *till the grantor does some act to avoid it*; and enables the grantee to pass a good title to another. A voidable deed *may be made good* by

4. The *re-delivery and cancelling* of a deed, before registry, will not avoid it, as between the grantor and the creditors of the purchaser, who may attach it as his; — but it will enable the former to make a valid conveyance to another person, who is ignorant of the first, or who bargains for it with the former purchaser.

The *alteration* of a deed, even in a material part, will not, like that of *an executory contract*, render it void.

No man can make another his grantee *without his consent*; but a deed, executed and registered without the grantee's knowledge, will pass the title, if afterwards accepted by him.

5. A conveyance to *an alien*, or one not a native or naturalized citizen of the United States, is voidable, whenever the Commonwealth shall choose to claim the land. Provided otherwise in Kentucky.

CHAPTER XII.

DEVISE.

A DEVISE is a disposition of *lands and tenements* by will. The general principles relating to wills and testaments, in which a devise is of course included,

---

some act or instrument of the grantor;[2] but a void deed is no foundation for any such ratification. Acts which affect only *private rights* are in general voidable, — those which *injure the public interest*, void.

[2] See p. 211.

have been already considered.[1] Those which apply peculiarly to a disposition by will of real estate will here be briefly noticed.

1. *Who may make, and the form of, devises.* Persons incompetent to *contract* or *convey* are also, in general, incompetent to devise. In Vermont and Maryland, *a feme-sole* may devise at the age of eighteen.

A will, to pass real estate, must be *written*, and in general *signed* or *acknowledged* by the testator, in presence of witnesses, who shall subscribe their names as such. In New York, he must *declare* it to be his will. In some of the States, three witnesses are required; in others only two; and in three or four none, provided certain other proof is furnished. If the testator's name be written *by himself* in any part of the will, this is generally held to be a sufficient *signing*, unless it appear that he intended, but for some cause failed, to sign at the end. In New York, the signature must be at the end of the will. The testator need not actually see, if he has the power to see, the witnesses sign. But he must have knowledge of the act. The witnesses need not attest in presence of each other, nor attest every page, nor know the contents, nor see the signing, — if the testator acknowledge it.

A devise to one who attests the will is generally void. But in New York, the witness, if an heir, shall have what he would have inherited, to the amount of the devise. *A creditor*, whose debt is charged by the will upon the real estate, is still, in general, a competent witness, although *interested* to establish the instrument.

---

[1] See p. 55.

If the witnesses to a will were *competent* at the time of attestation, so that they might then have been sworn to prove it, no subsequent *incompetency* will affect its validity, — as, for instance, where they have been convicted of some *infamons crime.*[1] In such case it will be sufficient to prove their *handwriting.* In New York, all the witnesses to a will must be examined; but generally, in other States, unless under some extraordinary circumstances, the testimony of one is held sufficient for probate of the will.

2. *What may be devised, and to whom.* Any interests in land, which can be *conveyed,* may also be *devised,* and also some, of a *contingent* character, which cannot be conveyed.[2] One *disseised* cannot devise his right, except, by way of release, to the *disseisor.*

By the English law, a devise can pass only such real estate as the testator is the owner of *at the making of the will*; — even though he expressly disposes of "all that he *shall die seised of.*" In this respect, a devise is regarded rather as a *conveyance* than a *testament.* In some of the States, the above rule has been changed; and, by a general disposition, all the lands will pass, which the testator owns *at his death.*

A devise to *the heir at law,* if it give the same interest which he would otherwise inherit, even though charged with *payment of debts,* — is void, and the heir will take *by descent.* When there is a devise to one *and his heirs*; — if the devisee *die* before the testator, it is the general rule, that his *lineal descendants* shall take. If there are none, the devise is void.[3]

3. *Revocation of devises.* The general principles relating to the revocation of wills have been already

---

1 See *Infamy.* 2 See p. 213. 3 See p. 65.

stated.[1] A devise is revoked, by any *conveyance* of the lands devised, subsequent to the making of the will; and will not be revived by a new purchase or acquisition of them, under another title. Even the *foreclosure*[2] of a mortgage has been held such a change as will revoke a devise of it. But a conveyance obtained by *fraud* is no revocation. And, in New York, an instrument merely altering the estate, is no revocation, except to the extent of such alteration.

4. *Republication of devises.* A devise may be *republished,* either by an express *re-execution* of the will, that is, by repeating the same formalities with which it was first made; or by *a codicil*[3] duly attested. The effect of republication is two-fold: first, to revive a will which has been *revoked*; second, to give the will an operation from the time of republication. Upon the latter ground, a republished will passes lands, acquired since the making, but before the republication. Thus, if the will devise "all my lands," it will cover no real estate purchased afterwards. But if, after such purchase, the will be *republished,* the whole estate passes by it. Every codicil, if executed in the form necessary to a devise of lands, is "per se," of itself, *a republication,* whether it refer to after-purchased lands or not;—unless its manifest and sole object was to make some new disposition of the lands originally devised, and not to pass those subsequently acquired.

5. *Construction of devises.*

Less technical phraseology is required, for *the limitation of estates,* by devise, than by deed; upon the ground that wills are often made in haste and by in-

---

[1] See p. 57. [2] See p. 176. [3] See p. 57.

experienced persons. Thus *a fee-simple* may pass, without the word "heirs"[1]; as where the devise is of "all my real estate whatsoever"; or where the devise is *general*, and *some personal charge*, such as the payment of a sum of money, is imposed upon the devisee in connexion with the bounty; or of *wild lands*, the clearing of which by *a tenant for life* would be waste. So a devise to "hold for ever"; or to a man *and his successors*; or "for his own use, and to give away at his death to whom he pleases" will pass the fee. An estate may even be created in a devise *by implication*. Thus, if one devise lands to his heir at law, *after the death of his wife*; the wife will take an immediate life-estate. The above liberal constructions, however, may be controlled by other parts of the will, indicating a different intent.

6. *Effect of devises.*

A devisee gains no title to the land, till after *probate of the will*; nor till after *entry* or some equivalent act, unless the estate is unoccupied. If a devisee *for life* refuse to accept the devise, the devisee *in remainder* may immediately take possession, but is not obliged to do so till the death of the former.

---

[1] In New Jersey and Virginia, the same words which in a deed pass a life-estate, will give a fee by devise.

BOOK VI.

PRIVATE WRONGS.

CHAPTER I.

REDRESS OF PRIVATE WRONGS BY ACT OF PARTIES, AND BY ACT OF LAW.

Having in the preceding books treated of *private rights*, both *of person* and *of personal and real property*; we shall, in the present, consider *private wrongs*, which are *the violation or infringement* of those rights, and the remedies provided by law for redress of the same.

Wrongs are usually redressed by application or *suit* to *courts of justice*; but sometimes in other modes, which will be briefly noticed in the present chapter.

1. *By act of one party.* Every man has a right to *defend* his person, property, or relatives from unlawful attack, by all the force necessary for that purpose; but, if he go beyond this point, he becomes in his turn an aggressor. Where *an officer*, having *a writ* or *process* against one person, attempts by virtue of it to seize the goods of another; the latter may defend his possession precisely as he might against any other trespasser. So a man may *retake* his property, wife, child, or servant, wrongfully abducted or detained

from him, wherever he may find them, if it can be done without disturbance or breach of the peace. Thus, if my horse is taken away, and I find him on the highway, I may lawfully seize him; but I cannot justify breaking open a private stable, or entering on the land of a third person, unless the horse were *feloniously stolen.*

Under the same head, may be classed *the right of entry upon land*, of which a party has been *disseised*;[1] and of *abating* or removing *a nuisance*,[2] — as, for instance, a house or wall, built so near his *ancient lights*, as to stop them, and which he may therefore peaceably pull down.

To this class of remedies belongs the right of *distress. Distress* is *the seizure of goods*, upon premises leased, for *non-payment of rent*; or of *cattle, doing damage*, — "damage feasant," — to one's land. The practice is unknown in New England, except in reference to the *impounding* of cattle; but prevails in most of the southern and middle States. In many of its principles, *distress* resembles the process of *attachment*,[3] hereafter to be considered. It therefore demands only a brief notice at the present time.

Articles cannot be *distreined* in a workman's or mechanic's shop, because they are presumed not to be his property; — nor in the highway. But, in general, whatever is found upon a tenant's land may be distreined;[4] and, if the property of a third person be taken, he must look to the tenant for satisfaction. But the cattle of a stranger cannot be distreined, when they stray upon the land through defective

---

[1] See *Entry*. [2] See *Nuisance*. [3] See *Attachment*.
[4] In Virginia and New Jersey provided otherwise.

fences, until after they have been "levant et couchant," or passed one night upon it; nor, if the tenant were bound to repair the fences, till after notice of the fact. In New York, the right of distress is laid under many restrictions; but rent is *preferred* to other debts.

The owner of property distreined may regain possession of it, and try the right of seizure, by the process of *replevin*, which will be noticed hereafter.[1]

2. *By arbitration.* *Arbitration* is where parties, having a controversy, instead of going to law, submit it to the judgment of *arbitrators* or *referees.* The decision of arbitrators is called *an award*, and is as binding upon the parties as the judgment of a court. It cannot indeed be enforced, like a judgment, by *execution*; but a refusal to comply with it will, like the breach of any other contract, subject the party to an action for damages. *The submission* is usually made, by *mutual bonds* to abide by the award. A suit may be brought, either upon the bond, or the award itself; but not till the latter has been made known to the parties. *A bill in Equity* will also in general lie, to enforce an award.

A submission may be *revoked*, by *act of God*, as by the death of a party or arbitrator; by *act of law*, as the marriage of a *feme-sole*; or by *express revocation* of one of the parties.

The most common form of arbitration, is by *a rule of court*, so called; by which the parties to a suit, pending in a court of justice, withdraw it therefrom, and submit the question to the judgment of referees. Such an award is *returned to court*, and *judgment* is rendered upon it, as upon *a verdict*. In causes which

---

[1] See *Replevin*.

involve long and intricate *accounts*, these are referred usually to *auditors*, — called in New York *referees*, whose judgment upon them is held conclusive, unless it be rebutted by strong contradictory evidence.

A submission by *rule of court* cannot be *revoked* by either party without the other's consent. Nor can the suit be *discontinued*; because, if it were, a new one for the same cause might be commenced; whereas an award and judgment in favor of the defendant are a perpetual bar. Such a submission operates as a waiver of all merely formal and technical objections, which might otherwise be made. The arbitrators may examine *interested witnesses*, who, in a court of law, would be *incompetent*; and, in general, may determine according to *equity and good conscience*. They have power to award *costs*; — but other referees have not.

An award, made by only *a part* of the arbitrators, is void; unless it was agreed to abide by such decision.

The form of an award need not be technical, provided it is a substantial decision of the question submitted. Thus, an award that the defendant *recover costs* is a determination of the case in his favor.

If referees *exceed their authority*, as to some of the parties or subject matters, and not others, the award may be good as to the latter, unless the part which is void be the condition or consideration for the fulfilment of the other. If demands in favor of only one party be submitted, and they award a sum in favor of the other, the award is void.

A time should in general be fixed, within which the award shall be made. If not, it must be made in *reasonable* time.

The court, to which an award is returned, may for good cause *recommit* it. Thus, if either party have not had sufficient opportunity to be heard; if the report vary from the submission; if either of the arbitrators have acted partially and corruptly; or if the award contain gross errors.

A mere *submission* to arbitration is no bar to *a suit* for the same cause of action. *An actual award* is a bar. But, though the submission be "of all demands," it has been held in Massachusetts and New Hampshire, that the award will bar an action, only upon such demands as were actually presented, and considered by the referees. Otherwise in New York. When it is meant to refer all disputes, the terms of reference should be "of all matters in difference between the parties;"—if only a particular cause, "of all matters in difference in the cause."

In addition to the modes of arbitration *at common law*, a special statute in Massachusetts provides a form of submission *before a Justice of the Peace.* The award, in such case, is returned to court, like one founded upon *a rule.*

3. *By act of law.* Remedies are sometimes effected, without any act of parties, by mere *operation of law.* This happens in two cases.

(1.) An executor or administrator, himself holding a debt against the deceased person, may *retain* from the effects enough to satisfy it. The reason is, that in order to recover the claim by action, he must sue himself. This proceeding is termed "retainer." In some of the States, if the estate is insolvent, it is provided that the executor shall not *retain* more than his proportion.

(2.) Upon a similar principle, where the rightful owner of land, who has been wrongfully dispossessed, and could recover it only by an action, has the freehold cast upon him by some subsequent defective title; he is *remitted* or sent back, by mere operation of law, to his old right. Thus, if A *disseise* or dispossess B, and die, leaving a son C; B cannot in general regain his estate, but by an action against C. But, if C make a lease for life to D, remainder to B, the latter immediately regains his former estate. An immediate voluntary purchase, however, would not have the effect of *a remitter*,—being regarded as *a waiver* of the better title.

CHAPTER II.

REDRESS BY ACTION IN COURTS.

A COURT is a place wherein justice is judicially administered.

Courts are either of *record*, or *not of record*. The former, is where the proceedings are *recorded* for a perpetual memorial and testimony; which record is of conclusive authority, cannot be denied, and is proved, if occasion require, merely by production and inspection of itself, or of a copy.[1] Most of the judicial courts in the United States are of this description.

---

[1] See *Record*.

Courts, in this country, are of various kinds and degrees. Suits brought to recover less than a certain sum, — varying, in the several States, from twenty to a hundred dollars, — are tried by *Justices of the Peace*; with a right of *appeal* to a higher court. In some States, justices have the aid of *a jury*; but usually not.[1]

For the examination of more important causes, each State has its superior and inferior tribunals; some limited, in jurisdiction, to a single *city* or *county*, and others embracing *the whole State*. An appeal usually lies from the former to the latter. A large proportion of actions are tried in these courts. In some States, the Senate is a final *Court of Errors*.

Besides the *State courts*, there are several tribunals, instituted by the constitution and laws of *the United States*. The jurisdiction of these courts is *definite and specific*, and not general; and it is therefore only in comparatively rare cases, that resort is had to them for redress of private wrongs. *The District Courts* are chiefly *Courts of Admiralty* for the trial of *maritime causes*. *The Circuit Courts* have jurisdiction of *appeals* from the former, and also of suits between *citizens of different States*; and, in some instances, a cause may be removed to them from the State courts. *The Supreme Court* has jurisdiction, chiefly *appellate*, but sometimes *original*, of cases, arising under the constitution, treaties, or laws of the Union; affecting ambassadors; in which the United States are a party;

---

[1] In general, a justice cannot try any question *of real estate*; nor, in New York, actions for certain personal wrongs, nor against corporations or executors. In New York, justices may receive *the acknowledgment* of debts to the amount of two hundred and fifty dollars. In Kentucky, a justice has jurisdiction, it seems, to the amountof five pounds, or a thousand weight of tobacco.

between two States; and in some other instances. In one instance, an appeal lies to this court from a State court.

Most of the courts in the United States are courts *of common law.* Some are not. Of the latter description are Courts *of Chancery, of Probate, of Admiralty, of Impeachment,* and *Courts Martial.* In *common law* courts, the proceedings are usually commenced *by writ,* and the trial is *by jury*; but in others, the proceedings are commenced by *bill, petition,* or *libel,* and the trial is *by the court or judge.*

In every court, there are at least three constituent parties, — *the plaintiff,* who complains of a wrong done; *the defendant,* who is called on to make satisfaction for it; and *the judge,* who is to examine the facts, and determine the law applicable to them. This is the general principle. There are certain *amicable proceedings,* instituted in compliance with some statute provision, which constitute an exception to it.

It is also usual, in courts, to have *attorneys,* and *advocates or counsel,* for the respective parties.

An attorney is bound to use care, skill and integrity in his client's service, but will not be responsible for a mere error or accident. Formerly it was held that he could recover no compensation for his services. But it is now settled otherwise.

Suits or actions are divided into three kinds, — personal, real, and mixed. *Personal actions* are those whereby a man claims *a debt or personal duty,* or damages instead of it; or else *damages for some injury* done to his person or property. The former are said to be founded upon *contracts,* the latter upon *torts* or wrongs.

Real actions are such as concern *real property*

alone, and whereby the plaintiff or *demandant claims a freehold title* to lands or tenements.

Mixed actions are those wherein *some real property* is demanded, and also *personal damages* for a wrong or injury. *Waste* is an example, — being an action to recover the place wasted, together with damages.

All persons interested in the subject matter of an action must, in general, be made parties to it.[1] If *a promise* is made *to two persons*, they must join as plaintiffs; and, if made *by two persons*, they must be joined as defendants. If *an injury* is done to the joint property of two, they must unite in the action; but joint *wrong-doers* may be sued together or separately.

When a person, for or against whom a cause of action exists, *has died*; his executor or administrator shall sue or be sued,[2] if the action is personal; and, if real, his heir. If *one of two parties* has died, the survivor alone can generally sue or be sued; unless the promise were *joint and several*. But the statute law, in some States, has made the executor of a *joint* promisor liable to suit. (In relation to suits for or against *femes-covert* and *infants*, see pp. 19, 26-27.)

The common law, wherever it gives a right, gives also a remedy or action for a violation of that right. And when *a statute* creates a new right, without prescribing a remedy, the common law will give one; but, if the statute designate a remedy, no other can be pursued. So, if the legislature authorize an act, the natural consequence of which is damage to one's property; he cannot maintain an action at common law, but must pursue the statute remedy.

---

[1] See p. 73. [2] See p. 68.

For the sake of clearness, simplicity, and precision, the law has appropriated particular forms of action to the redress of particular wrongs. But, where the circumstances of an individual injury do not fall within the more definite and specific remedies, a broad and comprehensive one is furnished, called "trespass on the case," or, more familiarly, "an action on the case," — that is, an action framed to meet the case which has arisen.[1]

CHAPTER III.

INJURIES TO THE ABSOLUTE RIGHTS OF PERSONS.

As the rights of persons are either *absolute* or *relative,* so the injuries done to those rights require the same classification.

I. *Injuries to the body.* *A threat or menace* of bodily hurt, through fear of which a man's business is interrupted or any other injury sustained, is a ground of action for damages.

An assault is an attempt or offer to beat another, without touching him; as by raising one's cane or fist, in a threatening manner. This is itself a sufficient ground of action, without proving actual injury.

A battery is the unlawful beating of another. The least touching of another's person, wilfully and in anger, is a battery. But this is in some cases lawful; as where a *parent or master* moderately corrects

---

[1] See *Action on the Case.*

his child or servant; or where one, being struck, or only *assaulted,* strikes *in self-defence*; or where a man strikes for the purpose of *defending his property,* or of *ejecting an intruder* from his premises. In the latter case, if the entry were *peaceable,* there must be a previous request to quit; if *forcible,* the intruder may be immediately ejected by force. This defence, from the words used in the plea, is called "molliter manus imposuit,"—meaning that the defendant *gently laid on his hands* to eject the plaintiff.

Mayhem is a species of battery, whereby *a wound* is inflicted, which deprives the party of some member necessary for his defence when attacked,—such as an arm, finger, or fore tooth. This is the only case, where the court have power to increase the damages awarded by a jury. It must be done, however, "super visum vulneris," on sight of the wound.

An *unlawful imprisonment* is an assault and battery; and every continuation of it is *a new trespass,* for which a new action will lie.[1]

For an assault and battery, an *indictment* or public prosecution lies, as well as an action for damages; and neither is a bar to the other, except perhaps where the act is of so atrocious a nature, as to constitute *a capital offence.* In New York, a person injured by *a felony,* for which the offender is imprisoned, receives satisfaction from his estate; and in no case, it seems, is a right of private action merged in the crime.

The above-described injuries are sometimes called *trespasses to the person*; and the form of action proper for obtaining damages is *trespass* "*vi et armis,*" with force and arms.

---

[1] See infra, IV.

II. *Injuries to health.* *Injuries affecting health* are where, by any unwholesome practice of another, a person sustains damage in his bodily vigor or constitution;—as, for instance, by selling bad provisions; by the exercise of a noisome trade, which infects the air in his neighbourhood; or by the neglect or unskilful management of a physician or surgeon. If, in the latter case, by means of the administration of improper medicine, the patient die, and the physician knew enough of its nature to induce a probable expectation of this result; it is *murder* or *manslaughter*. But, if the act was done through ignorance, and with an honest intention to effect a cure; the law will not adjudge it to be a crime.

III. *Injuries to reputation,*

1. *Slander.* *Slander* is the use of *false and malicious words,* tending to one's damage or derogation.

Words are *in themselves* slanderous, when they charge a person, either with some *heinous or disgraceful crime,* — as murder or perjury; with some *infectious disease,* which may exclude him from society; or with something that may *impair his trade or livelihood,* or is *derogatory to his professional character,* — as to call a trader "a bankrupt," a clergyman "a drunkard," or to say that a judge has given "a corrupt judgment." In all these cases, *an injury is presumed,* and no special damage need be proved. But other defamatory words are not actionable, unless they cause some *particular injury.* Thus, to call one "a rogue," or "a rascal," is not actionable, unless some pecuniary loss, — as the loss of a customer in trade, — result from it. And the injury must have resulted solely from this cause.

It is not, in general, necessary to prove *the precise words,* but only the substance of them. But any variance, however slight, *which changes the sense*, — as, for instance, an interrogation instead of a positive assertion, — will be fatal to the action. When the words used admit or require *amplification or definition*, to convey their meaning more precisely; this is done, in the writ, by "an innuendo," so called. For instance, if the words were, "he signs notes for other people," the writ sets forth these words, and adds, "*meaning* that the plaintiff forged notes." But *an innuendo* cannot give to words any other than their necessary and natural signification. Thus, if the words were, "he is foresworn," the innuendo cannot make this a charge of *perjury*, because it does not imply that the oath was *a judicial one*. If the remark were made in a conversation about some judicial proceeding, it would be actionable; and, in such case, that conversation is referred to in the writ, and is called in law "the colloquium."

There is no slander without *malice*. Thus words spoken *in a friendly manner*, by way of advice or admonition; or in the discharge of some *official duty*, — as by an advocate in Court, if pertinent to the cause; or in the form of *petition* to a public body, if in the usual and proper mode; — are not actionable. The same is true of words spoken *privately* to the person charged; — though *an indictment* will lie, for such communication of *a printed libel*, as tending to *breach of the peace*. Malice need not be expressly proved, but may be *inferred* from the nature of the words themselves. It is no proof of want of malice, that the words were spoken carelessly, wantonly, or in jest. To show malice, evidence may be offered of a previous malignant intention, and, in general, of other words than those for which the action is brought.

Words cannot be slanderous, if they are *true* ; and the truth is a common and legal defence to an action of slander. If not made out, however, it has the effect to aggravate the damages.

Another sufficient defence is, that the defendant declared merely what *he had heard from another person*, giving the name of that person at the time, as his authority, — provided it was done without malice. So it is a good defence, that the slander was procured *by the contrivance of the plaintiff*, for the purpose of bringing the action ; or that the defendant was *insane*, — if the insanity was such that the words could produce no effect on the hearers.

In mitigation of damages, the defendant may show the plaintiff's *general bad character*. And, on the other hand, *to increase them*, the plaintiff may give in evidence his own *rank and condition*. He may also offer evidence of his good character, in answer to *a plea of the truth* made by the defendant.

2. *Libel.* — *A libel* is *a malicious publication*, expressed either in printing or writing, or by signs and pictures, and with intent to blacken the memory of one dead, or the reputation of one who is alive, and expose him to public hatred, contempt, or ridicule. According to the above definition, expressions may of course be libellous *in print*, which would not be slanderous, *if spoken*.

Libels are a subject of *criminal prosecution*, as well as of private action for damages. In the former case, *the truth* of the publication, at common law, is no defence ; but the constitutions or statutes of most of the States have changed this principle, and allowed the truth, if published with good motives and for justifiable ends, to be offered as a justification.

Every new publication of a libel, is regarded as *a new libel*; and it is no excuse, as in slander, that the defendant only repeated what he heard from another. Greater strictness is required, in proving the precise expressions alleged, than in case of slanderous words.

The general principles of law relating to libel, as the subject of a civil action, are substantially similar to those already stated in regard to unwritten slander.

3. *Malicious prosecution.*—A man may be injured in his *reputation*, (as well as his *person and property*,) by having *a malicious and unfounded prosecution or indictment* preferred against him. For this the law provides a remedy; either by an action of *conspiracy*, where there are two or more concerned; or by an action for *malicious prosecution* against the party making the charge before any judicial tribunal. The latter is the more usual course. Any charge, which would be *libellous*, if preferred otherwise than in a judicial proceeding, is ground of action for malicious prosecution, when made in that mode.

The commencing of *a groundless civil action* is also a cause for suit, against the plaintiff in such action, by the defendant. Thus where one maliciously brings an action in another's name, without authority, and attaches the defendant's property. So where one partner, having access to the company's books, sues another for a balance, and the balance is found against him. If a groundless suit be submitted by the parties *to referees*, the submission will not amount to a waiver, by the defendant, of his claim for damages. This action cannot be sustained, without proving both *malice* and *the want of probable cause* for a prosecution. The latter implies the former; but the former may exist without the latter. Upon this ground, the plaintiff must show, at the outset, that he *prevailed* in the original suit or indictment; — a conviction or judgment against him being conclusive of *probable cause.* Contrary to the established rule, that *no man can testify in his own favor*, the defendant may sometimes give evidence of what he himself swore on the former trial.

The remedy for injuries to health, or to reputation, is an action of *trespass on the case.*

IV. *Injuries to personal liberty.*—These are effected by *false imprisonment*, for which the law not only provides a punishment as a *public crime*, but also *a private reparation*, both by removing the actual confinement, and giving an action for damages.

To constitute *false imprisonment*, there must be *a detention of the person*, and such detention must be *unlawful.* Every confinement of the person is an imprisonment, whether it be in a prison, or a private house, or by forcible detention in the street. To be *false*, it must be done without sufficient authority; — which authority generally consists of *some process or warrant* from a court or judicial officer,[1] though under special circumstances it may arise from other sources. Thus one, who openly commits a violent and aggravated crime, may be immediately seized by any person who witnesses it.

Whenever any person is detained, with or without due process of law, unless for *treason or felony* plainly expressed in the warrant of commitment, or unless he be *a convict*, or legally charged *in execution* or on *mesne process*, or committed according to the provisions of the constitution; — he is entitled to his writ

---

[1] See *Imprisonment for Debt.*

of *Habeas Corpus* for release. The nature of this writ has been already adverted to.[1] It is obtained, by summary application to some judicial officer, either in court or out. The effect of it is, to bring the party detained, immediately before the appointed tribunal, together with the true cause of commitment; so that, if insufficient, he shall be forthwith discharged, either absolutely, or on giving sureties, as the case may be. It is the intention of the Habeas Corpus acts, *to relieve against unlawful imprisonment*, and not to alter the law authorizing commitments. They, however, afford relief, not only from illegal confinement of a public nature, but from every unjust restraint of personal freedom *in private life*, though imposed by a husband or father.

If one be arrested on a process *void for irregularity*, — as, for instance, *a writ* not returnable[2] at the proper term of the Court, or *an execution* issued more than a year after judgment,[3] — *the creditor*, causing the act to be done, is liable to an action for *false imprisonment*. *The officer* who executes the process, is not liable, provided the Court had *jurisdiction* of the case. But if not, even *the Judge*, and every other person in any way concerned, is subject to an action. So, *the Clerk of a Court*, or *a Justice of the Peace*, who issues an execution contrary to law; and, in some cases, *the assessors of taxes*, which for any cause are illegal, may be sued for false imprisonment.

---

[1] See p. 12. [2] See *Return of Writ*. [3] See *Execution*.

CHAPTER IV.

INJURIES TO THE RELATIVE RIGHTS OF PERSONS.

INJURIES to *relative rights* may be offered to a person, in the capacity of husband, father, guardian, or master.

A husband may maintain an action, either for the *abduction*, *seduction*, or *beating* of his wife.

The first may be either by *fraud and persuasion*, or by *open violence*. But the law, in both cases, supposes force and constraint, the wife having no power to consent; and therefore gives an action of trespass "vi et armis."

For the injury of *adultery*, very large and exemplary damages are usually given, — varying, however, with different circumstances, such as the rank and fortune of the parties; the relation or connexion between them; the wife's previous character, &c. Evidence may be given, in mitigation of damages, of the husband's previous criminal conduct; or of his want of affection, and ill treatment, towards his wife. And proof that he consented to her infamy will constitute a complete defence to the action. So will proof of their having, by agreement, lived apart from each other; or, of his having abandoned her. In the case of adultery, *actual marriage* must be proved; though, in most other cases, *reputation and cohabitation* are considered as sufficient evidence of it. The confessions of the wife are no evidence *for the husband*, nor her letters to the defendant, *against him*.

But letters passing between the husband and wife, if strictly proved, are evidence of their intimacy and affection.

For the injury of *beating one's wife*, the husband may join with her in bringing an action of trespass; or, if she were severely hurt, he may recover damages alone, *for the loss of her society and service.*

Injuries to *parents and guardians* are substantially the same with those just described, and require no distinct notice.

A master may maintain an action against any one, who *entices away his servant*, during the time that he has agreed for his services; — either *with knowledge* of the previous contract, or *without*, if he retain the servant after demand. But no action lies, for inducing a servant to leave his master after his contract expires; although the persuasion be used before that time, and the servant had no previous intention of leaving.

So also an action lies for *beating* a servant. And, upon the principle of master and servant, a father may recover damages for *the seduction* of his daughter; alleging, as the ground of action, *the loss of her services*, "per quod servitium amisit." The daughter herself can maintain no action, unless there were also *a promise of marriage*;[1] in which case, seduction may be shown *in aggravation of damages.*

Where the daughter is a minor, the action lies, though she reside out of her father's family, — her services being presumed. Otherwise, if of full age. The daughter herself is a competent witness for the plaintiff.

---

[1] See p. 76.

CHAPTER V.

INJURIES TO PERSONAL PROPERTY IN POSSESSION.

Injuries to property may be either to *personal estate*, or *real estate*. The former are also divided into injuries to personal property *in possession*, and to personal property *in action*. The first class of wrongs will be considered in this chapter.

I. In case of *a wrongful taking* or *detention* of personal property, the owner may have an action *to recover the thing itself*, with *damages* for the injury. This is effected by the action of *replevin*; — the action of *detinue*, formerly in use, being now for the most part obsolete, and, in New York, expressly abolished.

Replevin differs from all other actions in some material points. In other actions, the plaintiff or demandant is not *put in possession* of the thing demanded, until after *a trial and judgment* in his favor. But, by virtue of a writ of *replevin*, the officer who serves it *takes the property* from the holder, and delivers it to the plaintiff, — the latter *giving bond* to restore it, if he shall fail in the suit. The defendant in his plea claims *a return*; and the plaintiff, if he prevail, has judgment only for the damages of detention, and costs, — the goods themselves being already in his hands. These circumstances have the effect of reversing the usual order of judicial proceedings; — giving to the plaintiff, in many respects, the posture of defendant, and "vice versâ." In New York, when the defendant disputes the plaintiff's property, the repleving officer keeps the goods till after trial.

In England, replevin is said to lie only for property wrongfully taken by the process of *distress*;[1] but, in Massachusetts and other States, it may be brought for any personal property either *taken or detained unlawfully*. The most common occasion of bringing this action, is where the property of one man has been seized *by writ or execution*, as *belonging to another*; in which case, the former *replevies* the property from the officer. Thus, when the owner of goods sells them, and, after the sale, they are seized by his creditors, upon the ground that the sale was *fraudulent and void*;[2] the purchaser may *replevy* them, and, in this form, the validity of the sale will be tried. So, when a merchant *consigns* goods, and they are seized by creditors of *the commission merchant*, as *sold* to him.

In order to maintain replevin, the plaintiff must have *the right of property* and *of possession*. Hence, if the goods were *leased*, the lessor cannot, while the lease is in force, replevy them from one who takes them out of the lessee's hands. But if, before judgment, the lease should expire, the defendant would have judgment *for costs only*, and not for *a return of the goods*.

The bond is considered a part of the replevin process. It is *a condition precedent*, and, for want of it, the defendant may stop the suit. If the defendant prevail in the action, he usually recovers, besides the goods themselves, as a satisfaction for having them

[1] See *Distress*. [2] See p. 90.

taken from him, a certain *percentage* on the penalty of the bond.

II. The usual remedy for an unlawful taking or detention of, or injury to, personal property; is a suit not for the property itself, but *for damages*.

1. *Trespass*. The action of *trespass "vi et armis"* lies only for *a wrongful taking*, and not *a mere detention*. This, however, need not be *a forcible seizure*; but may consist in any interference with, or attempt to dispose of, another's goods without his consent; or in advising or aiding such a wrongful act. And where a person takes another's goods by virtue of any *legal authority*; if he afterwards *abuse* or deviate from such authority, he becomes *a trespasser "ab initio,"* from the beginning. Thus, where a sheriff works a horse which he has *attached*; or sells goods, without having observed the legal formalities,—he may be sued in an action of trespass. Any abuse of an authority given *by the owner himself* can never have this effect; because he is in fault, for having reposed an improper confidence in the wrong-doer.

Besides this action, usually called "trespass," there is another form of the same remedy, called "an action on the case."

2. *Trespass on the case.*

To maintain trespass "vi et armis," one must have had *possession*, or *an immediate right to possession*, of the goods taken or injured. For injuries to *reversionary rights*,[1] the proper form of action is "trespass on the case." If an injury is *immediate*,—as where the defendant negligently or wilfully drove his chaise against the plaintiff's,—"trespass" should be brought; if *consequential*, as where the defendant threw a log

---

[1] See pp. 46, 178.

into the road, and the plaintiff's horse fell over it,—"case" is the remedy. In general, "trespass" is the form of action for *forcible injuries*, to things in their nature *tangible*, committed *by the defendant himself*; and "case," for injuries *without force*, to things in their nature *intangible*, such as health or reputation, or committed by the defendant's *animals or servants*.

In New York, "case" may now be brought whereever "trespass" would lie, except for injuries to *real estate*.

3. *Trover*. The action of *trover*, is a common form of recovering damages, for either an unlawful taking, or detention, of personal property. Although originally founded upon, and deriving its name from, the act of *finding* another man's goods, and *converting them* to the finder's use; it now lies against any one, who has had in his possession the personal goods of another, and has either sold or used them without the owner's consent, or refused to deliver them when demanded. The injury lies in *the conversion*, not in the finding; and the law presumes a conversion, if the defendant refuse to restore the goods on demand.

Trover lies, where goods are delivered by the owner, upon contract, for a particular purpose, and are misused or abused by the receiver. Thus, if one hire a horse to ride to a certain place, and he ride beyond it, or to a different place; it is an unlawful conversion of the horse, which subjects him to an action of trover; and a return of the property will merely go to mitigate the damages.

If goods be obtained *by fraud*, though with the consent of the owner at the time; it is *a wrongful taking*, and this action may be brought without a demand and refusal.

Trover is in most cases a concurrent remedy with trespass; a party having liberty to bring either action at his election. The same right of property is required to sustain both.

CHAPTER VI.

INJURIES TO PERSONAL PROPERTY IN ACTION.

UNDER this head, may properly be considered injuries to those rights which are *founded on contracts*, and the remedies therefor. The nature and several divisions of contracts have been already explained.[1]

I. *Express contracts.* These include *debts, covenants*, and *promises.*

1. *A debt* is a sum of money due by *certain and express agreement*, — as by a bond, a bill or note, or a lease; — where the amount is fixed and specific, and does not depend on any subsequent valuation to settle it. The non-payment of these is an injury, for which the proper remedy is by *action of debt*, to compel performance of the contract, and recover the specific sum due. This action, however, is now seldom brought, but upon contracts *under seal.* In other cases, the usual remedy is the action called "indebitatus assumpsit," to recover *damages* for non-performance of the contract; — in which the plaintiff will recover *according to his proof*, though it be less than he claims in the writ. The averment is, that the defendant,

---

[1] See pp. 72, 73.

being indebted to the plaintiff in a certain sum, for a certain cause, promised in consideration thereof to pay it, but failed, — laying the damages at whatever sum the plaintiff may see fit. In Massachusetts, and other States, it is the practice to annex *a bill or schedule* to the writ, and simply refer to it by the words "according to the account annexed."

2. *A covenant*, contained in a deed, is another species of *express contract*, the breach of which is a civil injury. The remedy, is the *action of* "covenant," for damages, the amount of which will be governed by the circumstances of each particular case. The nature and different kinds of covenants have been already explained.[1]

3. *A promise* is of the same nature with a covenant, but *not under seal*. For breach of this, the remedy is an action of "assumpsit" for damages. And any one, beneficially interested in the promise, may bring this action. Thus, a promise made to A, to pay B a sum of money, may be sued on by B. It would be otherwise with an action of *covenant* upon a sealed instrument; which could be brought only by A, and not by B.

II. *Implied contracts.* — The action of "assumpsit" is also the remedy for breach of *implied contracts*.

1. In this form, a person may recover *the fair value of work performed* or *goods sold*, "quantum meruit," as much as he deserved, or "quantum valebant," as much as they were worth; no price being fixed by the contract.

2. *Assumpsit* also lies, by one person against another, to whom he has "lent and accommodated," or

---

[1] See p. 205.

for whom and at whose request he has "paid," *money*, — the law *implying* a promise of repayment. Thus, *a surety*[1] may bring an action against his principal, for "money paid to his use," after satisfying the debt. The general rule is, that no action can be brought for *money paid*, till after *actual payment of money*; *the giving new security* is not sufficient. But, if a surety satisfy the debt by giving his *negotiable note*, this is regarded as a cash payment, and he has an immediate right of action for *money paid*. .If the surety pay the debt, though not legally liable; yet, if the principal were liable, the action will lie. As where the surety died, and, more than four years afterwards, the executor paid the note, though discharged by lapse of time.

This action also lies, *for one surety against another*, to obtain *contribution*, — the former having paid more than his share of the debt. If there be several sureties, and one pay the whole debt, and some of the rest have become insolvent; the person paying cannot recover *at law*, from any solvent co-surety, more than his proportional share of *the whole*: — but, *in Equity*, he may recover an additional sum *for the insolvent parties*. One nominally a surety, but really a principal, can have no action; nor will an action lie against one, who signed at the request of the plaintiff, the latter being also a surety. If the surety who paid the debt were *indemnified* by the principal, he must first reimburse himself from the property assigned to him, and can recover from the others no more than the balance.

Assumpsit for money paid, will also lie for one *joint*

---

[1] See p. 113.

contractor, who has paid the whole, against his fellow; but not for one *co-trespasser* or *wrong-doer*.

One who pays money for another *gratuitously*, without any request or legal liability, cannot recover it from the latter.

In the actions *for money lent and for money paid*, *interest* is recovered *from the time of payment*.[1]

3. *Assumpsit* "for money had and received," is a remedy even more common than "for money paid," and is the most comprehensive form of action known to the law; being applicable to almost every case, where one has received money, or money's worth, for which, in right and justice, — "ex æquo et bono," he ought to be accountable. It lies, to recover money paid the defendant, but *belonging to the plaintiff*; money due upon *bills or notes*, or for which these securities have been taken by the defendant for a debt due the plaintiff; money paid by *mistake*, *imposition*, *extortion*, or *illegal compulsory process*, as, for taxes wrongfully assessed, — though a mistake must be one *of fact*, not *of law*, every man being presumed *to know the law*; — money paid on a contract which has been *rescinded*, — as where *freight* is paid in advance and the goods are not carried; on *a consideration which has failed*, — as where a principal has put money into his surety's hands for security, and himself pays the debt; or paid *in trust* and misapplied, as where the plaintiff made partial payments upon a note, which the defendant did not indorse, but afterwards recovered judgment for the whole; but not money paid in pursuance of *an illegal contract*, — as for the *compounding* of a felony, unless

---

[1] See p. 100.

where the plaintiff is less guilty than the defendant, and oppressed by him, — as in case of *usury.* And where one *unlawfully disposes of my property*, so that *trespass* or *trover*[1] would lie, and receives the proceeds, whether in money, land, or otherwise; I may *wave the wrong*, and sue for money had and received.

The action "for money had and received" will not, in general, lie *for failure of consideration*, if there is another adequate remedy; as, for instance, to recover the price of land, the title to which afterwards fails, where there are *covenants* in the deed of conveyance. The suit must be brought *upon the covenants.*[2]

In this action, *interest* is recovered *from the date of the writ.*

4. The action of *assumpsit* may be brought for *use and occupation of real estate,*— in the absence of a lease under seal. But *a title to land* can never be tried in this form: therefore, *an adverse claimant*, of whom the tenant *did not hire*, cannot sue him for the rent, upon the ground of being the true owner; nor, in such suit brought *by the landlord*, can the tenant set up in defence *a third person's title to the land.*[3]

5. *Assumpsit* lies upon *a stated account*, between merchants or others jointly concerned in business;— the law implying a promise to pay the balance found to be due from one to another. The declaration is, in such case, that the plaintiff and defendant had *settled their accounts* together, and *a certain balance*

---

1 See *Trespass, Trover.* 2 See *Covenant in Deed.* 3 See p. 210.

was found due to the former. This is termed an "insimul computassent." To compel a settlement of accounts not yet made, another action is resorted to, viz. the action of "account." This, however, is now superseded, for the most part, by *a bill in equity*; in which *the oaths of the parties* are allowed, and by that means the details of accounts can be more easily and accurately adjusted, than by the evidence allowed in courts of law.[1]

6. *Assumpsit* also lies upon *the implied contract*, that every one, who undertakes *any office or employment*, will perform it with integrity, diligence, and skill. Any person, injured by the want of these qualities, may maintain an action for damages against the party in fault. Thus, the action lies against a sheriff, for neglecting to serve a writ committed to him; or against a mechanic of any sort, for not performing his work in a workmanlike manner. But an implied contract does not arise, unless the person assuming the work make it his *regular profession and business.* If otherwise, it seems necessary that there should be *a special engagement* in order to charge him.[2]

In cases of the above description, the more usual remedy, instead of *assumpsit*, as upon a contract, is *an action upon the case*,[3] charging the neglect or violation of duty, as a *tort* or wrong. And when a penalty is given by statute, and *an action of the case* provided for its recovery; an action of the case for *a tort* is intended, and not *in assumpsit*, no promise being implied.

---

1 See *Chancery*. 2 See p. 100. 3 See *Action on the Case.*

CHAPTER VII.

INJURIES TO REAL PROPERTY. OUSTER.

Injuries to real property are, 1st. those which *deprive the owner of his possession*, and usurp his right. 2dly. Those which only *disturb the enjoyment*, or *diminish the value*, of the land, without changing the possession. The former class will be considered in this chapter.

Dispossession of real estate is called in law *an ouster*, and is of several kinds.

Abatement, — where *the owner dies*, and *before entry of the heir or devisee, a stranger wrongfully enters.*

Intrusion, — where *an estate for life terminates*, and a stranger enters *before the reversioner or remainder-man.*

Discontinuance, — where a rightful occupant has *conveyed to a third person a larger interest than he himself owned*; as where *a tenant in tail* conveys for a longer period than his own life.[1]

Deforcement and *disseisin*, — where the owner is dispossessed in any other than the above modes. The latter term is generally used in this country, to denote any species of dispossession whatsoever; and is defined to be, "a wrongful putting out of him that is seised of the freehold."

Disseisin may be either of *corporeal* property or *incorporeal*; — of the former, such as houses and

---

[1] See p. 154.

lands, by *actual entry*; and of the latter, as for instance a rent, by disturbing the owner in his enjoyment of them. In the latter case, it is not usual to treat the injury as a *disseisin*; but the owner may so treat it at his election.

Upon a similar principle, the rightful owner of land may consider any one who wrongfully enters, claiming title, as a *disseisor* of his *whole interest*, although the latter expressly claim a less estate. A disseisor cannot *qualify his own wrong*; so as to prevent the owner from pursuing the remedies which the law has provided in cases of disseisin, and which are more specific and effectual than those for a mere *trespass*.

The remedy for a disseisin is *the restitution of possession* to the rightful owner, and, in some cases, *damages* in addition. This remedy is obtained in the following modes.

1. *Entry.*

An owner of land disseised, may make *a formal and peaceable entry* upon the land, and shall thereby be fully reinstated in his property.[1] No express declaration is necessary of his *intention* in making the entry; but it will be presumed to be the regaining of his estate, unless the contrary appear. Thus if, after entry, he remain in possession *with the disseisor*, claiming nothing of his original estate; or take the profits as *lessee at will* of the disseisor; or command a stranger to enter, or to put his cattle upon the land, — the estate will be revested. But an entry will not have this effect, if it was manifestly made for another purpose; — as where the owner

---

[1] In New York and Connecticut, a mere entry is insufficient, unless a suit be brought for the land within a year afterwards.

went into a house by invitation of the occupant, or as one of a jury to view the premises.

Where a man is disseised of different lands in *the same county*, he may enter upon one *in name of the whole*; if *in different counties*, or if there be several disseisors, there must be *several entries*. Entry should be made in presence of *witnesses*; the intention declared before them; and a memorandum made by them of the act. Entry must also be *peaceable*. The statute law of nearly all the States prohibits *forcible entry*, under a severe penalty; and provides a summary process, by which the party thus dispossessed shall be restored to his occupancy. The statutes apply as well to a *detainer* as an entry; unless the occupant have had possession for a certain time, — in Massachusetts, three years. But *a mere refusal* to deliver possession, when demanded, is not a foundation for this process. It must be attended with threats, violence, offensive weapons, a multitude of people, or some other *circumstance of terror*. The process does not lie, it seems, against any one who has entered *under the levy of an execution* upon the land, as the property of a tenant in possession; nor, in any case, in favor of the lessor, for ejecting his tenant. The latter alone can sustain it. In general, *no civil action for damages* can be brought by a wrongful possessor against the true owner, for forcibly regaining his estate, because *his title* would be a good defence. The only remedy is *by indictment for breach of the peace*, or the above-mentioned form of complaint. The infliction of *a personal injury*, however, would be a good ground of action. And, in New York, by the revised statutes, an action of trespass may be brought, and *treble damages* recovered.

No man can make entry upon lands after a certain period from the time when his right, or the right of those under whom he claims, accrued. This period is in most of the States *twenty years*; in Vermont and Connecticut *fifteen*; in Georgia and North Carolina *seven*; with savings, however, in favor of infants, *femes-covert*, persons *non compos*, imprisoned, or beyond sea, — who are allowed a certain time, either *in addition to the twenty years*, or *after their disability ceases*, to enforce their rights.[1] It is to be observed also, that a man's *right* does not *accrue*, nor the above limitation begin to run against him, while he has a mere *remainder* or *reversion*,[2] and not *an immediate estate*; as, for instance, during the life of *a tenant for life* who is disseised.

The right of *entry* is not applicable to those kinds of ouster, — viz. *deforcement* and *discontinuance*, where the first entry was *lawful*; but only to *abatement*, *intrusion*, and *disseisin*; the law not allowing *an apparent right of possession* to be overthrown by the mere summary act of the party. The right of entry is also "tolled" or taken away, by *the death of a disseisor and a descent to his heir*; provided the former had possession a certain time, — in Massachusetts five years, — and unless there were some *disability* in the owner during that time.[3] So an entry is not lawful upon *a third person* who has purchased from the disseisor; nor, in any case, upon the heir of an *abator* or *intruder*. The heir of a *disseisee* deceased has, in all respects, the same right as his ancestor.

Where a disseisor, notwithstanding the entry of

---

[1] See p. 83. [2] See p. 178.

[3] It seems, in New York, a right of entry is not *tolled* by descent.

the owner, still retains the possession against him, or where he resists his entry; — such detention or resistance is an ouster and disseisin, upon which *an action* may be maintained. Hence, when a demandant is entitled *as heir*, and the disseisor has died, not having been in possession five years; the former may either enter and then sue *upon his own seisin*, or, without entry, sue *upon his ancestor's seisin*, in the form hereafter to be mentioned.

2. *Writ of entry.*

Possession of land may be recovered, where *the right of entry* for any cause does not exist, *by an action,* — called *a writ of entry*; wherein the owner or *demandant* disproves the title of the possessor, by showing the unlawful means by which he entered or continues possession. The writ claims *restitution of the land*, which the demandant alleges to be *his right and inheritance*, or *his freehold,* — accordingly as he demands *the fee* or only *a life estate.* This is called "a real action"; and is the form, generally used in New England and some other States, for recovery of lands and tenements.

The form of action and course of judicial proceedings in writs of entry, are materially different from those, hereafter to be noticed,[1] in *personal suits*; and therefore require a brief, separate consideration.

It is common to speak of *the degrees*, within which writs of entry are brought. If brought against *the party himself* who did the wrong, they charge only him with it. This is called a writ of entry "in the quibus," — that word being used in the ancient Latin form of the writ. If there has been a *conveyance* or

---

[1] See ch. 9 *et seq.*

descent since the *ouster*, this circumstance must be alleged. One conveyance or descent makes the *first degree*; which is called the "per," because the form of the writ is, that the tenant "had not entry but *by*" the original wrong-doer; that is, that he came into possession under or by permission of the latter. A second alienation or descent makes another *degree*, called the "per and cui"; because the form in that case is, that the tenant "had not entry, but *by or under* a prior alienee, *to* whom" the first disseisor passed the estate. If there are more than two degrees, the writ of entry is said to be "in the post"; because it does not state any intermediate titles, but only that the tenant "had not entry unless *after*" the *ouster* done by the original dispossessor. And to make *a degree*, there must be a transfer of the seisin from one person to another either by *act of law*, as by descent, or by *act of party*, as by conveyance. No estate gained *by wrong* makes a degree. The party in such case comes in "in the post." So the estate of *tenant by the curtesy*, or of a purchaser *on execution*, is "in the post," and does not make *a degree*. It is otherwise with *dower*, — the wife is in *by* the husband.

In regard to *the description* of the property sued for, it must be so certain, that the tenant may understand what is demanded of him, and the sheriff deliver possession without any information from the demandant. And when the object of suit is to settle *a disputed line*, the utmost precision of description is necessary.

Where one is *actually seised* of lands, even by wrong; he may maintain a writ of entry against any person who dispossesses him without title.

If the demandant *die* pending his action, *the heir* may come in and prosecute it.

In a real action, *the freehold*[1] is demanded. Hence, if the defendant or *tenant* is not seised of the freehold, he may plead *non-tenure* or *a disclaimer*, and defeat the suit. If he does not thus plead, it is a tacit admission that he is tenant of the freehold. This plea cannot, in Massachusetts, be made to an action brought by *a mortgagee*,[2] because such suit lies against any one *in possession*, and does not settle the freehold title. In general, if the defendant is not in actual possession, but some third person under him; the latter must be served with a copy of the writ.[3] The demandant, if circumstances require, may *discontinue* the suit as to *a part* of the lands demanded.

As *an alien* cannot hold lands, *alienage* is a good plea to a real action; — but may be obviated by proving *naturalization* or some other fact which confers citizenship.

The plea of "the general issue" or "nul disseisin" is an acknowledgment of *actual ouster*, and raises merely the question of *title*.

In Massachusetts, where the tenant, or those under whom he claims, have had actual possession *for six years*, the jury, on his application, shall find the value of *the improvements* made upon the land, and also, on application of the demandant, what it would have been worth without them; and the demandant must either surrender the land on payment of the latter sum, or take it, and pay the value of the improvements or *betterments*. There is a similar law in Maine.

---

[1] See p. 152. [2] See p. 174.

[3] In New York, the defendant in *ejectment* is *the actual occupant.*

A demandant, having recovered *judgment*, may enter upon the lands without any *execution*. But the usual practice is, to take out an execution, and have it regularly executed by the sheriff.

To maintain a writ of entry, one must prove *an actual seisin*, either of himself or his ancestor, within a certain period; which varies, in the several States, from *forty years* in Virginia and Kentucky, down to *seven* in Georgia, Tennessee, and North Carolina.

3. *Writ of right.* — *The writ of right* is considered the highest writ in the law. It is *the last resort* of him who has been ousted of real property; and lies only for the recovery of an estate *in fee-simple*. It is generally resorted to, either where the right to maintain a possessory action is *barred by lapse of time*; or where *judgment* has been given in such action *against the demandant*. The time of limitation for this writ is, in Massachusetts, forty years; — hence it lies, after the right to *a writ of entry* is gone; and, contrary to the general rule, a judgment in the latter, though substantially the same question be tried, is no bar to the former, it being regarded as of *a higher degree*. In most of the States, however, the period of limitation for writs of entry and writs of right is now the same.

More technical strictness is required in writs of right than in writs of entry. The tenant may, however, offer any defence whatever, under the general denial of the demandant's title.

4. *Ejectment.* — In New York, *real actions* have been expressly abolished; and there, and in most of the middle, southern, and western States, *titles to real estate* are tried by the action of *Trespass and Ejectment*.

To lay the foundation for this action; according to the English practice, still adhered to in some States, the party claiming title *enters upon the land*, and there *gives a lease* of it to a third person, who, being *ejected* by the other claimant, or some one else for him, brings a suit against *the ejector* in his own name. The lessee, to sustain the action, must prove *a good title in the lessor*; and, in this collateral way, the title is tried. For the purpose of dispensing with the above-mentioned forms, this action has been made substantially *a fictitious process*. The defendant *agrees to admit*, on the trial, that a lease was made to the plaintiff, that he entered under it, and has been ousted by the defendant, — or to admit "lease, entry, and ouster," — and that he will rely only upon his *title*. An actual entry, however, is still supposed; and therefore ejectment does not lie, *if the right of entry* is gone.

In New York, by the late revised statutes, the above fictions are all abolished, and the writ of *ejectment* is made in substance like a writ of entry, setting forth *possession by the plaintiff*, and *an unlawful entry on the part of the defendant*. The action is also extended to all cases where *a writ of right* would lie. No actual entry is necessary. Within five years the defendant may obtain *a new trial*, if justice require it.[1]

5. *Trespass for mesne profits.* — In the above-described actions for the recovery of lands and tenements, only *the property itself* is recovered, or at most merely *nominal damages* in addition. To supply this

---

[1] In the same State a process is provided, by which an occupant of land for three years may call upon any adverse claimant to come forward and assert his title, or be for ever barred.

deficiency, and effect justice between the parties, *a subsequent action* is provided, by which the party, who has regained his estate, is enabled to obtain indemnity for *its detention, and the loss of the profits* while it was held by the disseisor. This is an action of *trespass*, — usually termed "trespass for mesne profits." It alleges, that the defendant turned the plaintiff out of possession, and kept him out and deprived him of the profits, for a certain length of time.

The right to bring this suit is a necessary consequence of a recovery in the action of *ejectment*; and that recovery is conclusive evidence of the plaintiff's claim, from the date of the lease which is set forth in the former action. The same *statute of limitation*, however, applies to this, as to other actions of trespass; nor, unless by statute provision, can it be brought against *the executor or administrator* of the wrong-doer, because it is for *a tort* and not for *a debt*.[1]

Recovery in a *real action* is not *conclusive* of a right to sue for *mesne profits*. It exists, only where the demandant, who has recovered the seisin, had *a right of entry* at the time of bringing his suit. Hence it does not lie after recovery in *a writ of right*, as this admits the tenant's *right of possession*. Nor can *a mortgagee*, who has recovered a judgment to *foreclose* the mortgage, sustain an action for the mesne profits, even from the commencement of the former suit.[2]

The damages, in this action, are not limited to *the rents and profits* actually received by the defendant,

---

[1] See p. 68. [2] See p. 174.

but may be enhanced by any circumstances of aggravation in the ouster, or any injury done to the estate even by accident. On the other hand, this is considered a liberal and equitable action, in which the defendant may claim every equitable allowance, — as for instance taxes and repairs, — especially where he came into possession under *a supposed legal title.* Whether allowance shall be made for *new erections* or *permanent improvements,* seems somewhat doubtful.

CHAPTER VIII.

INJURIES TO REAL ESTATE WITHOUT AMOTION.

1. *Trespass.* — This signifies *an unauthorized entry* by one man upon the land of another. The remedy is an action of *trespass* "*quare clausum fregit,*" *for breaking the plaintiff's close.* Every one's land is constructively, though not actually, *enclosed*; and the legal boundaries are broken by any unlawful intrusion. There is also *a constructive damage,* in all cases, which the writ always alleges, — viz. *treading down and bruising the herbage.*

Property, and possession or an immediate right to possession, of the soil, or the vesture and herbage, — are necessary to sustain this action. One *seised in law,* but *not in fact,* — as an heir after the ancestor's death, and before entry, — cannot bring *trespass.*

A man is answerable also for the intrusion of his *cattle* upon the land of another; who may either take and keep them, as "damage feasant," — doing damage, by the process of *distress*,[1] till satisfaction is made; or may bring an action against the owner.

Where the trespass is in its nature *continuous*, — as by the defendant's cattle remaining on the land, — the injury may be alleged as continued from day to day, or "laid with a continuando"; or else repeated acts may be charged, as done at different times within a certain period.

Under certain circumstances, it is no trespass to enter another man's land or house without permission; for instance, *a public inn*; or for the purpose of *paying or demanding money* which is there payable; or of *executing legal process*, such as a warrant or execution; or of *hunting ravenous beasts*. But, in all such cases, as in the case of personal property heretofore mentioned,[2] *any abuse of the right* will make the party *a trespasser "ab initio"*; — as where one remains in an inn an unreasonable length of time, and against the positive command of the landlord; or where one, having a right of common, cuts down a tree upon the land.

A rightful owner may enter upon *a wrongful occupant*, even by force, without being a trespasser.[3]

2. *Nuisance.* — *A nuisance* is any thing which works hurt, inconvenience, or damage. Nuisances are of two kinds; *public or common*, which affect the community, and are a subject of *public prosecution*, as, for instance, any obstruction to a highway; and *private*, which may be defined as any thing done to

---

[1] See p. 222. [2] See p. 242. [3] See p. 252.

the hurt or annoyance of the lands, tenements, or hereditaments of another.

Familiar instances of *private nuisance*[1] are the following, — building a house so near another, that the roof of the former overhangs the latter, and throws the water upon it; obstructing *ancient lights*, which have existed twenty years or more, even though at the time of erecting the building which obstructs them, they are not open; or practising an offensive trade, so near another's premises, as to make the air unwholesome, or the enjoyment of life and property uncomfortable. And where the owner of a house, divided into two tenements, leases one of them, it is a nuisance to the tenant to obstruct the lights, however short a time they may have existed, and though there is no stipulation against it. But the mere interception of a pleasant prospect, or diminution of light, enough remaining for comfort and practical purposes, — is no nuisance. So the obstruction of lights, which have been discontinued twenty years.

If *a ferry* is erected on a river, so near another *ancient ferry*, as to draw away its custom, it is a nuisance to the owner of the old one; because he is bound to keep his ferry in constant repair, and readiness for public use, and is therefore entitled to a peculiar protection, corresponding with his burden. As a general rule, however, all *competition* in business is allowed and even encouraged by the law.

The remedies for a nuisance are either *an abatement or removal* of it by the injured party himself, doing no wanton or unnecessary injury, after which

---

[1] See p. 43.

no action can be brought; *an action on the case* for damages, in which every continuance of the nuisance will be held a new one, and *exemplary damages* given for persisting in the wrong; or finally, *a specific writ,* now generally exploded, but still in use in New York, by virtue of which, judgment is rendered for *abating* the nuisance *by legal process.* A Court of Chancery sometimes interferes, in case of nuisance, by *injunction.*

The subject of nuisance has been treated, in the several States, as peculiarly proper for statute regulations; and many salutary acts have been passed, which differ in details, but are similar in their general objects and provisions. These statutes apply almost exclusively to such nuisances as affect the public at large.

CHAPTER IX.

JUDICIAL PROCEEDINGS FOR REDRESS OF PRIVATE WRONGS. WRIT, SERVICE, AND ENTRY.

I. *Nature and Form of Writs.* — The first step towards obtaining redress for a private wrong *by action,* is *to sue out a writ.*

Writs are *precepts,* issuing constructively from a Court, but in reality prepared by attorneys and counsellors, without special application to any judicial tribunal. The formal parts of the writ, being substantially the same for every case, are printed; and blanks left to be filled up by such allegations and complaints as the particular injury may require.

Writs issue in the name of *the Commonwealth, the State,* or *the people*; are *tested* or witnessed by a Judge, his name being either printed, or filled up by the attorney; and are signed by *the Clerk* of the Court. They are addressed, in form, *to the sheriff or his deputy,* or, if a sheriff is party to the suit, to *a coroner*; and command him, in general, *to attach the property,* or *take the body,* of the defendant, and summon him to appear, or produce him, at a particular *term* of the Court, then and there to answer to the plaintiff in *a plea,* for a certain *wrong* which is set forth in the declaration accompanying the writ; and to make *return* of the writ at the Court named. Attending the writ is usually *a summons,* which is to be delivered to the defendant. This is unnecessary when the service is by *arrest*; and in some cases *an attested copy* of the writ is used instead of it.

The above is the mode of commencing an action in the New England States and some others. Other forms prevail in many parts of the country. *The declaration* often forms no part of the writ, but is *filed in Court* by itself; and the filing of the declaration is *the commencement of suit.* In New York, a suit may be commenced before Justices of the Peace, by consent, without any writ.

A writ is often called in law *mesne process,* in distinction from *final process* or *execution.*

II. *Service of Writs.*

In New England, the usual *service* of writs is either by *attachment of property,* or *arrest of the body.* It is otherwise in *real actions,* and the action of *replevin*;

where the property itself is the specific object of suit, and no *security* is necessary.

Out of New England, *attachment of property* is for the most part unknown, — except in cases of *absconding*, *non-residence*, or *imprisonment*, of the debtor; and upon *affidavit* of the creditor.

In Massachusetts, New York, Kentucky, and Tennessee, *imprisonment for debt* has been substantially abolished; in Maine and New Hampshire, much restricted; but in Connecticut, New Jersey, Maryland, and Pennsylvania, the old laws, by which a writ alone, without other formality, authorizes an arrest, remain unaltered. In Massachusetts, by a late act, no person can arrest another, without first making affidavit that he apprehends his escape or avoidance, and has a just demand against him. A similar rule prevails in other States. Special exemption is provided for females.

In New York, actions are brought, either by a "capias" or arrest, which lies, in certain cases, both for debts and for *torts*; by *a summons*, against corporations; or by *filing a declaration* in Court, and serving a notice upon the defendant.

In general, the same writ cannot be served by both an attachment and an arrest. But, in Connecticut, after service of a writ in one way, and before the *return*, it may be served in the other. In Rhode Island, property is attached, only where the defendant cannot be found for arrest.

A writ cannot be served, either by attachment or arrest, by *breaking into the defendant's dwelling-house*. A man's house is "his castle," and the law will not suffer it to be invaded. But *an inner door* may be broken, after an entry through the outer one.

Any *alteration* of a writ after service renders it void.

III. *Attachment.*

1. *What constitutes, and the mode of proceeding in an attachment.* — For the purpose of making *an attachment*, the officer, on receiving the writ, may seize the property of the defendant and keep it in his own custody. The universal practice is, however, to allow the defendant to keep possession of the property, on giving *receiptors*, so called, for its forthcoming to meet *the execution*. To constitute an attachment, the officer must have the property *under his control*; and, if he leave it, it may be attached in some other suit, and the officer will be liable for the loss to the first attaching creditor. So delivering it up to a receiptor is, it seems, *an abandonment*, which authorizes a new attachment, and the officer must look to the receiptor for his indemnity. But the officer may appoint *a keeper*, whose possession will be equivalent to his own.

In New York, the officer does not seize the goods, but may take the defendant's *books and papers*.

An attachment being merely *for security*, and prior to any debt proved or judgment recovered against the defendant; of course the property cannot be *absolutely disposed of*, as it may *on execution*. In several of the States, however, to save the expense of *keeping* from the commencement of suit till final judgment, the property may be sold *by consent of parties*, and *the proceeds* remain in the officer's hands, as the goods themselves would, to satisfy the execution. And, if the goods be in their nature *perishable*, or require *extraordinary expense* in keeping, — as, for instance, live stock, provisions, &c. — they may be sold, after certain formalities, *on the application of either party.*

In New York, if goods attached are claimed by another person than the debtor, the officer *summons a jury to try the title.* In the same State, *vessels* are placed on a different footing, in respect to attachment, from other property.

2. *What may be attached.* — Both *real and personal estate* may be attached. And, in attaching the former, the officer is not bound, nor even permitted, in general, *to take possession,* as in case of goods; but the attachment consists merely in his noting the time of *receiving the writ,* and in *making a return* accordingly; and this incumbrance will have precedence of all subsequent conveyances. This is called *private attachment.* In Rhode Island and New York, *public notice* must be given. In the latter State, neither real nor personal property is *taken and kept*; but *trustees* are appointed, and an equal distribution, it seems, is afterwards made among all the creditors.

For the benefit of *poor debtors,* some articles are *exempted* from attachment; — not exceeding in value a certain and small sum, and being in their nature *indispensable for a family*; such as *furniture, fuel, clothing,* &c., and, in some States, *pews.* Similar exemptions are provided, in New York and elsewhere, from the process of *distress* and that of *execution.* Upon the same principle, *tools of trade* are exempted. In New York, the value of the latter is limited to twenty-five dollars, — in Rhode Island, thirty. The exemption applies to the tools used not only by the party himself, but by *journeymen,* if it is usual to employ them in the business. The term "tools," however, means implements used *by the hand of one man,* and not complicated and expensive *machinery*, such as printing types and forms.

In general, *private papers* and *account books* cannot be attached. Otherwise in New York.

Since an attachment requires *actual possession* by the officer, such articles cannot be attached, as would be destroyed or greatly injured by *removal*, — as, for instance, green hides in a vat.

In most of the States, special provision is made by statute, for the attachment of property in its nature *intangible* or *documentary*, and of merely *equitable interests*. Of the former description are *shares in incorporated associations*, and of the latter, *equities of redemption*.

3. *Effect of an attachment.*

By an attachment, the officer acquires a *lien* upon, and a *right to possession* of, personal estate; and may maintain an action against any one who wrongfully interferes with it. *The attaching creditor* gains no title whatever; nor does *the debtor* lose his right; — but, till after *judgment* and *execution* in the action, the general property is *in abeyance*, or uncertainty and suspension, and the special property of *a bailee*[1] in the officer. If the suit terminate *for the plaintiff*, the goods are held by the attachment for a certain period after judgment, — usually thirty days, — and sold *upon execution*, and the proceeds paid over to the creditor. On the other hand, *if the defendant prevail* in the suit, the goods shall be restored to him, or accounted for by the officer.

Real estate, after attachment, may be *conveyed* by the debtor, subject to the lien or incumbrance; and the purchaser will have a right to clear it off by paying the debt.

---

[1] See p. 97.

The same goods may be attached *in different suits* by the same officer;[1] and the creditors shall be satisfied in the order of their attachments. In New York, however, after an attachment by one creditor, others may become equal sharers by application to Chancery; and trustees will be appointed to take charge of the effects, as in cases of insolvency.

Goods held *by a United States collector*, as security for *duties*, are not subject to attachment by a creditor of the importer, though he offer to give such security.

To guard against *fraud and collusion*, statutes have been passed in some of the States, by which *a subsequent attaching creditor* is allowed to come into court, and contest the claim or debt of *a prior attaching creditor*, — the debtor himself making no defence. The application, in such case, sets forth a suspicion of *connivance* between the first attacher and the defendant, *to secrete the property* from other creditors. To sustain it, however, *actual* fraud is not necessary, but only *legal* or *constructive* fraud; as, for instance, when the first suit is brought upon a debt not yet due. Although this defence presupposes fraud in the defendant, yet his *admission of the debt* is received in evidence, subject however to be weighed by the jury.

IV. *Foreign Attachment.*

There are certain kinds of personal property, or certain situations in which it may be placed, to which the common process of attachment does not apply. For the purpose of reaching these cases, a distinct process is provided, called *the trustee process*, or *foreign attachment*. This exists in nearly all the

[1] In Connecticut, they may be attached by different officers.

States, and in some is the only kind of attachment that is known.

1. *Nature and form of the trustee process.*

To a trustee process there are *three parties* instead of two; — viz. *the plaintiff*; the defendant or *principal defendant*, as he is usually called; and *the trustee* or *garnishee*. The latter is *summoned* in the suit, as having in his hands "goods, effects, or credits" belonging to the defendant; meaning thereby, that he either *has possession of certain personal property* of the defendant, or else *is indebted to him*, which property or debt is designed to be secured in his hands, for the benefit of the attaching creditor. After service of a trustee process upon him, the trustee cannot safely pay the debt or deliver up the goods to the principal defendant, being accountable therefor to the creditor.

Upon a writ of foreign attachment, the defendant's property *in his own hands* may be attached as in other cases; but he cannot be *arrested*.

The question, whether the trustee shall be held accountable or not, — or, in legal language, whether he shall be *charged* or *discharged*, — is in general tried *by the Court, upon his answers under oath*; though, in some of the States, the parties may have *a jury*, if they desire it.

Foreign attachment is a very appropriate remedy in cases of supposed *secrecy and fraud*; and is constantly resorted to, to test the fairness of *assignments for the benefit of creditors*.[1] A trustee process takes precedence of the claim of any creditor, who signs the assignment after service of the writ. But the law so far favors assignments, that, if the trustee holds *per-*

---

[1] See p. 91.

sonal effects, which are trusteeable, and *lands or choses in action,* which are not; he will not be bound to pay other debts with the latter, so as to leave the former to be secured by the attachment.

2. *What may be attached by the trustee process.*

There are certain cases, where goods and credits are not subject to the trustee process.

(1.) A *contingent* or *conditional* debt cannot be thus attached. For instance, the wages of a sailor, or the rent of a tenant, cannot be attached, before the voyage is ended or the rent-day arrives; because the one is contingent upon the completion of the voyage, and the other upon the undisturbed occupancy of the premises during the whole term.

This exception does not apply, however, to a debt *absolutely due,* though not *immediately payable,* — "debitum in præsenti, solvendum in futuro." For instance, a bond or note not negotiable, payable in one year, may be secured by a trustee process, as soon as it has been executed.

Nor does the exception apply to a case, where the contingency relates *not to the debt or property itself,* but *to the person who may legally claim it.* For instance, one who has goods in his hands, the title to which is in controversy between the defendant and a third person, may be trusteed; and will be charged or discharged, as the title shall appear to be in one or the other of the claimants.

(2.) *Negotiable instruments* are in general excepted; because, if they were not, the maker, acceptor, or endorser of a bill or note might become *chargeable twice* for the same debt, — once to *the attaching creditor,* and again to *an indorsee.* A bill or note, *indorsed before it falls due,* is always good and available for the face of it, in the indorsee's hands. No objection can be made *for want of consideration*, and no *off-sets*, discounts, or counter-claims allowed, — as may be done, when a suit is brought by *the original holder*.[1] Consequently, it would be a great hardship to charge a party to such an instrument in the trustee process. These remarks are of course applicable to *bonds*, in those States where they are made negotiable by statute.[2]

The same reason does not apply to other debts. These may be *assigned*; but, as they are not negotiable, an assignee takes them at his own risk, and the debtor may make any defence which he could have made against the original creditor.[3] Hence, it would be a good answer to a suit by such assignee, that the debtor had been charged as the original creditor's trustee. And he is entitled to all *off-sets*, of which he could in any form have availed himself in a suit by his creditor, and shall be charged only for the balance.

To protect the rights of an equitable assignee, provision is almost universally made for bringing him into court as a party to the suit, when the trustee's answer discloses a probable assignment.

(3.) The general rule is, that such *effects* only can be attached in the trustee process, as might *be taken on execution*. Therefore *notes*, *account-books*, or *private papers* of the defendant, in another's hands, cannot be thus taken.

---

[1] See p. 109.

[2] In Connecticut and New Hampshire, negotiable instruments are not exempted from the trustee process, while they remain in the hands of the original holder.

[3] See p. 45.

(4.) One cannot be *trustee* for goods, of which he has merely *constructive possession*; — as, for instance, a ship at sea; because he could not *expose* it to be taken *in execution*, according to the requisition of that process.

(5.) In general, persons holding money or goods of another by virtue of *legal or official authority*, cannot be trustees. For instance, *an executor* is not trustee of *a legatee* or *heir*; nor *a sheriff*, of *a judgment creditor*, for the proceeds of his execution.[1] The reasons are, that property so situated is not "entrusted and deposited" *by the debtor*, according to the words of the statute; and also that, in such cases, the duties are imposed *by law*, and it will not authorize any impediment to their regular execution.

3. *Judgment and execution in the trustee process.*

The object of a trustee process, in reference to the supposed trustee, is to *substitute* the attaching creditor for the principal defendant, and not *to create any new debt or liability*. Hence, *a judgment* in this process is a complete *defence* to any action by the principal defendant against his former debtor. Upon the same principle, if the principal defendant has already *commenced a suit*, and the case is so situated that no new defence can be made; — the debtor cannot be trusteed, because he might thus be compelled twice to pay the same debt. The mere *commencement* of an action, however, has not always this effect. In Massachusetts, *the pleadings must have been closed.*

A judgment *for the trustee* is, of course, no defence against a subsequent suit by the principal defendant;

---

[1] Otherwise in New Hampshire.

because a man might thus defeat an honest debt by his own oath.

The execution, in a trustee process, runs against "the goods, effects, and credits" of the defendant *in the trustee's hands.* If he does not *expose* them to the officer, or satisfy the execution, a new writ, of "scire facias," issues against him alone, and the execution upon this writ runs, as in other cases, against *his property and person.*

V. *Arrest and Bail.* A defendant is in law *arrested,* after either a manual seizure by, or a voluntary surrender to, the officer; so that a subsequent *escape* will subject the latter to an action by the creditor for all the damages thereby sustained.

Upon grounds of public policy, the law gives *a privilege* from arrest to persons in attendance upon *courts of justice* or *legislative assemblies,* and in a few other cases.

After *arrest,* the defendant has the privilege of *giving bail*; that is, of obtaining a release by executing a bond with sureties, called *bail,* for his appearance to abide the event of the suit brought against him. The defendant himself must sign the bond, and, in relation thereto, is called *the principal.*

In New York and some other States, bail is of two kinds, *bail below,* and *bail above.* The former, taken at the time of arrest, become responsible merely for the defendant's *appearance at court. Bail above* are taken *in court* after the return of the writ, and are answerable for the defendant's *abiding the judgment* which may be rendered against him; that is, for his remaining within the county where he was arrested, so that he may be taken in execution unless he satisfies the debt. In New England, the only bail is that taken at the time of arrest; the obligation of which is the same as that of the bail above in New York.

The officer is responsible for *the sufficiency* of the bail at the time, but not for their future solvency. But, if he require *excessive and unreasonable* bail, and, for want of it, the defendant is imprisoned, he shall be released by *habeas corpus*.

No *action* can be brought against bail, till an execution has been issued against the principal, and a return of *diligent search* and "non est inventus," — *not to be found*, made upon it by the sheriff. The form of action is usually *scire facias*,[1] but sometimes *debt*, and it is brought in the name of the judgment creditor. Actions against bail are limited, in Massachusetts, to *one year* from judgment against the principal. A similar limitation prevails in other States.

Bail are *discharged* from their liability by any event which renders it absolutely *impossible* to surrender the defendant; for instance, by his death, if it occur before the *return-day* of the execution. But *a covenant* by the creditor, after taking bail, not to arrest the principal for a certain time, is no discharge of the bail; because it is a mere *collateral promise*, for breach of which damages may be recovered, and not an *actual release*. Bail are in general allowed to *surrender*, at any time before final judgment against them; and this may be done either to *the officer* or *gaoler*, or *in open court*.

Bail are understood in law to have the principal *in their custody*, and may therefore take him at any time

---

[1] *Scire facias* is *a writ of summons*, as the name imports, served *by copy*, and authorizes neither an attachment nor arrest. It is usually brought upon *judgments and records*.

without legal process. The circumstances which protect from *an arrest* are no protection against such a seizure. It may be made *on Sunday*, in a man's *own house*, or *in another State*.

There is no specified *time*, within which a creditor must take out execution against the principal, in order to charge bail. After receiving the execution, the officer is bound to use *due diligence* in finding him, and, if he return "non est inventus" without having used due diligence, although this return will justify a suit against the bail, they shall have their remedy against the officer for *a false return*. If such a return be made *by the creditor's instigation*, the fraud will be a good defence to the *scire facias*.

VI. *Return of Writs*. After *service* of the writ, it is the officer's duty to *return* it to court, with a brief indorsement of his proceedings. This is called the officer's *return*. In case of attachments, the return gives *a schedule* of the property, if it be *personal*; and, if *real*, merely states an attachment of *all the defendant's real estate* within the officer's precinct; or that he was *arrested and held to bail*, when such was the fact.

An attachment of all the defendant's interest "in a certain piece of land upon such a street," is valid, if he own but one piece; but if more than one, it is bad *for uncertainty*, and no verbal evidence will be admitted to explain it.

Upon obvious grounds of convenience and policy, the return of an officer *cannot be contradicted*, but must be taken for true. If untrue, any person thereby injured has a right of action against him for *a false return*; but, as affecting the rights of the parties to the suit, the return is conclusive. For instance, where two writs are given to an officer at different times, and he returns a first attachment upon the one which he received last; the injured creditor cannot claim to be first paid from the proceeds of an execution sale, but must resort for satisfaction to the officer himself.

By making a false return, an officer may often subject himself to the most severe responsibility. For instance, if, in advertising an equity of redemption to be sold on execution, he omit to mention *the place of sale*, but return that he did mention it, so that the sale is valid; a subsequent attaching creditor may recover from him the full value of the equity, although, if the officer had proceeded according to law, the whole would have been taken up by the first execution. The consequence is, of course, that the property pays debts to twice its value, at the expense of the officer.

A return may at any time be *amended*, according to the truth of the facts, by leave of court.

VII. *Entry and Appearance.* — The writ being returned to Court either at or before the time appointed, the action is *entered* by the attorney, by application to *the Clerk*, who makes a memorandum of the names of the parties upon a record kept for that purpose, commonly called *the docket.*

If the defendant does not *appear* by himself or his attorney to defend against the suit, he is *defaulted*, and judgment rendered against him *by default.* In some of the States, it is the practice, after default, to settle the amount of *damages*, by *a writ of enquiry*, so called. In most cases, however, this is unnecessary, a certain and specific debt being set forth in the writ and declaration, and judgment rendered accordingly.

On the other hand, if in any stage of the cause the plaintiff abandons or neglects to prosecute his suit, he is said to be *nonsuited*, and has judgment against him. This does not preclude another action for the same cause. A positive act of withdrawal, or *retraxit*, is a bar to any future suit.

For the purpose of defence, the defendant *appears* by his attorney, who enters his name on the docket, and thereby prevents a default.

After an appearance, the action is usually *continued* or postponed to a succeeding term of the Court. There are certain *pleas*, however, in their nature *formal and technical*,[1] and therefore not favored by the law, — which must be made at the first or *return term*, if at all. It is usual to apply at the first term, for leave to *amend* any defect in the writ, or to *plead double*, — that is, to make more than one distinct plea or answer to the action.

In order that there may be *a trial* between the plaintiff and defendant, the allegations of the former by his writ and declaration must be *answered* in some way by the latter, and a precise question or *issue* thereby raised. This leads us to consider briefly the important subject of *pleading*.

---

1 See *Pleading*.

CHAPTER X.

PLEADING AND ISSUE.

Pleading is the statement, in a logical and legal form, of the facts which constitute the plaintiff's cause of action or the defendant's ground of defence. In other words, it is the formal mode of alleging *on the record*, that which will be the support or the defence of the party *in evidence*.

The term *plea*, however, is usually applied only to the allegations of *the defendant*, in answer to those of the plaintiff. The statement of the ground of action, contained in the writ, is called the *declaration*. The plaintiff's answer to the plea, is *the replication*. Then follow the *rejoinder*, *sur-rejoinder*, *rebutter* and *sur-rebutter*, on one side and the other, if circumstances so require. Pleadings are rarely carried, however, beyond *the rejoinder*.

The general principles of pleading apply alike to all the degrees or stages above enumerated, including the declaration. Usually, however, less strictness is required in the latter, than in other parts of the pleadings. Much latitude is allowed to the plaintiff in his original statement, which, for the sake of precision and unity, must be narrowed down, before *an issue and judgment* can be had.

It is one of the first principles of pleading, to state only *facts*, for the purpose of informing the Court, whose duty it is *to declare the law* which arises upon them, and of apprizing the opposite party what is meant to be proved, that he may have opportunity to answer it.

No more should be stated than is *essential to the complaint or defence.* All the allegations, however, which are commonly inserted, are not equally essential. These are of three kinds. 1. The *gist,* or substance, which is all that it is absolutely necessary to prove, — for instance, in an action of trespass "qu. claus.," that the defendant *entered* upon the plaintiff's land. — 2. The *inducement,* which is merely formal or explanatory; as, for instance, in *trover,* that the defendant *found* the goods. — 3. *Aggravation,* which is something not necessary to sustain the action, but serves to *increase the damages*; as, for instance, in case of *a battery,* that the defendant was in consequence of it for a long time sick and disabled.

The allegations last mentioned, as they need not be *proved* by the plaintiff, cannot be denied or *traversed* by the defendant. And the want of them can generally be taken advantage of, if at all, only by *a special demurrer,* hereafter to be noticed.

There are some facts, which *need not be stated,* though their existence is necessary to sustain the action or defence. Of this description, are all *public facts,* of which the Court will "ex officio" take notice, without any suggestion, — as, for instance, the time and place of *holding Courts* or *legislative assemblies*; all *public domestic statutes*; *the almanac*; *weights and measures,* &c. If the action is founded *upon a statute,* and the same section which gives a right of action also contains *an exception,* the plaintiff must aver that the case does not fall within the exception; — but, if the exception is in another section of the act, it is for the defendant to take advantage of it.

A fact, which *the law presumes*, need not be stated, —as, that one is innocent of a fraud or crime; or that the defendant promised within six years, or was of full age when he promised. Fraud, crime, limitation, and infancy are matters not to be negatived by the party who denies them, but to be alleged and proved by him who would rely upon them.

Upon the same principle, facts need not be stated which are more peculiarly *within the knowledge of the other party*. For instance, where the plaintiff has occasion to show, that the defendant is *assignee of a lease*, and therefore bound by the covenants contained in it; he need not set forth all the intermediate conveyances through which the defendant's title is deduced.

A defect or omission in the declaration is sometimes *cured* or supplied by the defendant's plea,—which admits the fact omitted. For instance, in an action for *flowage of land*, if the declaration omit to aver that the flowage was caused by *a mill dam*; the defect will be cured by a statement in the plea of this fact.

There are many facts, which, though they need not be stated, yet, if stated, *must be proved*. Hence, all *superfluous allegations* are to be avoided. Thus, where the plaintiff is bound to state merely in general terms, that he has a *title* to certain land; if he undertake minutely to set out the particulars of his title, he must prove them as alleged, or will fail in the action.

But, where the matter unnecessarily stated is wholly *foreign and irrelevant* to the cause, it need not be proved. Thus, if the declaration should allege that a trespass was done *in the night-time*, this is termed surplusage, and may be entirely disregarded. So also, that the defendant committed the wrong *with a malicious intent.*

A declaration may contain *several counts*, that is, distinct and entire allegations or charges, either for *one* or *different* causes of action. Where there is but one claim or demand, the plaintiff may be in doubt as to some circumstance connected with it; as, for instance, *a date* or *the particular terms* of a contract. In such case, to avoid a *variance* between the declaration and the evidence, which would defeat the action, the plaintiff may make several counts, substantially alike, but varying in details; and, if the evidence agree with either of the counts, he will recover.

It will be no *variance* to omit the statement of such part of the *contract*, as is not the subject of suit. For instance, a note sued by the payee, though payable *to order*, need not be so stated. But *the entire consideration* must be alleged; and, in all actions upon simple contract, an omission to state a consideration will be fatal.[1]

Distinct causes of action may be joined in one suit by means of *several counts*. But the demands must be *of a similar nature*, — admitting *the same plea* and *the same judgment*. For instance, a note, an account, and a special simple contract may be joined; because "non assumpsit" might be pleaded to them all. But a note cannot be joined with a bond. Nor, in any case, *a debt* with *a tort*, the general issue to which is

---

[1] See p. 75.

"not guilty." *Misjoinder* of counts is ground for *demurrer*,[1] and will defeat the action; though sometimes the plaintiff may *amend* by *striking out* one of them.

In *personal actions*, the declaration must allege every *traversable fact* to have happened *on some particular day*. That day, however, need not be proved to be the true one, except when stated as *the date of an instrument*; in which case, the slightest deviation from the facts would be *a variance* and defeat the action. For instance, if the plaintiff alleges that the defendant "*on the first day of the month* promised to pay him fifty dollars," he need not prove it on that day; but, if he sets forth a note *dated* the first, and it proves to be dated the second day, the action will fail: because a judgment for the plaintiff would not prevent a new suit upon the true note, and the defendant might thus be held to pay the same debt twice.

A certain place, as well as time, is alleged in the declaration. This is termed *the venue*, and must be *within the county* where the suit is brought. Most actions need not be commenced in the county where *the cause of action arose*, but will lie wherever the parties, or one of them, may happen to be. These are called *transitory actions*. *Local actions* are such as must be brought in the county where the debt was incurred or the injury done. *Replevin* and all actions relating to *real estate* are of this description. Mistakes of *venue* are subject to *amendment*; but a local action, commenced in the wrong county, will be *abated* for that cause, and, in Massachusetts, *double costs* allowed to the defendant.

---

[1] See *Demurrer*.

In all actions upon *sealed instruments*, the plaintiff makes *profert*, so called, of the deed, by the words "here in court to be produced." The defendant may then in his plea claim *oyer* of it, that is, a hearing; may set it forth verbatim; and take the same advantage of any defect, as if the plaintiff had himself recited it at length.

In actions for *debts*, the declaration concludes by alleging *a breach* of the contract, as follows: "yet though often requested, the defendant has not paid said sum, but neglects and refuses so to do." This is termed "licet sæpius requisitus," and is, in general, mere form.

The defendant may *answer* the declaration, either *by a demurrer* or *a plea*.

A demurrer admits the facts alleged by the plaintiff, but denies that they constitute *a cause of action*, and submits this question, being a question *of law*, to the judgment of *the court*.

Demurrer is either *special* or *general*. *A special demurrer* excepts to some *formal defect* in the declaration, which must be particularly pointed out. In New York, if judgment be rendered for the plaintiff on special demurrer, it is *final* and decides the cause; but, in general, the defendant may make a further answer to the action.

A general demurrer excepts to *the substance* of the plaintiff's claim. For instance, in an action of *slander*, if the declaration sets forth words which are not in law slanderous, the defendant may demur generally, and will have final judgment in his favor.

A demurrer may be made to any subsequent part

of the pleadings, as well as the declaration. And judgment will always be against that party who commits the first error in pleading. Thus, if the plaintiff demur to the plea, and the plea is bad; yet, if the declaration is also bad, judgment will be for the defendant.

The usual answer to the declaration is *a plea.* Pleas are of two kinds. *A dilatory plea* or *plea in abatement* is in its nature *formal,* and either denies *the jurisdiction* of the court, or excepts to *some defect in the writ.* Pleas in abatement, like special demurrers, are regarded unfavorably by the law, as captious and technical. They must, in general, be offered at an early stage of the cause, and sometimes verified by *affidavit*; and the utmost nicety is required in the form of them. If the plaintiff denies or *takes issue* upon a plea in abatement, and prevails, he has *final judgment*; but generally, after failing in this, the defendant may plead anew *to the merits.*

A plea to the merits, is either *the general issue,* which is a direct *denial* of what is alleged in the declaration; or *a special plea,* which *admits* the declaration, but sets forth some new fact *to avoid the effect of it.* For instance, in the action of *assumpsit, the general issue* is *non-assumpsit,* — never promised; but *the statute of limitations* would be *a special plea,* inasmuch as it admits the promise, but relies for defence upon its having been made more than six years ago.

It is to be observed, however, that the practice is, especially in modern times, to dispense with special pleas in many cases, and allow matters of defence to be *proved* under the general issue. For instance, under the plea of non-assumpsit, the defendant may prove that, although he did make the promise, yet the plaintiff has since *discharged* him from it; or that he was *under age* when he made it. In actions before *Justices of the Peace*, special pleading is very rarely used; and it is not generally required of defendants, who justify their acts under some *official authority*.

There are some pleas, which admit *the whole claim* of the plaintiff, and merely question his right *to bring a suit* upon it. Such is the plea of *tender*, which alleges that the defendant *offered to pay* the debt when it became due, has been ever since and is still ready to pay it. In this case, the money is *brought into court*, to be taken by the plaintiff at his pleasure. The effect of the plea, if sustained, is merely to throw *the costs* upon the plaintiff. By a law of the United States, certain coins are designated as making *a legal tender*; but it is generally held, that any *current money* will be sufficient, unless specially objected to by the creditor. After a tender, the defendant must have been *always in readiness* to pay — "tout temps prist"; and a subsequent *demand and refusal* will, therefore, avoid the effect of the plea.

Where there has been no tender, the defendant may *pay into court* the amount justly due. And, if the plaintiff proceed with the suit to recover more, and fail, the defendant shall have *costs* from the time of payment.

The defendant may *admit* the plaintiff's demand, and yet defend against it by an *off-set* or *set-off*; that is, by some counter-claim in his own favor. The right applies, in general, only to *specific debts*, and not to *indefinite damages for tort*. In New York, no demand can be *off-set*, of which the defendant took *an assignment* since the commencement of suit. And, in Massachusetts, *an indorsed note* can never be off-set. If the defendant in one suit is plaintiff in another, the *judgments* may be set-off; excepting, however, *the costs* in both, which belong rather to *the attorneys* than the parties. Provision is also made, in general, for off-setting *executions* in the hands of the officer or sheriff.

Special pleas are divided into those of *justification*,—as where *an officer* is sued for seizing and confining a person, and *justifies* by virtue of *a writ* against him; of *excuse*,—as where one is sued for going upon the plaintiff's land, and sets up *a license* from a third person, who is the true owner, in defence; or of *limitation*, which has been already explained.[1]

The replication either *denies* the plea; or alleges *new matter contradictory to it*,—as where the plea to a suit upon *an arbitration-bond* is, that *no award* was made, and the replication avers *an award*, and states what it is; or *new matter consistent with the plea*,—as where *the statute of limitations* is pleaded, and the plaintiff *replies* that the demand is *an account between merchants*;[2] or *an estoppel*,—as where, to an action *for rent*, the defendant pleads that the plaintiff *had no title* to the land, and the plaintiff *replies*, that the defendant *signed a lease*, and is thereby precluded or *estopped* from such defence;[3] or *makes a new assignment*,—as where the plaintiff sues for *a trespass* upon "his farm" generally, the defendant pleads that he entered upon *a particular spot* of the farm *which he owned*, and the plaintiff then *replies*, that the entry was *upon another spot* which he did not own.

---

[1] See p. 82. [2] Ib. [3] See p. 210.

In every stage of the pleadings, when either party alleges *new matter*, he concludes as follows,—"and this he is ready to verify." On the other hand, when either party *traverses* or denies what has been alleged on the other side, he *tenders an issue*,—that is, submits himself to trial, by the words "and of this he puts himself on the country." Upon reaching this point, the case is ready for *trial*; and the only matter to be tried, is that which is finally asserted on one side, and denied on the other.

Questions of fact are tried *by jury*. *A jury* consists of twelve men, *returned* or sent to the Court from different parts of the county where it is held, to try such questions as may come before them. The mode of selecting jurors is a subject of statute regulation in the several states, and need not be particularly described. In New York, a list is made out by *the clerk of the county*, and, in Massachusetts, they are chosen by *the selectmen* of each town. Two juries, or twenty-four persons, are returned, together with a number of supernumeraries, to guard against the sickness or other disability of the rest.

A jury, when seated in order for the commencement of a trial, is said to be *impanelled*, and is sometimes called "*the panel.*"

Either party may *challenge*, that is, object to, the whole jury, if improperly and illegally returned; or, which is more common, some particular juryman, as under the influence of partiality or interest, or in some other way disqualified to serve.

If, for any cause, the panel cannot be filled from the regular jurors, the vacancy may be supplied from persons casually present, who are then called "tales-men."

The jury are *sworn* to try all causes "according to the law and the evidence."

The cause is *opened* to the jury, after reading the declaration and pleadings, by the plaintiff's *counsel*, who states briefly the nature of the action, and the evidence which will be offered to sustain it. After this evidence has been heard, the defendant's counsel pursues the same course; and the cause is then *argued* to the jury on the one side and the other, upon the testimony which has been given.

The important subject of *evidence* will be considered in the next chapter.

CHAPTER XI.

EVIDENCE. NATURE AND GENERAL PRINCIPLES OF EVIDENCE.

All facts and circumstances, from which any reasonable inference can be drawn, as to the truth or falsity of the *issue* or disputed fact, are admissible in evidence. They must be proved, however, by legal and competent means, the nature of which will be hereafter considered.[1]

Evidence is either *direct and positive*, where witnesses swear to the very fact in issue; or *circumstan-*

---

[1] Ch. 12.

tial and presumptive, where other facts are proved, from which this may be inferred, as usually or necessarily connected with them.

Presumptions are either *of law* or *of fact.* The former are inferences, *uniformly and necessarily drawn, by the Court*, from facts proved. Thus, if an indorsee have put into the post-office a letter, containing notice to the indorser[1]; it is *a presumption of law*, not open to dispute, that the latter received it. In other words, such a proceeding is constructive and legal, though not always actual, notice.

Presumptions of fact are inferences *usually* but *not necessarily* drawn, from facts proved, *by the jury*; and are open to explanation and contradiction by other evidence. Thus, in the action of *trover*,[2] *demand and refusal* are strong evidence of *conversion*, but not so conclusive, that the Court can draw from them *a presumption of law.* They must be left to the jury.

Although *presumptions* are the chief foundation of judicial proceedings, yet there are certain facts or statements, which, while they have some tendency to prove the point in issue, for peculiar reasons are not admitted in evidence. This exclusion is founded upon one of two considerations: first, that the proof proposed is *indirect and uncertain*; or, second, that its admission is *improper and impolitic.*

I. 1. Upon the former ground, *hearsay evidence* is in general inadmissible.

Hearsay evidence consists of *declarations*, either verbal or written, *made out of Court.* These are not regarded as *facts*, but as mere *statements*, liable to

---

[1] See p. 111. [2] See p. 243.

vagueness and uncertainty, and, above all, wanting the solemn sanction of *an oath*, and the important test of *cross-examination*. For these reasons, a witness will not be allowed to testify *what another person said*; nor will any *written paper* or document be received as evidence of the facts which it contains.

There are many exceptions however to this rule. (1.) *Public documents* of any kind, — such as proclamations, statutes, and records, — though strictly *written declarations*, are respected, as being constituted by proper authority for the perpetuation of important facts, and therefore received in evidence.

(2.) Whenever the declaration is in itself *a fact*, and a part of the "res gestæ," it is admissible in evidence. In other words, a declaration is admissible, the truth of which does not turn upon *the veracity* of the person making it, but may be judged of from *its connexion with the other facts of the case.* Thus, where one person claims certain goods against the attaching creditors of another, who has absconded; the declaration of the latter, accompanying the act of showing the goods to the plaintiff, *that they were the plaintiff's*, is admissible. The declarations even of *a party himself*, and in his own favor, if *accompanying acts*, have sometimes been received. As where a person, on receiving an injury, immediately complains of it, and charges the defendant with its commission. So, where a horse was sold to the plaintiff, and afterwards attached by creditors of the vendor, upon the ground of a fraudulent transfer;[1] evidence was received, to repel this imputation, that the plaintiff informed the keeper of the

[1] See p. 90.

horse that he owned him and would pay for the keeping.

(3.) There are certain peculiar cases, where hearsay evidence is received, under the form of *reputation and tradition.*

In questions of *character*, this evidence is of course admitted;—because character itself is nothing but *reputation.* In all *criminal trials,* the defendant may offer evidence of his good character, which however will weigh but lightly against positive testimony; but, in *civil actions*, such evidence is inadmissible, until the character is impeached. *A witness* may be *discredited* by evidence of bad character *for truth and veracity*; and to this particular the enquiry must be strictly confined. After such an attempt, evidence is admissible, to support the witness' character, of his *general good conduct.*

Common reputation is also admissible to prove *a pedigree*; that is, *the state of a family,* in regard to *the relationship* of its different members, their births, marriages, and deaths, — more especially those which are so ancient as to preclude direct testimony of their occurrence. Upon this principle, the habitual association of a man and woman, and their practice of addressing each other as husband and wife; a pedigree hung up in the mansion, or entered in the family bible; a monument with its inscriptions; a parish register; and the declarations of persons connected with the family, since deceased, — are received in evidence.

Reputation and tradition are also evidence of *prescriptions* and *customs.*[1] But only on the following

---

[1] See p. 197.

conditions. First, the right or privilege claimed must be shown, by the common proofs, to have been exercised *at a recent date*; and then, for the time *beyond living memory*, old persons may be called to testify, what they have heard others, since dead, say on the subject.

Secondly, the right must be *a public*, not *a private one*. Thus, it must relate to parishes, commons, highways, or public boundaries, which concern a large number of people; and not to individual persons or estates, because the latter are not likely to be a subject of general knowledge and remark. And, upon the same principle, a particular *fact* cannot be proved in this way, — as, for instance, that a piece of land belonged to a particular estate. Authentic *histories* however are usually admitted to prove facts; and *ancient deeds* and other documents, found in their proper repositories, are received as evidence of title, after *a recent possession* of the premises has been proved, consistent with, and naturally explained by them.

Thirdly, this evidence, being in its nature fallacious and exceptionable, is not admissible, where the declarations were made "post litem motam," — that is, after the subject became matter of *legal controversy*, and was therefore liable to excite *prejudice and partiality* in those acquainted with it.

(4.) The objection to *hearsay* of course does not apply to *a party's own admission against himself*. This is received as strong evidence, but not in all cases conclusive. For instance, after admitting *his signature to a note*, one may still offer evidence that it is *a forgery*. And an admission must always be taken in connexion with any accompanying declaration *favorable* to the party, which however may be disproved by other testimony, and will be received with great caution. The admission of one *joint contractor* may be used against all; but the joint concern must first be shown by other proof. An offer to pay money, by way of *compromise*, cannot be used as an admission. Nor will a party's admission as to *the legal effect* of his contract have any operation whatever. For instance, an admission that one is bound to pay *the debt of another*, because he promised *verbally* to do it, would not prevent him from showing the promise void under the *statute of frauds.*[1] An admission, contained in *a sealed instrument*, is termed *an estoppel*; and is so conclusive of the fact admitted, as to constitute a distinct kind of *replication* in pleading.[2] For instance, the sureties in *a bail-bond*[3] are *estopped* to deny that the principal was arrested; and those in *an administration-bond*, that the principal was appointed administrator.[4]

(5.) *Hearsay* evidence is admitted of such facts, as could be *known only to a few persons*, particularly if the declaration is *against the interest* of the party making it. Thus the entry of a steward, in his accounts, of *the receipt of rents* is admissible to prove such receipt; the party himself being dead or absent. So, in an action by *a bank* against *a depositor* who has *overdrawn, the bank books* are admissible, on proving the handwriting of the clerk, who is dead or insane.

By immemorial usage, in most of the States, *books of account* are admitted, to prove the sale and delivery of goods and merchandise. They must be

---

[1] See p. 79. [2] See *Replication.* [3] See *Bail.* [4] See p. 61.

verified, however, if the charges were made by the plaintiff, by his *suppletory oath*. He is sworn to make true answers to questions *relating to his books*; and is then interrogated whether they are his *original entries*, made *at or about the time* which they purport, and whether they are *true*. No book will be received, which bears suspicious marks upon the face of it; and the *credit* of a book, when received, is always open to the jury. If the first charges were made in a way which renders it impossible to produce them, — as, for instance, upon a slate or cart, they being afterwards copied and rubbed out, — it has been held in Massachusetts, that *copies* are admissible, but in Pennsylvania otherwise. In Tennessee, the party's own oath is not admitted to prove any account of more than two years' standing; and, in many of the States, book accounts are subjected to a shorter *limitation* than other *simple contracts*. Where the person who made the charges has died or become insane, the books are generally admissible without his suppletory oath.

(6.) Declarations, made under the apprehension of *impending dissolution*, are admissible, the solemnity of this situation being held equivalent to the sanction of an oath. They are of course inadmissible, if made by one whose oath would not be received, — as, for instance, *a convict*.

Upon a similar principle, evidence is received of what a witness swore at a former trial, he having since died.

2. Upon the ground of *indirectness and uncertainty*, the law excludes mere *opinions* as evidence. There are some cases, however, where witnesses may give their opinions instead of swearing to *facts*. These

are questions of *scientific and professional skill*, which ordinary men are not supposed capable of perfectly understanding. Thus, upon an indictment for murder, a surgeon may give his opinion, whether death was caused by the blow or wound in question. So a professional surveyor may give his opinion, whether certain marks upon a tree or stone were designed for boundaries. And, in questions of *handwriting* and *identity*, opinion is received, as all that the nature of the case admits of.

3. Evidence, unobjectionable in other respects, is often excluded because it is not *the best evidence*; that is, the best *which the case admits of.*

This rule does not exclude any evidence *in the abstract*, but only *by comparison* with better proof that might be had; and it proceeds upon the ground, that the party fraudulently keeps back the best evidence, because it would show something adverse to his cause. Thus *the copy of a deed* is always inadmissible, until some good reason has been given for not producing the original, or *a counterpart*, if there is one; — for the latter might contain something, which would defeat its operation. So *the declaration* of a person can never be proved, when he himself might be called as a witness.

Upon this principle, a contract *put in writing* cannot be proved by *verbal testimony*, unless the absence of the written instrument be first accounted for.

Upon the same ground, *parol* or verbal evidence is not admissible, to *alter or contradict a written agreement*, whether sealed or unsealed.

An ambiguity, however, in a written instrument may sometimes be *explained* by parol evidence. Ambiguities are of two kinds, — *latent* and *patent*. A *latent* ambiguity is one which arises, not from *the instrument itself*, but from some *extrinsic fact.* For instance, if an estate is devised to A B, and it turns out that there are two persons of that name; this is a latent ambiguity, and may be explained by parol evidence as to the individual referred to by the will. A *patent* ambiguity is one which appears *by inspection of the instrument*; and this is not open to explanation by parol evidence. For instance, if a devise be made of certain property, and *a blank* be left for *the name* of the devisee; the whole is *void for uncertainty*, and no evidence in explanation can be received.

Ambiguities may in general be explained by *the acts of the parties* under the instrument in question, — as, for instance, the occupation of a certain piece of land under a deed. And such evidence has been allowed to control even express courses and distances.

A written contract, though it cannot be *varied* or *explained* by any thing which took place *before or at* the making of it, may be *subsequently altered or discharged* without writing;[1] because the latter transaction does not *control or avoid* the former, but is rather something *independent and additional.* So *the date* of an instrument is not conclusive as to the time of signing it; and *receipts* may be explained or contradicted by parol evidence.

Upon the principle of requiring *the best evidence,* the *subscribing witness* to an instrument must always be produced to prove it, unless there is some special reason to the contrary. This rule of law is very

---

[1] See pp. 83, 84.

strictly enforced. Even *the admission* of a person, that he signed the paper in question, is improper evidence, where it is attested; because this is the mode of authentication adopted by the parties, and supersedes every other. So it is proper to prove *an ancient deed,* which ordinarily *proves itself,* by the subscribing witness, if he is living. But where *a copy* is admitted, the original being lost, it need not be thus proved.

If a witness swear that he has no recollection of attesting the instrument, but knows the handwriting to be his;—it is sufficient proof.

When the subscribing witness cannot be had, or for any cause is incompetent to testify, his *handwriting* may be proved, if the instrument is one that the law requires to be attested; or, if not, the handwriting of the party himself. But strict proof will be required of the witness' absence or incompetency.

Handwriting is proved, either by witnesses, who *have seen the party write,* or held *a correspondence* with him, in which their own letters were regularly replied to; or, in some States, by a mere *comparison* of admitted signatures with that in question,—by the jury.

Notwithstanding the best evidence is strictly required, it is not necessary, in every case, to offer *the fullest or most direct possible proof.* Thus a fact, *witnessed by many persons,* may be satisfactorily proved *by one*; and no unfavorable inference arises from the absence of the rest. So a purchase of goods may be proved without producing *the bill of parcels.*

The rule of course does not apply, where the better evidence, although once existing, is now *lost or destroyed,* or *cannot be procured* by the party.

Thus if a paper is shown, by positive or strong presumptive evidence, to be lost, *a copy* is received; so, if it is in the hands of the adverse party, who refuses, on notice, to produce it.[1]

It should also be observed that, in many cases, upon the ground of public policy, the law will *presume a right or authority, from an act*. Thus, where one assumes to act as sheriff or constable; in a suit between third persons, this will be sufficient *primâ facie* evidence of his authority, without proving his regular appointment. So *cohabitation* is ordinarily sufficient proof of *marriage*.

II. Another ground, upon which evidence is sometimes excluded, is that of *public policy*.

1. It has been already seen,[2] that *a husband and wife* cannot be *witnesses* for or against each other. Upon a similar principle, some other evidence, though in itself free from suspicion, is excluded, because its admission would *defeat the ends of justice*, or *injure the community*. *An attorney or counsellor at law* cannot be called upon to divulge what his client has communicated, even though he be willing to state it. This is his client's privilege, not his own. The principle does not apply to other confidential communications; except perhaps, in some instances, to consultations and instructions passing between *departments or members of the government*, which the public interest does not permit to be divulged. In New York, confidential confessions to *clergymen*, and those which are in their nature professional to *physicians*, are also protected.

---

1 In New York and some other States, the Court have power to compel the production of a paper. Courts of Chancery always have such power.

2 See p. 19.

2. Upon the same principle, that of *public policy*, is founded the rule, that no man shall *allege his own turpitude*. A plaintiff cannot support his action, nor a defendant his defence, by showing *the illegality of his own conduct*.[1] Upon a similar ground, one who has *given credit to a negotiable instrument* by indorsing it, cannot be admitted a witness to prove that it was *void*, for usury or other cause, *in its creation*. The exclusion does not apply to *other instruments*, nor to circumstances which occur *after the making*.

CHAPTER XII.

INSTRUMENTS OF EVIDENCE.

EVIDENCE is *obtained*,—first, *by witnesses*, who make their statements *upon the stand*, or in open court, to the jury; or, secondly, *by written documents*.

I. 1. *Attendance of witnesses*. The attendance of witnesses is compelled by a *subpœna*; which is a *judicial summons*, commanding the witness to appear at the trial and testify what he knows, accompanied by a tender of such *fees* as the law provides for his travel and attendance. If the subpœna is wilfully disobeyed, the court on application will issue an *attachment*, *capias*, or *warrant*, for his compulsory seizure.

The law *protects* witnesses *from arrest*, "eundo, morando, et redeundo,"—in going, staying, and re-

---

[1] See pp. 77, 78.

turning. And the privilege applies to all examinations and trials, whether strictly *judicial* or not. Whether it can be claimed by one who attends *without a subpœna* is an unsettled point. It extends to the witness *at his lodgings*. If he voluntarily *submit* to an arrest, he cannot afterwards complain of it as unlawful. A witness may either guard himself by *a writ of protection*, which however is merely *a notice to the officer*, and cannot protect one not fairly entitled to it; or, when arrested, he may be discharged *by motion to the court*. The privilege has been said to be that of *the court*, and not of *the witness*.

In New York, exemplary damages are provided for wrongfully arresting a witness. A penalty is also imposed of fifty dollars for non-attendance upon summons.

2. *Testimony of witnesses*. To secure *the veracity*, and determine *the ability and knowledge*, of witnesses, the law has provided two general tests, — viz. *an oath* and *cross-examination*.

A judicial oath, is "a solemn invocation of the vengeance of God upon the witness, if he do not declare the whole truth, so far as he knows it."

Cross-examination is the examination of a witness by the party *against whom* he testifies; and takes place, after he has been examined by the other side, or *examined in chief*. The object of it is, in general, to detect the ignorance or falsehood of the witness, by minute inquiry into the details of what he has broadly stated. Thus, when the veracity of another witness is in question, and the witness on the stand states that his *reputation for truth* is bad; the other party may ask, on cross-examination, from what individuals the witness has derived his information on this point.

3. *Incompetency of witnesses.*

Notwithstanding the above-named securities for truth, there are several causes which render a witness *incompetent* to testify. *Competency* is to be distinguished from *credit*; the former is a question for *the court*, the latter for *the jury*. An incompetent witness the court will not suffer to testify at all; but, though competent, the jury are still to judge whether he tells the truth.

(1.) *Religious belief.* No one can be a witness, who does not believe in *a God*, *a future state of rewards and punishments*, and *the future punishment of perjury.*[1] With this qualification, persons of all sects and nations, Jews, Mahometans, Gentoos, &c. may be sworn, each in the form of his own country which he holds the most solemn, — a Jew upon the Pentateuch, a Turk upon the Koran, a Catholic by kissing the book. *Quakers*, and in Massachusetts all other persons who have conscientious scruples in regard to an oath, may be *affirmed* instead of being sworn; the form concluding "under the pains and penalties of perjury" and not "so help you God." In many States, the practice is to *kiss the Gospels.* The objection from belief is usually taken from the witness' own statement, or "voir dire."[2]

(2.) *Infamy.* Any person who has been convicted of some *infamous crime*, is not a competent witness. But conviction *in a foreign country* or *another State* goes merely to *the credit* of the witness; upon the

---

[1] In Massachusetts and New York, disbelief in future punishment goes only to the *credit* of a witness. In the latter State, the question is, whether he believes *in a God, and in the punishment of perjury.*

[2] Otherwise in New York.

same principle, that *a foreign judgment* in civil actions is not *conclusive evidence of a debt* in our courts.[1] Infamy is proved by *the record of conviction.*

(3.) *Incapacity. Children,* and persons of *weak intellect,* are not absolutely incompetent, but may be examined by the court to ascertain their capacity, and admitted or rejected according to the result of such examination.

(4.) *Interest.* No mere bias, partiality, or prejudice comes under the legal definition of *interest.* Thus, all *relatives,* except husband and wife, may testify for each other. *Interest* is in its nature *pecuniary*; and must be *a certain and direct concern,* either in *the event of the cause,* or in *the record* for the purposes of evidence. Thus, where one *assigns* to another an account or other contract not negotiable, and an action is brought upon it, as it must be, *in the name of the former*; the latter is an incompetent witness for the plaintiff, being interested *in the event of the cause.* On the other hand, if a *general custom* or *right of common* is claimed, in a suit by one; others who are not *parties,* but have *a share in the same right* if it exist, cannot be witnesses to prove it, because *the record* or judgment in this action might be used by them *in their own cause.*

A mere *honorary obligation,* on the part of a witness, to indemnify a party if he lose the case, will not in general render him incompetent to testify. And where there is *a balance of interest,* the witness is competent. For instance, if a man sells goods, and afterwards they are attached by his creditors upon the ground that the sale was *fraudulent*: in a suit

---

[1] Infra II.

between the purchaser and the attaching officer, *the seller* is a good witness; for, if the sale was valid, the property cannot go to pay his debts; and, if void, he is liable to refund the price to the purchaser.

The inquiry, whether a proposed witness is legally *interested*, gives rise to many nice and subtile distinctions. Where there is any doubt, however, the courts lean in favor of the witness' *competency*, leaving his *credit* to the jury.

Interest is no exception to a witness, if acquired, either maliciously or wantonly, *since the event happened*, which is to be proved, — as, for instance, by laying *a wager* upon the subject matter, — because this would be a fraud upon the party.

Necessity gives rise to another exception from the general rule, in the case of *a servant or agent*, who transacts his master's business, and, in the usual course of affairs, is the only person to be resorted to for proof. Thus a servant, employed to carry money and pay it, may prove the payment, although he thereby clears himself from blame or liability.

By special statutes, *the members of public corporations*, such as towns, &c., are in general made competent to testify in favor of the corporations, although interested.

Even *a party* himself may in certain instances be a witness; but only where *he alone* can be supposed to *know the fact*. The most common instance is in proving the *loss of a paper*, in order to introduce parol evidence of its contents.

When a witness is objected to as *interested*, the usual course is to examine him upon the "voir dire," in regard to his interest; that is, to prove it by his own statement on oath of his connexion with the party or subject matter. Or it may be proved, in the ordinary way, by other witnesses. This cannot be done, however, after an examination on the "voir dire"; though the testimony will be rejected, if the interest be made apparent in any stage of the cause.

4. *Examination of witnesses.*

In the examination of a witness, *leading questions* are not allowed, — that is, questions which suggest to him the answers he is to make, or questions to which the simple reply of "yes" or "no" would be sufficient. Violations of this rule, however, are sometimes necessary, in order to *direct the witness' attention* to the particular subject of inquiry. And less strictness is required, where he shows an evident disposition to conceal the truth or favor the other party.

Where a witness has made *a memorandum* of certain facts, he will be allowed to *refresh his memory* by referring to it, but not to use it as the original source of his information.[1]

On application of the adverse party, witnesses shall be examined *apart from each other.* This, however, is rarely done.

After the examination in chief, or even after the witness has been sworn but not examined, the adverse party has the privilege of *cross-examining.* And he may propose *leading questions.* Although the chief object of cross-examination is to detect some misstatement, yet the party cannot question a witness upon matters *collateral* or *foreign* to the issue, for the purpose of contradicting him on those points

---

[1] In South Carolina it has been held otherwise.

by other testimony, and thereby destroying his general credit. Any such question may be objected to as irrelevant, and, if answered, the answer must be taken for true.

Where a party has called a witness who is interested against him, the other party may cross-examine him upon the points in which he is interested in his own favor.

A witness is not bound to answer any question, a reply to which will expose him to *criminal punishment* or *penal liability*. But the danger of incurring a mere *pecuniary charge*, or in any other way injuriously affecting his interest, will be no excuse.[1] Thus a witness may be asked, whether *he* did not agree to pay the debt in question. It is the province of *the Court* to judge, whether any direct answer to the question proposed will furnish evidence against him. If it may disclose a link in the chain of evidence necessary to conviction, he need not answer it. Whether the rule applies to questions, an answer to which may subject the witness to *disgrace and shame*, — as, for instance, "if he has not stood in the pillory," seems somewhat unsettled.

The party who called a witness cannot *re-examine* him, after cross-examination, except on the points therein touched upon. But it is to be observed, that the strict rules on this subject are in practice often dispensed with, either by consent of parties or indulgence of the Court.

5. *Impeachment of witnesses.*

The credit of a witness may be *impeached*, either by *contradictory testimony*, by *disproving his general*

---

[1] Held otherwise in Connecticut, Tennessee, and Louisiana.

veracity, or by his own previous *inconsistent declarations.* The latter however cannot be shown, without first asking the witness himself, whether he ever made such declarations. Only the *general reputation* of a witness for truth, and not *particular facts* or *conduct*, can be shown to discredit him; because no man would be prepared to meet such testimony, and its admission would burden every cause with a mass of collateral points, foreign from the issue. The proper question to be put to one witness respecting another is, *whether he would believe him on his oath*, or *what is his character for veracity*; but, in North Carolina and Kentucky, it has been held that the inquiry may extend to the witness' *general character*. And any fact may be proved, which, while derogatory to the witness' character, tends to show *a want of knowledge* or *recollection*, — as that he was *drunk* when the event in question took place.

A party cannot *discredit the testimony of his own witness*; because there would be unfairness, in giving him the benefit of it if favorable, and, if otherwise, allowing him to disprove it. Still, however, where a witness is called to prove a particular fact, and unexpectedly denies it; others may be examined for the same purpose; — as where an *attesting witness* denies his signature. And where a party is required to prove a writing by the subscribing witness, who, on cross-examination, swears to other facts, the party may discredit him in any way except by impeaching his general veracity. In one case, the three witnesses to a will joined in testifying to the testator's incapacity; and yet the will was set up upon other testimony. If a witness, upon cross-examination, contradict a deposition formerly given by him, the party cannot call other witnesses to support his general character.

II. Facts may be proved, not only by the testimony of witnesses *on the stand*, but by *written instruments*. Under this head, we may consider; 1st, *the nature and authentication* of written evidence, and, 2dly, its *legal effect*.

1. (1.) *Depositions*. A deposition is a *written statement of a witness' testimony*, taken, for special reasons, *out of court* and before the trial, by or in presence of some officer authorized for that purpose. This kind of evidence is not favored by the law; which regards the visible demeanor of a witness on the stand, as one very important means of enabling the jury justly to appreciate his testimony. Depositions are usually allowed to be taken, in a pending cause, where a witness *is sick, lives remote from the place of trial*,[1] or *intends leaving the State*; and, *for the perpetuation of evidence*, — "in perpetuam rei memoriam," may also be taken, although no actual controversy have yet arisen. Provision is invariably made for *notice* to the opposite party.

(2.) It has already been seen,[2] that *written declarations* are not admissible in evidence; falling under the same class, of *hearsay*, with oral declarations. This exclusion applies chiefly or wholly to documents in their nature *private*. *Public* documents, or those which partake of a public character though in some sense private, are received as evidence; and may, in general, be proved *by copy*.

---

1 In New York, it seems, this is no ground, provided the witness is *within the State*.

2 Ch. XI. (I.)

A very important class of written instruments are *the records of Courts.* These are usually proved by *copies attested by the clerk.* If also bearing *the seal of the Court* and *certified by the presiding judge*; — according to the constitution and laws of the United States, they have the same credit in every other State, that they would have in the State where they belong. A Justice of the Peace may certify, that he is the presiding judge and clerk, that his court has no seal, and that the attestation is in the usual form; — and the copy thus authenticated will be received in every State.

A copy should be of *the whole record*; or of so much at least as concerns the matter in question.

In general, the judgment of *an inferior Court,* which keeps no formal records, is proved by the customary minutes of its proceedings. Thus a license to keep an inn, may be proved by the *minutes* of the Court of Sessions, containing merely the name of the party, written under the head of "Licenses," — these being its only records.

Where the law *entrusts a particular officer with the making of copies,* it also gives credit to them in evidence without further proof. This principle applies, in Massachusetts and other States, to *copies of deeds* made out by *the Register.* Upon the same principle, *certificates* or *entries* made by those who are expressly or by implication authorized to make them, are *primâ facie* evidence of the facts to which they refer. Thus the certificate of a clergyman as to a marriage. So that of a register of deeds, as to the time of recording a deed. And all public documents, which from their nature cannot be removed, and for copies of which no particular provision has been made, may be proved by a copy *sworn* to have been *examined with the original*, — called *a sworn copy*. Another rule is, that when the original, if produced, would *prove itself*, — a sworn copy is admissible. The original however must be shown to have been *in its proper repository*; and its contents will not be taken as evidence of this fact. In the case of *ancient* or *lost* records, copies not sworn are sometimes received; or even parol evidence of them. A clerk's certificate is no evidence of the loss of a record; — it must be proved, like other facts, by oath.

In regard to *statutes*; those which are *public*, — relating to the community at large or considerable portions of it, — require no proof, being part of *the law of the land*; and *printed copies* are used, not as evidence, but mere *memoranda* to refresh the memory. The same practice prevails, although not strictly conformable to law, in regard to the printed statutes of other of the United States, if published under public authority.

Private statutes, — relating to individuals, — are no part of the general law, and must therefore be *proved*, like other facts. Still, in practice, the printed copies are often admitted as evidence.

All other *acts of state*, done by any department of the government, may be proved by the official printed copies. As, for instance, *messages* from the President to Congress. So the *printed journals* of Congress have been received as evidence of its proceedings.

Public registers of all kinds, though not designed for the purposes of evidence, are admissible to prove the facts contained in them, and may generally be verified by *sworn copies.* Thus navy registers, log-books, prison books, bank books, &c.

2. The *legal effect* of written evidence demands no distinct notice, except in reference to *records* or *judgments.*

The record of a judgment is *conclusive evidence, that such a judgment was rendered,* and also of *all legal consequences* resulting therefrom; as, for instance, the consequence, that one convicted by such judgment of an infamous crime can no longer be a good witness. But, in regard to *the facts which a judgment involves,* or upon which it is built; — it will or will not be evidence of those facts, according to circumstances.

It is a maxim of the law, that *the public good requires a termination of controversies,*— "reipublicæ interest, ut sit finis litium." Hence, the same question *cannot be twice tried and adjudged* between the same parties, — "nemo debet bis vexari pro eâdem causâ;" and *the record* of a former judgment will be a conclusive bar to a *second suit* for the same matter. The general rule is, however, that such judgment must be specifically relied on as *an estoppel*[1] or bar; — if offered *in evidence,* it will be *merely evidence,* open to examination, — like any other proof.

The above principle precludes a second action, by or against *the same party,* and *for the same cause,* for or against whom, and for which, a suit has already been decided.

(1.) In general no one is bound by, or can avail himself of, a judgment, unless he was *a party* to the suit, or *in privity* with the party, or *possessed the*

---

[1] See *Estoppel.*

power of making himself a party, — even though the question be the same. Because, if the judgment were *unfavorable*, he has thereby lost the right of *cross-examination*, not being present at the former trial; and the testimony there given, with the judgment itself, is as to him *mere hearsay*: or, if *favorable*, not being a party to that suit, he may have been a *witness*, and thus indirectly *testified in his own cause*. Thus, where the question is, whether two defendants are *partners*, the plaintiff cannot, to prove them such, offer a judgment against them in a previous suit brought by another person; nor can the defendants, to disprove that they are partners, offer the judgment in that suit in their favor.

A suit between different parties is termed in law "res inter alios acta."

Judgments, however, are binding upon *privies* no less than parties. *An heir* is bound by a judgment against *his ancestor*; an *assignee* by a judgment against his *assignor*. And there are some cases, where, by virtue of *privity*, persons not parties to a former judgment are bound by it "sub modo," — for certain purposes. For instance, if *a sheriff* is sued for some *wrongful act of his deputy*, and damages are recovered of him; this judgment will be evidence, in another action brought by the sheriff against the deputy, of the *amount of damage*, though not evidence of *the deputy's misconduct*. So where one, having *a warranty deed* of land,[1] is *evicted* or dispossessed by the suit of an adverse claimant; the judgment is evidence, in an action upon the warranty of *the eviction itself*, but not that *the adverse title was*

---

[1] See p. 205.

good. In both cases, however, if the parties ultimately liable *had notice* of the first suits, the judgment will be no less conclusive against them, than if they were the nominal as well as real defendants. The matter is no longer "res inter alios."

For the reasons above assigned, a judgment either for or against a person in *a civil action*, is no evidence in *a criminal prosecution* for the same act. The converse is also true. *The parties* are not the same; *intention* comes in question in one and not the other; and the injured party may *be a witness* in one and not in the other.

(2.) The judgment in a former suit will not be a bar, unless *the fact in issue*, as well as the parties, were the same. But *the form of action* may be different, provided *the merits have been tried.* For instance, after an action of *trover* for *wrongfully taking* one's property, the plaintiff cannot sue in *assumpsit* for *the proceeds* of it. On the other hand, *if the merits have not been tried*, but the former judgment was rendered *upon some technical ground*; it is no *estoppel* to another suit. The same is true with a judgment rendered upon a *non-suit* or *discontinuance*, instead of *a verdict.* [1] And where *distinct demands* are included in the same suit, one of them may be *withdrawn*, so that the judgment will not bar a future suit upon it. It would be otherwise if the whole were left to the jury. So where the plaintiff's claim is in its nature *indivisible*, judgment for part of it will bar another suit for the rest. For instance, if a horse and chaise were sold for so much *by one contract*, and the seller sued and recovered judgment for the price of the

---

[1] See pp. 278, 318.

horse alone, — he must lose the price of the chaise. "A personal contract cannot be apportioned," so as to make several suits out of one cause of action. [1]

Sometimes the same question *of right* is presented in both suits, while *the facts* are different. For instance, if one bring an action against another for trespassing upon his land, and the defendant plead *a title* in himself to the land, and upon this issue judgment be given for the plaintiff; — it seems the judgment is conclusive as to the title.

A former judgment is no evidence of such matters, as were *not directly* but *collaterally* decided by it, — or matters *of inference* merely. For instance, where the issue was, whether a party taking a conveyance had knowledge of a former one, [2] and the verdict was that he had such knowledge; this does not settle the validity of the first conveyance, but it may be disputed in another suit between the same parties.

Judgments are either *domestic* or *foreign*; that is, rendered by our own Courts, or those of some other State or country; and, in certain points of view, there is an important distinction between these two descriptions of judgments.

It is to be understood, that a judgment may be used for two purposes; as *a ground of action*, or *a ground of defence*. For instance, one who has recovered judgment upon a note of hand, may enforce that judgment by *a new suit*, — an action of *debt* or *scire facias*; — although the usual mode

---

[1] In many States, when there are several actions pending between the same parties, the Court may order a "consolidation" of them into one suit.

[2] See p. 201.

is *an execution.* On the other hand, if, in the suit upon such a note, the defendant made a defence and prevailed, and the plaintiff then brings another suit upon the same note; — the defendant may produce *the former judgment* as *a bar* to the present action.

When used for the latter of these purposes, — as *a defence,* — the better opinion seems to be, that a foreign judgment, rendered by a court of competent jurisdiction, is no less conclusive than a domestic judgment; provided it be shown to have been *final.*

On the other hand, when one who has recovered a foreign judgment, *seeks to enforce it by an action* in our Courts; the judgment is *not conclusive,* but, like all other evidence, *open to explanation or contradiction.*

Before the formation of the Constitution, each State was held *a foreign State* in all the others, with regard to the validity of judicial decisions. But, by that instrument, and a subsequent act of Congress, the judgment of a Court in one State has the same effect in every other, which it has in the State where it was rendered; provided the Court *had jurisdiction of the subject matter and of the party.* For instance, if a certain Court has jurisdiction of all debts under a hundred dollars; a judgment of that Court for a debt of more than a hundred dollars would not be conclusive in another State, because the Court had no jurisdiction of *the subject-matter.* On the other hand, if the defendant in the suit were not *an inhabitant of the State,* and never were actually *notified* of it; — the judgment will not be enforced in another State, because the Court had no jurisdiction *of the party.* Special provision is made, in most of the States, for securing debts due from persons, who *live out of the State* but *own property within it,* by an attachment of the property, and giving public and long-continued notice in the newspapers or some other satisfactory way. Of course, if these proceedings are adopted, a judgment against an absent defendant is perfectly valid in the State where it was rendered; so far as to give a claim *upon the property.* But, if that proves insufficient to satisfy the judgment, and a suit is afterwards brought upon it *for the balance, in the State where the defendant resides*;—the former judgment is held not conclusive, because the Court had no jurisdiction of *the party.*

It remains to consider a certain class of judgments, which, from their peculiar nature, are *conclusive,* not only *upon the parties,* but upon *all other persons,* in reference to the point which they decide. These are called "judgments in rem"; because they relate to *a single fact* of a general and public, and at the same time very important, character. Judgments of this description are rendered by some Court of *peculiar and limited jurisdiction.*[1] Such is a Court of *Admiralty,* acting upon a question of *prize*; or a Court of *Probate,* upon a question as to the validity of *a will,* or a question of *guardianship. The conclusiveness* of such judgments depends not only upon *their specific nature,* but their *mode of proceeding,* which is, to give *public notice* to all persons interested, instead of *the private process* practised in common law courts.

A decree of *restitution,* in the United States Dis-

---

[1] See p. 228.

trict Court, *of a vessel* which has been *seized by revenue officers*, is conclusive evidence, in an action by the owner against the officers, that the seizure was illegal. And judgments in *Admiralty*, whether domestic or foreign, are generally though not uniformly held conclusive, as to the *neutral or hostile character* of a ship. This question very often arises, and this evidence is used, in actions *upon policies of insurance*, containing *warranty of neutrality*.

The *probate of a will* is conclusive, in all the States, *as to personal property*; but not in all of them as to *real estate*, — the English law, which gives no jurisdiction of real estate to the *Ecclesiastical* or Probate Court, being still wholly or partially adhered to in Pennsylvania, Maryland, and New York.

It is to be observed, however, that judgments "in rem," like others, are not to be regarded, if the Court pronouncing them had *no jurisdiction*. Thus, *a prize judgment* must have been rendered in the Court of *a belligerent* or *ally*, constituted according to the law of nations. So the judgment of *a Probate Court* will be disregarded, if the Court had no jurisdiction.

Nor do such judgments establish any fact, not strictly *necessary as the foundation of them*.[1]

Judgments, like all other acts, are *vitiated by fraud*; and this more especially in regard to *third persons*, who have no opportunity of exposing the fraud, and obtaining redress, by any *appellate* proceedings in the suit itself. Hence, when a fraudulent judgment is set up against one not a party, it may be declared *void*, and treated as a nullity.

In cases where *hearsay evidence*[2] is admissible, —

---

[1] See p. 314. [2] See p. 292.

those of *prescription, custom,* and *pedigree,* — a judgment, though between other parties, is also received, as falling under the same general head.

A *verdict*, though usually followed by a judgment, is no evidence, when offered in a subsequent suit, unless the judgment also be produced; because the verdict may, for various reasons, have been *set aside* or *avoided*, and the cause have terminated in favor of the party who suffered a verdict against him.

CHAPTER XIII.

VERDICT, JUDGMENT, AND EXECUTION.

I. *Verdict.* When the evidence and the arguments have been closed on both sides, the presiding judge *charges the jury,* — that is, presents to them a summary view of the cause, and instructs them what are the rules of law by which their decision is to be governed. The jury then retire, unless the case is a clear one, for private deliberation, taking with them all the papers which have been offered; and remain together usually until they come to a unanimous result or *verdict.* After a long and ineffectual attempt, however, to agree, the case will be taken from them and reserved for a new trial.

When the jury have agreed upon a verdict, they return into Court, and one of them, called the *foreman,* openly declares that they have found the issue either for the plaintiff or defendant, and in the former case a certain sum for damages. This is a *general* verdict. They may find a *special* verdict; which consists in stating *the facts* as they find them proved, and leaving *the legal conclusion* resulting from them to the Court. The verdict, on being declared, is *recorded* by the clerk, and in some States the record is handed over to the prevailing party.

Judgment will be rendered of course after verdict, unless there be some special cause for *suspending* or *arresting* it. Such cause however may often exist, and will furnish ground of *motion, for a new trial,* or *in arrest of judgment*; or for a *repleader.*

1. *A new trial* will be granted, for such errors or defects in the trials, *as do not appear by the record.* The usual occasions of it are, where *illegal evidence was admitted,* or *proper and legal evidence rejected,* by the Court; for *improper instructions or omissions* by the judge in *his charge*; for *interest* or other incompetency in *a juror,* or any attempt to *influence the jury,* or any *misconduct* on their part. *Excessive damages* are sometimes a ground of new trial. But only where the case is of such a nature, that the damages admit of *precise computation,*—as in most debts and contracts, — and the verdict disregards this standard; or else, in other cases, where the amount is so *exorbitant,* as to indicate the operation of passion, prejudice, or corruption. A new trial is sometimes granted, where the verdict is *against the evidence.* But, as the jury are instituted to judge upon questions of fact, the Court will not interfere for this cause, unless there be a very clear case of error and injustice. So if the verdict is *against law*; or *new evidence* has been discovered since the trial,

which the party could not previously procure,— there shall be a new trial.

2. A motion *in arrest of judgment* is made for some error or defect, which appears *upon the face of the pleadings*, or upon *the record*. That is, it is made for the same causes which would justify *a demurrer*, the nature of which has been already explained.[1] There are some defects, however, of an *incidental* or *technical* nature, which are *cured by the verdict*, and therefore, though they might have been taken advantage of on demurrer, do not furnish ground for *arrest of judgment*. If a declaration or plea omit to state some particular circumstance, without proving which the action or defence could not stand, or the jury could not have found a verdict,—as, for instance, that a trespass was done *on a certain day*; the defect is cured by verdict. But if the thing omitted is essential,—as, where the plaintiff states *a defective title*, and not merely a good one in a defective manner,—judgment will be arrested.

3. Where, by mistake, the issue was joined upon a point that is *immaterial*, the Court will not render judgment, but will award *a repleader*, or new course of pleadings. For instance, where *an executor*, to a suit brought against him as such, pleads that *he* did not promise, instead of pleading that *his testator* did not promise, and issue is joined upon this plea;— there shall be *a repleader*, because the verdict does not decide the merits of the case.

The above-mentioned grounds for suspending or arresting judgment usually involve nice points of law,

---

[1] See p. 284.

which are not decided immediately, but reserved for future and deliberate argument and adjudication.

II. *Judgment.* *A judgment* is *the sentence of the law*, pronounced by the Court, upon the matter contained in the record; and may be rendered upon *default, non-suit,*[1] *demurrer,*[2] or *verdict.* Judgment consists, ordinarily, not in any formal or open decision of a cause, but merely in a certain *entry* upon the docket, and a subsequent *record* of the case, made by the Clerk.

A judgment is either *interlocutory* or *final.* The former is a decision in some *intermediate stage* of the cause, which does not finally settle it; — as, for instance, a judgment of " respondeas ouster," upon *a plea in abatement,*[3] — that is, that the defendant shall not prevail by this plea, but make *a further answer* to the action. A *final* judgment *ends the suit,* unless *an appeal, review,* or *writ of error* is resorted to, for the purpose of reversing it.

An appeal is the process of carrying a cause *from a lower Court to a higher*; and is effected by *bond* or *recognizance,* usually with sureties, entered into before the lower Court. By an appeal, the whole case is opened for a new trial. To prevent *frivolous* appeals, such provision is usually made in regard to *costs,* as to operate by way of penalty upon the party in fault.

Writs of error and *writs of review* are new writs, brought for the purpose of reversing a judgment; and are rather the commencement of another suit, than, like an appeal, a continuation of the original cause. These processes are variously regulated by the statutes of the different States. In general, *a*

[1] See pp. 277, 278. [2] See p. 284. [3] See p. 285.

writ of error, like *a demurrer* or *motion in arrest*, lies only for some error *apparent on the record*.

In the nature of a writ of error, is *a certiorari*. A certiorari is the process, by which a higher Court revises such proceedings of inferior tribunals as are not *according to the course of the common law*,[1] — as, for instance, the laying out of roads, or the imposition of militia fines. A certiorari does not generally issue without *leave of Court*, granted on petition and for good cause.

In general, the prevailing party recovers *costs*. The nature and amount of *taxable costs* are subjects of statute regulation, and vary greatly in the several States. They include a reasonable allowance for the expenses of counsel, witnesses, jury, Clerk, &c. Costs make no part of *the verdict*, but only of *the judgment*. In some cases of peculiar hardship, *double costs* are awarded; as, for instance, in Massachusetts, when one brings an action in *a county* where neither the plaintiff nor defendant resides. On the other hand, it is usually provided, that if a plaintiff recover less than a certain sum *in a higher Court*, as a penalty for not bringing the suit before *the inferior Court* provided by law for such cases, he shall recover only a certain proportion of the debt or damages as costs.

A judgment may be *enforced*, either by *an execution*, which must issue within a certain period, — in general, one year,[2] — after judgment; or by *a new action* of *debt* or *scire facias*, to which no defence can be made, that might have been made to the original action.

---

[1] See p. 228.

[2] In New York, *two years*.

III. *Execution.* *An execution* is the writ or process, by which a judgment is carried into effect or *executed*; and is issued, on application of the prevailing party, by the Clerk. An execution is directed to the sheriff or his deputy, and commands him to satisfy the judgment by taking the debtor's property, or else to commit him to gaol.[1] In many States, however, the right of imprisoning is now done away.[2] In Massachusetts, execution shall not issue against the body, provided the defendant *make oath*, before judgment, *that he has no property*; nor for debts *under ten dollars*; nor against *females*. Similar exemptions prevail elsewhere.[3] A person committed on execution may obtain *the liberty of the yard*,— which, in some States, embraces the whole town, and, in others, the county,— by giving bond against his escape. If he go beyond the limits, his sureties become liable for the debt. At the end of a certain period,— usually thirty days,— the debtor shall be released, on making oath that he has no means of satisfying the debt. After this proceeding, his body cannot be again taken, but the debt remains good against his property.[4]

Substantially the same articles are *exempted* from execution, which have already been mentioned[5] as *exempted* from attachment.

Where the debtor's *property* is seized to satisfy an execution, the statute law of the several States pre-

---

1 In New York, the same execution does not run against both the body and property, but after return of an execution against the one, a second may issue against the other.

2 See p. 265.

3 In Ohio, *revolutionary soldiers* are exempted.

4 In New York, after commitment, no new execution, except in special cases, can issue against property.

5 p. 267.

scribes the mode in which it shall be disposed of. *Personal property* is *sold* by public auction, after being advertised. In general, *real estate* cannot be taken, but for want of personal. In several States, real estate, taken on execution, is absolutely sold; but, in New York, generally through New England, and in some other States, it is *appraised*, and *set off* or specifically allotted to the creditor, and the debtor is allowed to *redeem* it within a certain time, — usually one year.

In New York, and many of the middle, southern, and western States, *a judgment* constitutes *a lien* upon the debtor's real estate, so that it may be seized on execution notwithstanding any *conveyance* subsequent to the judgment. In New York, the lien extends even to after-acquired land, and continues ten years. In Kentucky and Mississippi, it commences with delivery of the execution. In New England, the purpose of such lien being answered by *attachment*, the right is not known.

It is the duty of the officer, after *service* of an execution, to return it to court, with an indorsement or *return* of his proceedings. This return constitutes *the record title*, by which the creditor or purchaser holds the property that was sold or set off. Where the property was such as is subject to execution *at common law*, the title is good, although *the legal formalities* were not strictly observed; but, if the proceeding was authorized only by *statute*, the slightest irregularity avoids the sale.

If an execution is served against the debtor, after the judgment has been *satisfied* or *discharged*, the law provides the writ of "audita querela" for redress of the wrong.

CHAPTER XIV.

CHANCERY.

THE proceedings for redress of private wrongs, described in the foregoing chapters, are those which are practised in *the courts of common law.*[1] In addition to these, there exists in several States a Court of *Chancery* or *Equity*; to which resort may be had in many cases for the same object. In New York, New Jersey, Delaware, Maryland, and South Carolina, there is a distinct Court of Chancery; and, in nearly all the other States, the courts of law are invested, some of them with full, and others with partial, *Chancery jurisdiction.*

The general purpose of a court of Chancery, is to provide a remedy for certain cases of wrong, which *the common law* fails to reach; and, as the term *equity* imports, to administer that justice between the parties, which in another tribunal strict and technical rules may hinder them from attaining. It is not to be understood, however, that Chancery decides each case as it arises, upon its own circumstances alone, and without regard to precedent or analogy. Equity has its *rules and principles,* more liberal perhaps in their character, but not less inflexible in their application, than the rules of the common law; and nearly or quite as little is left to private, individual discretion in the one case as in the other.

---

[1] See p. 228.

The mode of proceeding in Chancery is essentially different from that in a Court of law. The suit is commenced, as has been already stated,[1] by *a bill*, instead of *a writ*. But the most striking and important distinction relates to the method of *proof* and of *trial*. Instead of relying upon the *testimony of witnesses*, *the defendant himself* is made to *answer upon oath*, in reference to the matters alleged against him; and the trial is in general not *by jury*, but *by the judge or chancellor*.

The mode of *proof*, practised in chancery, renders its interference peculiarly appropriate, where there is a *defect of evidence* to sustain the plaintiff's claim, and it is therefore important to draw the truth from the defendant himself. Such are cases of *mistake* or *accident*, *fraud*, *account*, and *trust*; the last of which was the original source in England of the exercise of Chancery power.

Chancery also exercises jurisdiction, for the *protection of infants and heirs*; to remedy *the loss, informality*, or *imperfect execution, of papers*; *ascertain boundaries*; relieve against *penalties* or *forfeitures*, as in case of bonds and mortgages;[2] compel the *delivering up of void deeds*; and *vacate fraudulent judgments*.

Another important branch of Equity jurisdiction is that of *injunction*. *An injunction* is a process, by which Chancery interferes to prevent *fraud and mischief*. By this means, it may *stay proceedings in other courts*; restrain *infringements of a patent*; stop the commission of *waste*; *abate nuisances*; and, in gene-

---

[1] See p. 228. In Massachusetts, a bill may be inserted in a writ.
[2] See pp. 71, 175.

ral, check any gross invasion of private right, for which the damages in an action at law would be a tardy and ineffectual remedy.

Chancery may also enforce the *specific execution of a contract*, where damages for the breach of it would be an inadequate remedy.

Although Chancery, in many instances, furnishes *a remedy* which cannot be had at law; yet *the rules of property, of evidence*, and *of interpretation*, are the same in both tribunals; and it has become a familiar maxim, that "equity follows the law." For instance, the statute of limitations is not considered binding *as a statute* in chancery; but still is adopted, by analogy, for determining the period within which a claim may be enforced.

A bill in Chancery is *a petition to the Court* for relief, upon the ground that the complainant has no remedy at law. The bill usually calls before the Court all parties who are in any degree interested in the case; and a *subpœna* is then issued to require their attendance. In cases of urgent necessity, *an injunction* may be awarded immediately upon the filing of the bill. If the defendant does not appear on subpœna, it may be followed successively by various degrees of compulsory process.

If the defendant *appear*, the mode of *pleading* is substantially the same as in a court of law. The usual defence is his *answer on oath*; in which he can do nothing more than pray to be *dismissed* from the Court. If he has any *relief* to demand of the plaintiff, it must be done by *a new bill* of his own, called *a cross-bill.* If rendered necessary by the answer, the plaintiff may add *new parties* or *new matter* to the bill.

There may also be a bill of *revivor*, where one of the parties *has died*.

The plaintiff usually *replies* to the answer, that *his bill is true*, and offers to prove it. This is done by *depositions*, taken, in answer to *written interrogatories, out of court*.

Where any *point of fact* is strongly controverted, — as, for instance, a question of *sanity*, — the court order *a jury* to try it. This order is called *an interlocutory decree*. For the purpose of bringing the question distinctly before the jury, *a fictitious issue* is framed, which presents only the single point of inquiry.

If the case is found to involve long accounts and minute details, these are referred to *a Master in Chancery*, who is to report upon them, and his report to be either accepted or rejected by *the Chancellor*. After all issues and references are finished, there is a final *hearing* and *decree*. There may, however, be a petition for a *rehearing* or a *review*. A decree will be *enforced*, by *commitment of the defendant's person* or *sequestration of his property*.

INDEX.

42

S.

PROPOSED AMENDMENTS IN THE LAWS OF MASSACHUSETTS.

THE following amendments of the existing law, relating to the subjects treated in the foregoing pages have been proposed by the Commissioners and Committee of the Legislature appointed to revise the Statutes of Massachusetts.

Book III. ch. 1. Husband and Wife.

p. 14. Parties living in Massachusetts cannot evade our law of marriage by celebrating the marriage in another State.

p. 15. Seventeen and fourteen to be the ages of lawful marriage. Cohabitation, after coming of age, shall render the marriage of infants valid.

p. 16. Marriage not to be void for want of any formality, if the parties believed it legal. Consanguinity or affinity to render a marriage absolutely *void*. Divorce for confinement in the State-prison.

p. 18. Marriage void, "ab initio," may be declared so by sentence of *nullity*; and, on the other hand, either party may obtain *affirmation* of a valid marriage. Where a marriage is void for incapacity of one party, the children to be the legitimate issue of the other. So, where there is a second marriage, while the former husband or wife of one party is living; if this fact was unknown, the children to be the lawful issue of the other.

p. 20. The proceeds of a wife's lands, taken for public purposes, to be secured for her use.

Ch. 2. Parent and Child.

p. 21. Subsequent marriage and acknowledgment to legitimatize children. But they cannot inherit to the parents' relations.

Ch. 3. Guardian and Ward.

p. 24. A testamentary guardian to *give bond,* unless the will direct otherwise.

A fixed compensation allowed to guardians.

If the parent is alive, he or she to have the care of the child's person and education, though there be a guardian.

Ch. 6. Corporations.

p. 33. *Towns* may convey *by deed.*

p. 39. *Receivers* to be appointed to settle the affairs of a dissolved corporation.

Book IV. ch. 4. Testament and Administration.

p. 55. Every person, not under eighteen years of age, may make a will, excepting married women.

p. 57. A will void as to real estate from *incapacity* of the testator, shall also be void as to personal property. Instrument of revocation shall have three witnesses. (A suggestion that the same formalities be required for a *bequest* as for a devise.)

Ch. 5. Executors and Administrators.

p. 61. A special administrator provided for in certain cases.

p. 62. An executor may sell *mere rights* of the deceased to real property, as well as actual interests; also, within four years from his death, lands fraudulently conveyed by him.

Ch. 7. Contracts.

p. 82. *Merchant's accounts,* as such, not excepted from the Statute of Limitations. *Judgments* outlawed in twenty years.

Ch. 9. Bailment.

p. 97. Mortgagor of chattels may redeem within sixty days after breach of condition.

Book V. ch. 1. Mills.

p. 146. The owner of land *flowed* to have a *lien* upon the mill for the annual damage assessed by a jury.

Chap. 9. p. 193. One of joint mill owners to have a *lien* upon the rents and profits against another for his share of the cost of *repairs.*

Ch. 2. Life Estate.

p. 159. *Any pecuniary provision,* by way of *jointure,* to bar dower, if assented to by the wife ; or, if not, unless she elect otherwise within six months from the husband's death.

p. 163. Only *single* damages for *waste.*

Ch. 5. Mortgage.

p. 175. *An entry for condition broken,* either to be acknowledged by the mortgagor in writing, or proved by a sworn certificate of two witnesses, — the acknowledgment and certificate to be recorded.

p. 176. A suit by the mortgagee, after *foreclosure,* for the *balance of his debt,* to revive the right of redemption.

Ch. 6. Remainder.

p. 181. The alteration of the rule in "Shelly's Case," to embrace *deeds.*

Ch. 10. Forfeiture. Prescription.

p. 196. Forfeiture of *particular estate* abolished. No *expectancy* to be defeated by any act of the particular tenant, unless it be an *estate-tail,* or the instrument which created it so provides.

p. 198. *Twenty years' use* to give a right to easements, unless there have been a written license from the owner, or a public notice of his intention to dispute the claim.

Ch. 12. Devise.

p. 218. One *disseised* may devise his interest. *After-acquired lands* to pass under a general clause.

p. 219. Devise not to be *revoked* by a subsequent disseisin.

p. 220. The testator's *whole estate* to pass, unless he expressly will to the contrary.

Book VI. ch. 5. Detinue.

p. 240. *Detinue* abolished.

Ch. 7. Real Action.

p. 253. Right of *entry* not to be barred by a *descent* or *discontinuance*. Such *right* alone, without actual entry, required to sustain a writ of entry.

p. 256. The "improvement law" extended to all cases of *bonâ fide* occupancy under a title supposed good.

p. 258. *Mesne profits* to be recovered as damages in the real action itself.

Ch. 9. Attachment. Bail.

p. 267. Real estate attached shall be described with precision in the officer's return. (A suggestion that such attachment shall be publicly *recorded*.)

Bulky articles may be attached by leaving a copy of the writ with the *Town Clerk*.

p. 269. The defence of a *subsequent attaching creditor*, shall defeat only the attachment, and not the suit, of the first attacher. The latter may be a witness.

p. 274. Bail-bond to be *returned* with the writ.

Trustee Process.

p. 270. Other evidence than the *answers* to be received, in the form of *depositions*, and referred either to the Court or jury. Principal defendant may be a witness.

p. 273. *Executors*, &c. made trusteeable.

Ch. 10. Tender. Set-off.

p. 286. The right of *tendering*, and of *bringing money into Court*, extended to *involuntary trespasses.*

An *assigned* demand may be off-set, if taken, and notice given the plaintiff, before the commencement of his suit. Plaintiff cannot *discontinue* the suit without the defendant's consent.

Ch. 12. Evidence.

p. 299. Confidential communications made to a clergyman, physician, or fellow church member, shall not be offered in evidence.

Ch. 13. Execution.

p. 324. *Mere rights* to real estate may be taken in execution.

REPRINTS OF LEGAL CLASSICS PUBLISHED BY THE LAWBOOK EXCHANGE, LTD.

LEGAL EDUCATION

Hicks, Frederick C. *History of the Yale Law School to 1915.* With a new introduction by Morris L. Cohen and a new index. New Haven: Yale University Press, 1935-1938. 301 pp. Illustrated. Reprinted 2001 by The Lawbook Exchange, Ltd. LCCN 2001016436. ISBN 1-58477-175-5. Cloth. $75.

* The only history of the early years of Yale Law School, a chronological history from its founding to 1915, with historical information and colorful anecdotes not found elsewhere. Hicks, the author of *Materials and Methods of Legal Research*, was the librarian at Yale Law School from 1928-1944. From 1935-1938 Yale University Press issued the work in four paperbound volumes that were not widely distributed. This edition combines the four volumes (*The Founders and the Founders' Collection; From the Founders to Dutton 1845-1869; 1869-1894 Including The County Court House Period; and 1895-1915 Twenty Years of Hendrie Hall*) into one, and is prefaced by a new introduction by Morris L. Cohen, who was Professor of Law and head of the law libraries at Harvard and Yale, and is the author of many well-known works including *Bibliography of Early American Law*.

Hilliard, Francis. *The Elements of Law; Being a Comprehensive Summary of American Civil Jurisprudence. For the Use of Students, Men of Business, and General Readers.* Boston: Hilliard, Gray, and Company, 1835. xv, 345, v pp. Reprint available 2002 by The Lawbook Exchange, Ltd. LCCN 2001041395. ISBN 1-58477-188-7. Cloth. $75.

* Hilliard [1806-1878] was a New England lawyer and prolific legal writer whose works set the standard for later law texts. "At the time that he wrote, judges and lawyers lacked legal treatises which cited American decisions and showed how far the English common law had been followed by American courts or modified to suit new conditions. Textbooks presenting cases from all states were needed in order to encourage the development of national judge-made law rather than particularistic local doctrines. Hilliard was one of the first and most voluminous of the authors who met these needs." *DAB* V:53.

His vast legal knowledge is aptly employed in this important early textbook which provides a summary of the basic principles of American law. His success with this first work, which went into a second edition, led Hilliard to go on to write numerous other well-regarded treatises, many of which went into numerous editions, including *The Law of Torts* (1859), the first English treatise on the subject. *Dictionary of American Biography* V: 53-54. *Catalogue of the Library of the Law School of Harvard University* (1909) I: 925. Cohen, *Bibliography of Early American Law* 5393.

Kalman, Laura. *Legal Realism at Yale, 1927-1960.* Chapel Hill: University of North Carolina Press, 1986. xii, 314 pp. Reprinted 2002 by The Lawbook Exchange, Ltd. ISBN 1-58477-203-4. Cloth. $85.
* The history of the concept of legal realism as it evolved at Yale University Law School is in fact a history of the development of legal education in this country during the years 1927-1960, as Kalman shows in this important study. The realists' attention toward the importance of the role of litigation, the practitioner, judges and judicial reasoning, and the judiciary in a societal context represented a departure from the scientific casebook method espoused by C.C. Langdell at Harvard University Law School in the 1870s, and later supported by Roscoe Pound.

Kilbourn, Dwight C. *The Bench and Bar of Litchfield County, Connecticut 1709-1909: Biographical Sketches of Members. History and Catalogue of the Litchfield Law School. Historical Notes.* Litchfield, Conn.: Published by the Author, 1909. xiv, 344, [3], viii pp. Illustrated. Reprint available 2002 by The Lawbook Exchange, Ltd. LCCN 2001038974. ISBN 1-58477-213-1. Cloth. $80.
* Litchfield Law School, the first American law school, was founded by Tapping Reeve in 1782. The work is composed of materials relevant to the school and related personages, and contains historical notes, biographies, photographs, accounts of important trials, and the following reprints: Litchfield County: Historical Address Delivered at Litchfield, Conn., On the Occasion of the Centennial Celebration, 1851, by Samuel Church; Sketches of the Early Lights of the Litchfield Bar by David S. Boardman (1860); Fifty Years at the Litchfield County Bar by Charles F. Sedgwick (1870); and Reminiscences of the Litchfield County Bar, Delivered at the Centennial Banquet, November 18, 1898, by Donald J. Warner.

Langdell, C.C. *A Selection of Cases on the Law of Contracts. With References and Citations. Prepared for Use as a Text-book in Harvard Law School.* Boston: Little, Brown & Co., 1871. xvi, 1022 pp. Reprinted 1999 by The Lawbook Exchange, Ltd. LCCN 99-28293. ISBN 1-58477-001-5. Cloth. $120.
* The landmark work that introduced the revolutionary idea of the "case system" to legal education, which Langdell [1826-1906] instituted in his position as Dean at Harvard law School. A response to the European educational practice of the expository textbook as the basis of study, Langdell invented herein the use of original authorities to teach legal principles in his classes at Harvard. He posted lists of leading cases on the bulletin boards or announced them in class beforehand. The students prepared for class by going to the library, taking down the reports, and studying them. The process was both injurious to the library collection and inconvenient for the students. It was very soon apparent to Langdell that having done away with the traditional textbook, the law library was not a satisfactory alternative. No library had, or could afford, the number of duplicate volumes of the court reports that were required so that all students could have easy and equal

access to the cases. Langdell's solution was the casebook. This innovation in legal education publishing led to the proliferation of casebooks that continue today. Walker, *Oxford Companion to Law* 714. Marke, *A Catalogue of the Law Collection of New York University* (1953) 423. *Dictionary of American Biography* V:585-586.

Lieber, Francis. *On Civil Liberty and Self-government. Enlarged edition in one volume.* Philadelphia: J.B. Lippincott & Co.. 1859. xix, [15]-629 pp. Reprinted 2001 by The Lawbook Exchange, Ltd. LCCN 99-056928. ISBN 1-58477-070-8. Cloth. $100.

* "In these volumes Lieber presented the first systematic works on political science that appeared in America... he retains credit as a notable pioneer with wide influence in more than one generation." DAB VI:236-238. Widely read and used as a textbook, this is the best known of Lieber's work. Lieber [1800-1872], a German scholar and political activist who suffered persecution from the Prussians, was early associated with the historian Niebuhr. He immigrated to the United States in 1827, and his writings, among them an encyclopedia that was the foundation of the *Encyclopedia Britannica*, advanced his reputation. He became professor of history and political economy at South Carolina College, and was later appointed to the same chair in Columbia College. In 1865 he moved to Columbia Law School, where he was known to be a prominent political philosopher and consultant to the Union government, due to his influential writings on military law. Enlarged edition in one volume, having first been published in two volumes in 1853. Cohen, *Bibliography of Early American Law* 3369. Sabin, *A Dictionary of Books Relating to America* 40974. *Catalogue of the Library of the Law School of Harvard University* (1909) I:1176. *Dictionary of American Biography* VI:236-238.

[St. Germain, Christopher]. *The Doctor and Student or Dialogues Between a Doctor of Divinity and a Student in the Laws of England Containing the Grounds of Those Laws Together with Questions and Cases Concerning the Equity Thereof Revised and Corrected by William Muchall, Gent. to which are added two pieces concerning Suits in Chancery by Subpoena.* Cincinnati: Robert Clarke & Co., 1874. xiv, 401 pp. Reprinted 1998 by The Lawbook Exchange, Ltd. LCCN 98-11338. ISBN 1-886363-49-8. Cloth. $65.

* Written originally in Latin in 1523, this work contains two dialogues between a doctor of divinity and a student of English law, and is known for putting into popular form canonist learning regarding the nature and object of law, the religious and moral standards of law, the foundations of the common law and other discussions regarding the jurisdiction of Parliament. A very important work in the development of equity, *Doctor and Student* appeared in numerous editions. It was frequently cited and influenced generations of legal writers down to Blackstone and later. Marke, *A Catalogue of the Law Collection of New York University* (1953) 38. *Catalogue of the Library of the Law School of Harvard University* (1909) II:516-517.

Stevens, Robert. *Law School: Legal Education in America from the 1850s to the 1980s.*Chapel Hill: The University of North Carolina Press, [1983]. xvi, 334 pp. Reprinted 2001 by The Lawbook Exchange, Ltd. ISBN 1-58477-199-2. Cloth. $85.

* Comprehensive history of over a century of legal education in America. Examines the law school institution and its impact on the legal profession and the society it serves. This highly lauded work won a Certificate of Merit from the American Bar Association upon its original publication. Stevens' distinguished career in education and law includes his seventeen-year term as professor of law at Yale University and nine-year term as president of Haverford College, during which tenure this work was published. Well-annotated and indexed, with a thorough bibliography.

Walker, Timothy. *Introduction to American Law. Designed as a First Book for Students.* Ninth Edition. Revised by Clement Bates. Boston: Little, Brown, and Company, 1887. Reprint available 2002 by The Lawbook Exchange, Ltd. LCCN 2001038955. ISBN 1-58477-214-X. Cloth. $120.

* A systematic outline of American law, written to fill a void in this area, and "...for many years was used as a textbook for American law students." Marke, *A Catalogue of the Law Collection at New York University* (1953) 250. Based on lectures given by Walker [1802-1856] while a law professor at Cincinnati College.

Warren, Charles. *History of the Harvard Law School and of Early Legal Conditions in America.* New York: Lewis Publishing Company, 1908. Three volumes. xiv, 543; iv, 560; 397 pp. Illustrated. Reprinted 1999 by The Lawbook Exchange, Ltd. LCCN 99-29193. ISBN 1-58477-006-6. Cloth. $275.

* The definitive history. Warren provides a fascinating account of law studies, lawyers, legal practice and legal conditions in America from 1640 to 1817--the year of the foundation of the Harvard Law School. This is followed by a comprehensive history of the Harvard Law School from 1817 to 1908. Volume three contains a complete, detailed biographical Alumni Roll for the Harvard Law School, with selected class pictures and an alumni index. Marke, *A Catalogue of the Law Collection of New York University* (1953) 201. **The set is also available in handsome quarter calf with raised bands, gilt-stamped lettering-pieces and gilt embellishments, over marble boards for $750.**